MW01659493

Trish Sheppard

Motherhood

Dear Jill,
Think some of the situations in here will bring back memories!
Have a happy Christmas 1989 and lots of love,
Carol

Christmas 1989

Trish Sheppard

Motherhood

There's only one thing worse than having children . . . not having them!

ANGUS
& ROBERTSON
PUBLISHERS

ANGUS & ROBERTSON PUBLISHERS

Unit 4, Eden Park, 31 Waterloo Road,
North Ryde, NSW, Australia 2113;
16 Golden Square, London W1R 4BN,
United Kingdom

This book is copyright.
Apart from any fair dealing for the purposes of private study, research, criticism or review, as permitted under the Copyright Act, no part may be reproduced by any process without written permission. Inquiries should be addressed to the publishers.

Every effort has been made to trace the copyright holders of quoted material and apology is made for any unintended infringement.

First published in Australia
by Angus & Robertson Publishers in 1989
First published in New Zealand
by Angus & Robertson NZ Ltd in 1989
First published in the United Kingdom
by Angus & Robertson (UK) in 1989
Reprinted in 1989

Copyright © High Adventure Productions Pty Ltd 1989

National Library of Australia
Cataloguing-in-publication data.

Sheppard, Trish, 1942-
Motherhood : there's only one thing worse than having children — not having them.

ISBN 0 207 15998 X.

1. Motherhood — Australia — Case studies. 2. Mothers — Australia — Interviews. 3. Mother and child — Australia. I. Title.

306.8'743'0994

Designed by Leonie Bremer-Kamp

Typeset in 11pt Garamond
Printed by Australian Print Group, Maryborough, Vic.

THIS BOOK IS DEDICATED to the more than two and a half billion women in the world, each of whom carry within them, at the time of their own birth, the eggs of at least eight hundred other human beings.

CONTENTS

Beginnings

Starting Out

The Good Times

The Horror Years

Letting Go

All around me men were dying. Being burnt alive.
Screaming in agony. Calling out for their mother.

ARGENTINE SAILOR WHO SURVIVED THE
BRITISH ATTACK ON SS BELGRANO.

AT TIMES OF SUCH fundamental despair we cry out not for the flesh and blood woman who gave birth to us but to the eternal energy to which we all yearn to return and for which there is no more adequate word than Mother.

Introduction

When our last child left home we waved her off as she was driven away by a friend in an orange-coloured BMW convertible, ran back down the drive, and made love on the dining-room table.

During the following week I converted her bedroom into an office. By the end of the month we had indulged ourselves with a two-seater car (farewell to four-door family cars and the constant arguments about who is going to sit in the back seat, farewell to ice-cream-sticky fingers and in later years cigarette burns on the seats, and farewell to their choice of music on the car radio). And within two years we had sold the family home, buying one, which in addition to stupendous northerly views, has no spare bedrooms — just in case they have a change of heart or, more likely, run out of money.

None of this should be taken to mean that we don't love our children, that we don't enjoy being parents. Every night as I turn out the lights I smile at the photographs of them on the wall and wish them sweet dreams, health and happiness. Its just that eighteen years of close contact loving was enough, and on occasions more than.

So now this book: a collection of anecdotes, reminiscences, dreams and the day-to-day realities of sharing your life with your children. It's a self-indulgence really. I've heard the view expressed that having children is a self-indulgence — some indulgence! But this book is. It's my merit badge, self-awarded, for having survived, battle worn, bruised and occasionally bloodied.

It's a sharing of the fears and tears and love and joy, written in the hope of helping you keep a sense of perspective, because laughing at it all is the only way to stop from smashing yourself over the head with a hairbrush or kicking in the cupboard doors (I have a girlfriend who does both).

And it is unashamedly about mothering, not parenting. With a great sense of sisterhood it is for women about women. It's not anti-men, just pro-women, because I am a woman and because that means that although I can relate to being kicked in the testicles I can't experience the sensation first-hand. Whereas I do know what it feels like to have another being growing inside me, for my body to open up and pop it out, to have it clamped to my breast, and to feel so intimately related to this flesh of my flesh that still when the phone rings in the middle of the night my mind screams to the surface with the waking horror that one of them is in trouble. (Is it any wonder then that I am terse with the callers who, thankfully, invariably turn out to be Americans returning our business calls and who always express surprise that it's 3.00 am in Sydney when it's 1.00 pm in Dayton, Ohio?)

It is not a sociological treatise. I am not an expert on childraising, all I've done is raise my own. The same goes for the fifteen women in this book, to whom I want to say thank you for sharing their experiences through me with you. I have divided the book into five areas: 'Beginnings', that is, pregnant for the first time; 'Starting Out' with toddlers; 'The Good Times' when they are between five and twelve; 'The Horror Years' with teenagers; and 'Letting Go', the time we all eagerly anticipate but when it arrives we're not so sure.

For each of the women in this book, as for all mothers, mothering is the most important aspect of their lives. As I listened to them all it became very apparent that whether they put it into words or left it unsaid, whether indeed it was even a recognised emotion or was simply just there, every one of them was driven to motherhood by an overriding desire which could not be resisted. Being a mother came before everything else. One simple expression of this is the fact that not one of them, not one, said to me when I first asked them if they would like to be included in this book that they would first of all have to discuss it with their partner! Mothering, it seems, is the one area of life where we feel we do not need to defer to the male of the species.

It is written from my own background, calling on my own experiences. But it is written in the belief that mothers share a common bond. It's a bond that crosses all barriers: race, language, religion. Recently I was fortunate enough to make a working visit to the USSR. In Yalta, on the Crimea coast, I was interviewed by a radio journalist. We discussed the American Star Wars program, the Soviet response to it and the unimaginable horror of world war. I knew that she had two boys, a couple of years older than my own children, and after juggling verbally with a few of the usual bland, ineffectual generalisations about the fact that all warfare is unacceptable, I commented on how awful it would be if one day our sons found themselves in opposing forces, convinced that they had to kill one another. There was a pause, tears filled her eyes and she reached across and put her hand on top of mine. We knew.

So this is a celebration. It's to let you know that you are not alone and give you a little light reading on those nights when you can barely wake up to breastfeed and then lie wide awake for hours afterwards, anxious to hear that little warm snuffle as reassurance she is still alive; right through to those equally long nights when you lie awake stewing in anger and anxiety, having lent her your car to drive to a party on condition she doesn't drink and is home by midnight. At 2.30 am the telephone number at the girlfriend's house where you had been told the party was being held doesn't answer and the tone of reproof from the constable at the local police station with whom you have checked three times makes it too embarrassing for you to call again. What sort of mother are you anyway, you keep flagellating yourself, to allow such things? (She of course arrives home at 2.45 am blithe spirited, unintoxicated and blathers on about how the petrol must have been drained from the tank while she was at the party so the car had run out and she had had to walk for miles to an all-night service station. She thinks you came down in the last shower and you won't notice that her blouse is incorrectly buttoned!) In fact you are probably the same sort of mother as me, learning on the run and stumbling along in a miasma of self-doubt, just hoping that doing your very best will turn out to be good enough.

But when it comes to the bottom line you would no doubt agree with my dad, whom I remember quite distinctly telling me when I visited him with my first child while heavily pregnant with the second, that there is only one thing worse than having children and that is not having them! And having raised six of them he should know. So here's to us that have them!

BEGINNINGS

Trish

Janet Brennand

Julie Agius

Jenny Giannikouris

Trish

I came to motherhood in a less than cerebral manner. I met the man I wanted to spend the rest of my life with and I wanted to have his baby. Simple as that. Except that of course nothing can be that simple!

You've heard people say, 'I remember the first time I met him as if it was only yesterday,' and you've thought, yuk! How gushing, how impossibly unlikely, like some Mills and Boon novelette.

Well, sorry about that, but for me that's how it was. I remember, as clearly as if it were today, being shown around the offices of Radio Hong Kong by my new boss, following him into a room, and there *he* was. And I thought, that's *the* one. Lust, that's what it was (and still is!).

The fact that we both were married was what made it not so simple. But I have to admit that this was barely a deterrent for me. It was far more of a deterrent for him, and rightly so, because he had a son. Two years later, after heartbreak and despair had driven us both through a patch of complete insanity, we left the island together loaded down with guilt which took years to dissipate. Twenty-three years later the only justification for the unhappiness we inflicted on our partners is that we are still together in a happy, loving and constantly growing friendship.

I had gone to Hong Kong to escape — my past, England's future and the bloody climate, political and actual. The idea to desert must have been in my subconscious for some time but I remember the moment that it broke free, demanding to be acknowledged. It was a late afternoon towards the end of October. It was drizzling. The slim, very high heel of my new shoes (I've always been into shoes) got stuck in a crack in the pavement as I was hurrying along Oxford Street towards Bond Street tube station. As I stood there in light which was already dim, even though it was only 4.00 pm, balancing on one shod foot and examining the bruised heel of the other shoe, the drizzle seeped down inside my collar and I could smell the collective unwashedness of the gathering rush-hour crowd. And I thought, there has to be somewhere better than this.

I was born in Bristol, but when asked where I come from I say Midsomer-Norton, because that is my spiritual home, my Dreamtime. It's where my dad, Allan Clark, was born, and my gran and gramps. It is a coal-mining village in the west of England where it seemed as though everyone was either a Clark or a Gould (my gran's maiden name). My parents were never married. Dad had married when he was seventeen, just before he left to fight the war to end all wars in the mud of Flanders. Not surprisingly he returned a changed man and though they tried to keep the marriage going, even to the lengths of adopting a son, my older brother Bob, it became a sham which Dad finally escaped by going to work in the United States.

When he returned to Bristol after several years, having saved enough money to start up an engineering business of his own, he met my mother, Kathleen Hamlett, who had been married and already had a daughter, Mary. The two of them had myself and my younger sister, Sara. In a modern bungalow in a quiet cul-de-sac they lived together without blessing of church or state and with the disapproval of families and former friends.

Kathleen was without doubt the great love of my father's life. She was tiny, not quite five feet tall, with long red-gold hair which she wore in either a bun or plaits looped around her head. I remember watching Dad brush it for her as it cascaded down her back and her laughing as he whispered in her ear. I remember her laugh so well, her generous mouth and even teeth and her high cheekbones and blue sparkling eyes.

I have only a few memories of the woman in whose womb I grew, but at least they are all happy. Even when she was dying, and we more or less lived in some rooms which were part of the little private hospital, I have good memories of helping the nurses to push the tea-trolley around the wards and of my mother reading to me as I sat restless beside her bed playing with her long hair. We spent over a year in that hospital. I have been back there since; it hasn't changed. When she died of cancer, having had both breasts removed, she was thirty-nine. I was seven. Nowadays she probably would not have died; the cancer would have been detected earlier and they wouldn't have done such radical surgery.

But when she died my father blamed himself and for some time afterwards he got drunk quite frequently and us kids went to stay with various relatives. The business which Dad had built up over the years and which now included a garage started to go downhill. The neighbours gossiped and the social welfare people called on a few occasions. As fast as Dad employed housekeepers we got rid of them by frightening them with our outrageous, wild, rude behaviour. We didn't want a replacement mother.

Then he found one who had been through so much horror and grief herself that she was not about to be terrorised by a covey of hooligan kids. Ingrid was a refugee from Germany. Only twenty-nine, she had lived through the fire bombing of Hamburg and had two children of her own. She had survived Hitler, the loss of family wealth, two husbands and the American occupation. She was so glad to be in England that nothing, us kids, the stares and foul comments of the neighbours and relatives, the weekly check-in at the local police station, none of it made her determination waver.

She was extremely glamorous, always immaculately groomed and coiffed. I guess as a reaction to what she had been through she was fastidiously tidy. I liked and respected her a great deal. She had a sharp, perceptive intellect, she read widely and was interested in politics, religion, philosophy and social issues. But I couldn't love her, not in an immediate responsive daughter to mother way. She was too cool for that. Too collected and reserved. I never sat on her knee or cuddled her. She turned her cheek to be kissed. But nor did I ever resent or dislike her because as I grew older I read and came to understand something of what she must have suffered and because she saved my old man's life.

She dragged him back from the pit of despair and self-pity. She put the business back on its feet and, in her own cool manner, she loved him. At some point she moved from being our housekeeper to being his lover. Her children came from Germany to live with us, her daughter, Erika, a couple of years older than me and her son, Harald, the same age as me. They spoke no English and had to handle the understandable hostility of a people who saw them and their mother as the recent enemy.

We moved from the house, I think probably because Ingrid wanted to escape reminders of my dead mother, into the small flat on top of the garage. Here we all became teenagers. I took the dreaded Eleven Plus exam at the local junior school, threatened and bullied by the head teacher, Mr Weldon, into bed-wetting and winning a scholarship to the best private girls' school in the city, Red Maids.

All I wanted to do, all I've ever wanted to do, was to write. My plan was that by the time I was twenty-one I would have published my first book. I would also have put the world right; not single-handed, I was monomaniac not megalomaniac. The world did not seem right at all. There were a few haves and far more have-nots. I didn't feel comfortable with an education which automatically placed me in the top 2 per cent of the population. Red Maids had rubbed off. The worst was that when I visited my village I was treated as though I was 'from out'.

Dad and Ingrid sold the business and they designed and built their dream home on the River Stour near Christchurch on the south coast. The nearest place where I could work was Bournemouth, for me the last resort, a place which epitomised everything I found unacceptable, prig that I was, in British society. London beckoned, full of soul mates and publishers. But not before I had my obligatory affair with a twice-married man who had seven children and won top marks as a chauvinist.

He is the only lover I've ever had of whom I am ashamed. He was also my first. I was eighteen. He was thirty-six. An intellectual,

How in my wildest dreams could I even begin to imagine that from the moment of her birth, whatever else I am or become, whatever else I do, all of that, all of it, is secondary to what I became then, a mother.

talented and very bright European Jew who blitzed me through that rite of passage with breathtaking intensity. He gave me lists of books to read and then questioned me on them. He took me to art shows, galleries, concerts, operas, jazz clubs, theatres and bookshops. He introduced me to worlds and people I had dared only to dream of. He bought me clothes and jewellery and when he tired of my eager innocence he dumped me, distraught and pregnant, performing the abortion himself and leaving me suicidal.

Bournemouth has open-topped buses for the tourists and I must have scared the hell out of the poor man on whose car bonnet I landed after throwing myself from one of them into the rush-hour traffic! I am ashamed of my first lover because it's a poor comment on me that I was attracted to a man who was without doubt a deadshit. But in self-defence I add that this was the only one; all the others have one thing in common — they're good guys.

London was a great release. I found a room with a family in a tiny side street off Earls Court Road. For three pounds fifteen shillings a week I had a single bed, a wardrobe, a small table and chair and a row of shelves. The window looked out over rows of grey roofs. Paradise! I put out my books, stuck up posters showing statuesque women aglow with the fervour of revolution suckling large infants while commanding troops of threshing machines, and cooked my meals of mince and beans in the small communal kitchen.

The owners of the house lived with their two sons in the basement and let two other rooms apart from mine. These were filled with a succession of young women who were so different from anyone I had ever met that they might as well have come from another planet. In fact they came from Australia. They were so large. Well, I suppose that's not literally true, but in my memory they remain large because of the way they moved and took up so much space. They exuded confidence. They spoke loudly and laughed a lot. And they all wore ridiculously tiny shorts, which exposed great expanses of brown legs, as well as walking boots and thick socks. They were forever going out of the front door with huge back-packs and calling casually over their shoulders as they left, 'See you in Turin . . . Monte Carlo . . . Hydra . . .' or some other exotic and to me totally unknown place. Photographs of me taken fifteen years later, hitchhiking with the children through Africa, reveal me as identical to those women I had secretly admired in London. Perhaps it's something in the Sydney water!

If I couldn't make a living writing, the only other prospect which I could view with any pleasure was working in a bookshop, preferably my own. Even now it still has great appeal. The idea of spending all day surrounded by books and people who read is immensely pleasing. So I began work at Foyles, The Largest Bookshop in the World, in Charing Cross Road. Even though the pay was appalling, nine guineas a week (the snobbery still existed that those who worked with their hands were paid in pounds while those who worked with their minds were remunerated in guineas), and Foyles is far too large to be a caring retail outlet for any product, most of all books, I still loved working there.

London, like all big cities, and smaller ones too, can be an overwhelmingly lonely place. But I did then what I have done so many times since in new places where I don't know anyone; I joined interest groups and went along to their meetings. At Communist Party meetings I met the usual loose affiliation of intellectuals, no-hopers, idealists, misfits and loony tunes who wash up with equal ease on the shores of political parties of all persuasions. I joined the CND and went on Aldermaston marches. At anti-apartheid gatherings I sat on the floor eating boiled mealies as a sign of solidarity in front of two-bar gas fires fed by shillings in the slot. At the apogee of my time as a literary groupie I lived with a black South African writer, a political refugee whose back bore the salted scars of white oppression and fear and who took out on me his anger and hatred of whites. He eventually married a woman whose skin was even paler than mine.

After six months at Foyles I went to work for Haldanes, an extremely left-wing bookshop, named after A.M. Haldane, one of the founders of the Fabian Society. The shop was crammed into tiny premises off Charing Cross Road in a street colloquially known as Tin Pan Alley, the centre of London's music publishing scene. The street was brimming with would-be rock stars, which in turn meant that new avenues opened in my social life.

The money at Haldanes was just as lousy. But I was good at making what little there was go a long way. On Fridays — payday — the choice was either to take the tube to work or spend that ninepence on the week's issue of the *New Statesman* and walk. Unless the weather was extremely foul, I walked. I managed despite being poor to get el-cheapo seats in the gods at the opera and to go to the ballet and to concerts. Often I went to these occasions with a current lover but I almost always paid my own way, a habit developed in childhood which has stuck with me so that even now when I have a lunchtime sandwich with my ex-husband I still pay my share. On Sundays I took the *Observer* and the *Sunday Times* to the Paris Pullman in Chelsea, arriving early along with scores of other hopefuls to sit in the seat before the show started, pretending to read but in reality deciding which of the anticipated offers I would take up!

I think what all this meant is that I was looking for someone. I wanted to share my life with someone. I remembered lying in bed at home in the early morning and being able to hear the indistinct murmurs of Dad and Ingrid talking in bed. She would get up and make him a cup of tea, rinse her face, clean her teeth, comb her hair and drift around in a long extremely feminine negligee waiting for the kettle to boil. (Having been always a naked sleeper I recall asking her why the hell she got so dressed up to go to bed. She just smiled.) I would lie there listening to them, unable to hear what was being said but basking in the obvious warmth of the conversation and daydream about having a man of my own on whose chest I could nestle my head while we talked: philosophy, politics, sex, life, love, the whole damn thing. (Even now there are few things I enjoy more than lying with my head on his chest while he reads to me.)

Marriage, no. I've never wanted to be sanctioned by church or state. It's the ultimate put-down of women. The great con. The soft option. The height of patronisation. But commitment, yes. So when I sold this good-looking sort a book on chartered surveying and he asked me out and after the obligatory stasis of several dates we got it together in my single bed and he asked me above the noise of the rain falling outside my window to marry him, I said, 'Yes. Except I don't want to marry so let's just live together.' He was gentle and warm and funny.

But he had a mother who was a harridan and a widow and who had lumbered him with all the guilt of being the only son of a woman on her own. We lived together for some months but his mother demanded weekly visits to her place in the Home Counties on the grounds that the back fence needed painting, the dry rot needed looking at, or her deaf, blind, smelly spaniel needed attention and then she would take him aside and lecture him about the heinous crime of cohabitation, after which she would invariably have a spectacular asthmatic attack. So we got married. Outside the Kensington Registry Office my father said to him. 'You'll need steel balls for this one boy.' And I said, 'Dad!' and knew he was right. We went to France for a honeymoon. I lost my wedding ring in the ocean and, unused to real sunlight, we both suffered sunstroke and to recover we had to lie, red and blistering, in a darkened room for two days.

We spent a terrible English winter of evenings crouched over an electric blow-heater while he studied for his final exams and I recovered from the daily blows of a new job. I had been invited to help open the London office of Pergamon Press, owned by the then only slightly famous Robert Maxwell. My left-wing friends were all in agreement that I could not in good conscience take the job because the man, though professing to be a socialist, was in fact a rampant capitalist. I weighed these views carefully, for about half an hour, accepted the job, which paid an unheard of nineteen pounds a week, and went out and bought a pair of bright green, patent leather, very high heeled shoes from a tarts' shop in Soho.

But my friends were right and the shoes no compensation! The final decision to leave came after I went with my new boss in his chauffeur-driven car — was it a Roller or a Bentley? I can't recall — up the M1 to attend a party political meeting. Just outside the town where the meeting was to be held, we pulled into a garage, climbed out of the car and squeezed into a Mini, in which we travelled on to our destination.

Perhaps it was just the weather but it felt as though Britain had become a soggy morass of dodgy values: Profumo, Keeler, Ward, Wilson, my boss and to top it off my mother-in-law. Time to move out. We were among the last Colonial Office intake to travel to a posting by sea. At the docks in Southampton my dad said I couldn't go on board the P&O liner *Chitral* wearing jeans, 'They'll think you're a navvy'. They probably thought worse than that when they played The Queen before dinner and I remained seated.

But none of this mattered because at each port where we stopped, Port Said, Aden, Colombo, Penang, Singapore, I became increasingly goggle-eyed with wonder at the magic of the world. To think that I had lived twenty-one years in one spot when all this had been out here waiting! Finally Hong Kong, where less than a week after landing I walked into that office and saw him standing there.

I shared an office with him for a year, driven crazy because he never showed more interest in me than he did in any of the other women in the office. We were all treated with charm and consideration which for me was not enough. I played the last card in my hand and changed jobs. It worked. The year of our open affair was an amalgam of intense pleasure and the painful knowledge that we were both causing our spouses great hurt.

When we sailed from Hong Kong together we left everything behind. A wife and his seven-year-old son with enough money to take them back to Australia. A husband. Friends. Secure careers, one of which would shortly have provided a six-month holiday on full pay including tickets to any part of the world. Households full of furniture. Cars. And a sizeable chunk of our own self-respect. All we took with us was a suitcase of clothes each, our love for each other and enough guilt and unhappiness to fill our hearts, choke our throats and frequently make us weep. The year of our open affair had been crazy enough but this next six months was total madness.

We sailed via Japan and Hawaii to the West Coast of the USA, where we hoped we would be able to find work. We had so little money that after a month of bizarre experiences and no employment success in Los Angeles we hitchhiked all the way up the West Coast to Canada where as Commonwealth citizens we hoped to be able to work without the problem of Green Cards. We arrived the day before Christmas Eve with $2.40 between us!

I don't know why but I never once had any doubt that somehow or other everything would work out. All I wanted was to live with him forever and have his baby (women!) and so I stopped taking the pill. My father wrote accusing him of being a cad, of worming his way into a friendship with my husband and then betraying that trust. His parents wrote and dismissed me as a 'flash in the pan red-haired hotpants'. One of his friends wrote saying that when he got over this madness they'd have a drink and a laugh over it all. Heavy stuff.

We pawned a ring and a camera and stayed in a dosshouse where the snow came up to the windowsill. The clothes I had were so lightweight that I wore them all at once. The letters from our deserted spouses kept arriving. Full of pain. The guilt was fine-tuned torture.

When the phone call came telling me that my husband had attempted to take his life I felt I had no option but to return and nurture him through. I couldn't get on with my new life without attempting to clean up the mess I had left behind. The guilt I felt made it impossible to move forward. A friend paid for the ticket. When I stepped onto the coach which was to take me to the airport in Vancouver I stepped also into a hole in space, a time warp, where I existed as in a vacuum. I walked and breathed and ate and talked and no doubt looked perfectly normal to other people. But I felt at a great remove from everything and everyone. I surrendered myself. Gave up. What happened, happened.

The day after I got back, my period started. It meant I wasn't pregnant with his baby. I was very upset. But I didn't go back on the pill. And we lived together again as husband and wife. His hurt was as distressing up close as it had been at a distance and what was worse was I knew if I stayed I would hurt him more. I wrote to my lover every day and he wrote daily to me.

Within a month I was pregnant. But even that remained remote to me. It was as if I was separated from the rest of the world by a glass wall. I could see it but it couldn't touch me and I couldn't reach it. There's probably somebody reading this who recognises all the symptoms of a crack-up. Eventually, when I was five months pregnant, my husband recognised this too and told me that he would understand and could now cope with me going off with my lover. We cried a lot over the decision. Because I loved him and love him still. But he said that I looked like a bird trapped in a cage and that was indeed how I felt. We agreed that we would always stay friends and we have.

I flew back to Vancouver and stepped out of the time warp into the arms of my lover. I promise this is the end of the down-market version of *Dynasty*. From now on it becomes Dad and Doris! He of course knew I was pregnant and had written that it made no difference at all to the way he felt about me or his hope that we would spend our lives together. At the time I accepted this as I accepted all else about him. It is only over the years that I have fully recognised this as a mark of the generous capacity of his soul.

He had found work as a freelance radio journalist with the Canadian Broadcasting Commission and when I returned he had just the day before come back from the Dominican Republic, which was in the throes of a revolution. There he had filmed and recorded heaps of great material for a one-hour radio documentary and a half-hour film for CBC.

He had also already paid an enrolment fee for a three-month television production course in New York beginning that autumn and as soon as we had finished editing the two programs it was time to take off in our Volkswagen with only $300 in our pockets to drive 5000 kilometres across the continent. This was my first experience of camping out. Each night we took out the back seat to sleep on it under a piece of green plastic, which we stretched out from the side of the car. I had also never travelled in a large country and was on occasions overcome by agoraphobia — could any country keep stretching away into infinity? Where was the ocean? Help! It was September and so cold in the mountains that we woke one morning to find an inch of ice covering our pail of water, but I was kept warm with love and an ever-growing belly.

The journey took six weeks and cost us all of our $300. We sold our V-dub in Toronto for $300 and arrived in Manhattan with this money, our cat, who had enjoyed the car trip, no job, no place to stay and me more than eight months pregnant with no contacts, let alone a doctor, but, for some reason, without a qualm.

We found a basement bed-sitter on West 74th, just off Central Park West, for $26 a week. We paid $52 as a fortnight's advance on that and another $100 as a fortnight's advance on the production course. That left us with $150. Then we just got into it.

He found a job as a night guard at the Australian High Commission's office a few blocks from the college; so he would go to school from 9.00 am to 5.00 pm and then literally run to the High Commission office, always arriving ten minutes late and out of breath, to take up guard duty. He would work there until 1.00 am, come home to catch a few hours' sleep before getting up at 7.00 am to begin again.

We found a doctor, a wonderful woman called Margot Ammon who was somewhat bemused to find that I had had no previous prenatal care and that we both wanted to be there for the delivery, which I wanted to be as natural as possible. This was 1966 when the fashion in births was a spinal block, no father present, and no breastfeeding. I think Dr Ammon took to us because we were an oddity.

Between college and the job we found time to approach the BBC and the Australian Broadcasting Commission (as it was then) with story and interview ideas for their radio programs. It was a matter of being in the right place at the right time. They couldn't get enough. So while he was at school I researched and lined up interviews which he then rushed out and did either in the lunch hour or at weekends. He edited them on our portable Uher tape-recorder in the evenings, while he was supposed to be guarding Australia's interests!

We were so busy surviving I hardly had time to notice I was pregnant. For the first and only time in my life (except for during my second pregnancy) my hands and feet, which even on hot sunny days are always cool to cold, were warm, which was just as well because the weather was bitter and we couldn't afford gloves or warm shoes. My belly became so large that it was uncomfortable to wash the pale-coloured linoleum floor of our little apartment, which quickly became soiled with Manhattan grime. So he would do it and I would lie in a deep bath watching him work his way on his hands and knees backwards from our bed around the stove and fridge and into what passed as the bathroom. 'Thirty,' he would say, 'and still washing floors!' and laugh as he squeezed into the tiny space left in a bath already overflowing with me and mine.

Within six weeks we were earning enough money from the interviews to be able to take the calculated risk of giving up the evening guard duty and concentrate on the radio material. And I gave birth to my first baby. I was twenty-three.

It was a first for all of us. The first time I had popped out a human being, the first time he had been present at a birth and the first time Dr Ammon had presided over a natural delivery. It took fourteen hours of sweating and groaning, of him rubbing my back and of me getting niggly if he couldn't sense immediately when and where I wanted to be rubbed and at what pressure, of building to a crescendo of pain which was only acceptable because it was productive and of becoming high on that pain as if it was a drug, of wondering if it would ever end and just then it did.

And of course it was a miracle. Every birth is a miracle. To see in the mirror above the bed a head coming out from my body, to feel it struggle and strain to get out in order to make a claim on life, to see her tiny body, silken, shiny and slippery, perfect, held up still attached to me, flesh of my flesh, and then to have her at my breast; tiny delicate features, so fragile and yet so immensely strong, little wiggly fingers and toes so complete they even had nails! Everything in miniature. Already full with promise. If I told you she was the most beautiful piece of creation I had ever seen would you believe me? Shall I boast and tell you that on a chart the hospital kept for all its births she scored nine out of ten and no baby has ever scored ten? (Perhaps they are waiting for a second coming, you never can tell with Americans!)

He enjoyed the birth with such intensity that for months, even years, afterwards I would listen while he talked about it to people, and it sounded as if it was his body, not mine, which had brought forth a human being. (This is just one of the reasons why I love him.) We had no family or really close friends for him to share the experience and his happiness with so when he finally left me he went to the nearest bar and told anyone who would listen!

Margot Ammon was so delighted to have enjoyed a natural birth that she was barely fazed when we told her that we had been a tiny bit deceitful in not telling her that the man she had assumed was my spouse was not the legal father of the baby and that the birth certificate she signed would have to be in the legally correct names. Her assistant, a male doctor, came to visit me the day following the birth to apologise for not giving me an injection before the small episiotomy which had been necessary to prevent my flesh from tearing. I assured him that I hadn't even felt the incision, or the few stitches, that I hadn't wanted the injection and that the whole birth had been a pleasure beyond words. He couldn't allow himself to believe me without sacrificing some of his belief in his own worth. So he went away unconvinced that any woman could possibly enjoy birthing. Poor man.

The one friend we did have in New York, a Chinese scholar who had known us through the desperate days in Hong Kong, came to visit bringing us presents: an American football (for Zara) and *The Lord of the Rings* trilogy (for me), and sat for hours on my bed while I told him of my wonderful experience. All these years later he still recalls my enraptured expressions.

I shared a room in the hospital with a black woman who'd given birth to a son, Mickey she called him. He was very long-limbed and beautiful but I remember she was most distressed that he wouldn't open his eyes. It was as if she was worried that they would be blue! She and I were the only women in the maternity wing of the Roosevelt Hospital who were breastfeeding their babies. It was never said in so many words (but you know how nursing staff have a way of getting across to their patients what they think without needing to resort to words) that there was something not very nice about breastfeeding. This nasty habit which we shared was the reason why we were put in a room together. Out of the sight of those who might be shocked by seeing such an activity. My room companion they treated differently from me. She was black, so the fact that she breastfed was okay. But I shouldn't be doing that sort of thing! We joked about it, my room companion and I, and one night I told her that the milk she bought in cartons from the supermarket came from cows' udders. Until then she had assumed that it was manufactured in some other quite mechanical way and had nothing whatsover in common with what we were doing when we fed our babies! Her Mickey would be the same age now as our daughter and judging by the length of him he might very well be a basketball star.

I wanted to call our daughter Kathleen, after my mother, the woman to whom I felt the closest emotional link, but I couldn't do that without taking the risk of upsetting my stepmother. I didn't want to do that even though we were still persona non grata with all the families. So we chose Zara, after my younger sister. It is a Hebrew name, the name of Lot's wife, the one who was turned into a pillar of salt. It means princess. And to me, ardent republican though I am, this was what she was. I was quite overwhelmed by the immediate love I felt for her. How did that happen? Where did that come from? The day before she had been a lump of bone and blood, even her sex had been unknown. Now here she was nuzzling at my breast, already making emotional claims far and above what anyone else had ever demanded. There was a presumption about her that they would without doubt be met. And even more amazing—they were, without any reservations whatsoever. Only twenty-four hours old and already a person for whom I would give up whatever was required. For whom I would kill; for whom I would lay down my life.

Her existence changed everything for me. This wasn't something I had anticipated. I had been just getting on with my own life, assuming, when I thought about it at all, which wasn't often, that the birth of my baby would make very little difference. How in my wildest dreams could I even begin to imagine that from the moment of her birth, whatever else I am or become, whatever else I do, all of that, all of it, is secondary to what I became, a mother.

Janet Brennand

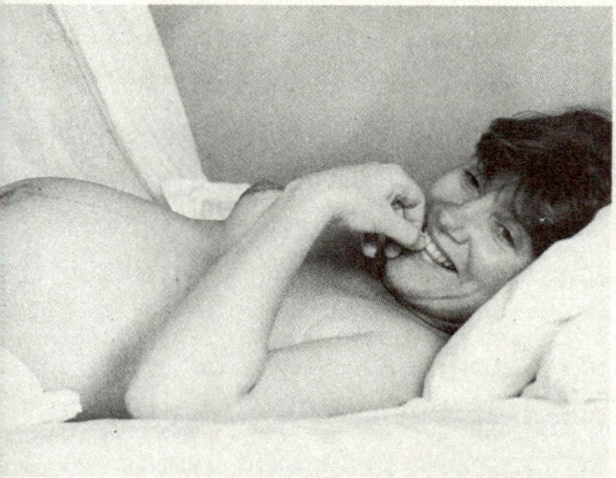

I've become quite fascinated with pregnant women. I think a pregnant woman is very voluptuous and sensual, not sexy, but immensely attractive.

'I'm the youngest of a family of seven, five girls and two boys. All except one of them are married with children. I have thirteen nieces and nephews. My sisters married young and by the time I was fourteen one of them was separated and had come back home to live bringing her three-year-old and one-year-old with her so there were eleven of us living in a three bedroom cottage. I remember thinking to myself, my god, I don't want this.'

So Janet kept putting off having children through a number of steady relationships while other pursuits took priority, and then ironically it was the over-population and poverty in India which sparked her final decision to become a mother. 'We spent three months travelling there in 1985 and what we experienced and saw, the handicapped children, the disease and poverty, quite contrary to what you would expect, made me feel I wanted a child. I wanted to be part of the cycle of life and death.

'I had to be sure I wasn't being driven by my hormones, you know, all this talk about the biological clock affecting women once they reach thirty' — Janet is thirty-three. 'It was important to me that it was an intellectual decision. I think of myself as practical and in control and didn't like the idea of being pushed by something ungovernable. But even so it was still an emotional reaction. India is so real, so raw, so intense. I wanted to be part of it and that meant having a baby. An astrologer I met by chance told me that there were many decisions to make that could be shared with others but there were two which were vital to make independently: having a child and a change in career. He was very right.'

But it wasn't all as easy as that. Returning to Australia, the decision made, Janet found that the bad dose of what she had assumed was Delhi-belly was a far more severe amoebic dysentery, plus a debilitating virus which affected her blood. 'When I mentioned to the doctors I saw that I was wanting to have a baby they all said I would have to wait until I had completely recovered because there was a very real danger to both the baby and me.' It was more than a year before she was given a medical all-clear. 'But looking back I am glad I had that space, it gave me time to fully adjust to the idea and what was involved so that by the time it happened I was ready for it. Well, as ready as any woman can be. I approached pregnancy in a very cerebral manner. I read a lot about it, rather like a study project; it's the way I approach everything.

'I put the idea of pregnancy at a manageable distance, that is until I became pregnant. Right from the start I was aware of changes in my body and though I went for a serum test at six weeks there was no doubt in my mind I was pregnant. Violent attacks of morning sickness made me close the books finally and give in to what was happening to me. All this must be very different for each woman. They must all have their own individual story. I know it was very different from my mother's experience.

'I was born in Bolton, Lancashire. I feel very positive about that. Those roots are important to me. I come from the heart of the British industrial north.' She has the accent to prove it and though five years in Australia have softened the vowels, you mention this fact at your peril.

'My family are working class. My dad went down the pits at fourteen and left the mines in his mid-fifties to start his own central heating business. My mum had all her children born at home, on the settee. Dad was there for all the births and he delivered the last four, including me. There was a local midwife and a big support network of other women and it was all far more intuitive, more natural in a way, than it is now. Maybe it would be better to be like that but you can't turn back the clock, we are more conscious about all our natural functions now.'

Janet left home at sixteen, '. . . determined to get away from the claustrophobia of family life. I went to Rhodes, where I found work stripping and painting four-poster beds, the latest fad of the "artistes" who lived on the island, and as a nanny to a number of Greek families. Out of the frying pan into the fire. Looking back now I can see this as a contradiction, the same as I can see that I went into teaching because of the need to nurture, which I turned outward instead of inward. Being pregnant has helped to put all that in perspective.'

After a year in Greece Janet returned to Bolton and in one year knocked off her A levels, the equivalent to the HSC, a feat which for the average person takes at least two years. I tried living at home again but there was no place for me any longer so I took to the road and spent a year following the crops, picking potatoes, vegetables and fruit as they came into season. By then I had decided to teach so I spent the next three years at Elizabeth Gaskell College of Education, an all-women's college in Manchester. I enjoyed the learning but loathed the silly social restraints, having to be in by 11.00 pm and that sort of thing. But I stuck it out.'

This doesn't come as a surprise. Tenacity is the word which springs to mind as a first description of Janet. She is barely five feet tall (153 centimetres if you must) and although she doesn't look in the least like a terrier that is what she always makes me think of, because she is so tenacious. So emphatic. Looking you straight in the eye with an unwavering gaze. Even when she asks how you are it would be foolish to give a bland, polite reply. Janet is not interested in being merely sociable. And she is always so busy it makes mere mortals feel like wimps. Until the last month of her pregnancy she was teaching full time. Even now, with just ten days to go, she is still doing two days a week. But straight teaching would be too undemanding for Janet, she teaches handicapped kids, the majority with spina bifida and other neural tubular defects, as well as psychologically disturbed children. More than teaching the children, she helps the parents adjust to the difficulties that inevitably come from having an unusual child. This means home visits, which in turn means driving many hundreds of kilometres a week.

Work is far from all Janet does. She is a voracious reader. I have known her to have three books on the go at the one time, bounding from a historical biography to a psychology textbook to a classic Australian novel and back. She swims 1500 metres a day, lapping up and down in a neat rhythmic style, attends meetings of groups pushing for a Nuclear-Free Pacific, goes on frequent bushwalks in the Blue Mountains and takes weekly classes in Chinese language and culture. But she has paid a price for such a frontal attack on life.

'For five years, from when I was sixteen through to twenty-one, I was anorexic. And when I was thinking about having a baby I was anxious that being big, looking fat, would upset me. But it hasn't. Not at all. I have really enjoyed it. Loved it. Naturally I have had a few anxieties. Working with the kind of children I teach has made me far more aware than most people of what is involved in having a problem child; of the pressures that puts on the whole family. So early in my pregnancy I had a protein test which shows whether or not a woman is carrying a baby with a predisposition to spina bifida. I showed up in the normal range and although that doesn't totally rule out the possibilities of any problems I decided that if there is something wrong with my baby it will just be the luck of the draw and from this perspective recognised my anxiety as one all would-be mothers face. After I had crossed that admittedly huge barrier I became contented with myself and my pregnancy.'

As with everything Janet gives the impression of having thought this all through logically. It has been how she has approached her entire life so far. 'I left college with a teaching certificate but failed to complete the final, fourth year which would have given me my B.Ed., which had been my original intention, mostly because I'd had enough of the silly unnecessary rules and regulations. I taught in Manchester for two years choosing to work at a community school in a run-down area. I was very committed to the project. We opened at 7.00 in the morning and didn't close until 9.00 in the evening at the earliest. The children would have breakfast, lunch and an evening meal at the school. Their parents were either working, or if they were out of work they were down at the pub. In the evenings we ran courses for anyone who wanted to come. There was a tremendous feeling of community and of caring.

'At the time I was living in a shared house with a group of people one of whom was a woman with strong political and feminist ideologies who made a big impact of my life. She opened doors for me into new worlds, raised my consciousness and encouraged my growing confidence in myself and what I thought was right but until then hadn't been able to feel at ease with. But at the same time this was happening to me I was very drawn by my own beginnings and by trying to be what my parents wanted; I lived in a schizoid world.

'The result was that between the ages of eighteen and twenty-three I became engaged three times! Each time to a village bloke from my area. One was in the building trade, one worked in an electrical factory and one worked down the pits. Part of me was trying to conform. Dad and Mum had always pushed and encouraged me to go and get my degrees but I felt they also wanted me to retain my basic roots. Of course none of the engagements went on to a marriage. It would have been disastrous for those men as well as for me if they had. The men in that area do not want to marry self-achievers. And fortunately the greater part of me did not want to conform. As it is I am still good friends with them, they are all married and have families and have stayed close to the area where we grew up. They appear to be happy and no doubt look at my life as unsettled and in some ways not normal, and perhaps not nice.'

One of the ways in which Janet's life would be, in the eyes of many people, 'not nice' is that she and the father of her baby are not married and have no intention of being so. 'Because I find the ceremony so artificial.' But does she see the relationship as a lifetime commitment? There is a pause, a consideration is under way and then, 'No. I cannot perceive of anything as being forever. Though of course,' she laughs gently, 'this child is. Still, marriage is something which never enters my head. I feel confident and very okay about myself so I don't need a marriage to make me feel more secure. I've worked bloody hard at establishing my own emotional and psychological strength and a marriage wouldn't add to it. Perhaps it wouldn't detract either. It's simply a non-issue.'

But is it a non-issue with their families? 'With mine it is. The subject has never been raised. His mother would probably like him to get married, but probably not to me because I'm working class. All in all it's good to be over here away from them all. We've just come back from spending six weeks with them and it's great to be on our own again. A large family can be very overpowering. They still see me as the youngest member of the family even though I am now thirty-three and have spent almost half my life living away from home, so they felt it was their role to give me advice. No doubt most of it was good but my need for independence surfaced very strongly.

'My one regret about my family is that my mum died of cancer when she was fifty-four and I was twenty-five, so she won't see my baby. We had been through plenty of conflict over the years and we were just coming together again and getting a good relationship going when she died. That makes me sad because I am sure that relationship would have grown better and stronger. I had a very happy childhood and in one way I am still close to my dad who is now sixty-nine, though because of the pressure of working for himself he has become an alcoholic and his drinking gets between us. It's destroyed the stability of the family. But fortunately I can remember him from before when he used to tell us stories and organise treasure hunts. He was a great dad when I was little and that's been a good foundation for me as an adult woman and the way I relate to men.'

Janet and her partner have been in Australia for five years, they are both Australian citizens. 'When he said he was going to Australia and asked me to come with him I had to make a few big decisions. I was at a crossroads in my life. I had spent the previous four years going to night school four evenings a week to get my B.Ed. At the same time I was teaching full time in this extremely demanding situation as well as being very politically active, which meant chasing up and down the country to attend meetings and demonstrations. At almost the same time as he asked would I come to Australia I was offered a job as head of Language Development in the school. It was a choice between following my head or my heart. I had worked very, very hard to get to where I was and I didn't want to throw it all away, but at the same time I was very tired, exhausted really, and there was the challenge and excitement of a new country. So I told myself I would take a holiday in Australia and see how things worked out. So here I am. Pregnant and happy.'

*For the first time in my life
I can really love being on
my own and just sitting,
perhaps thinking, perhaps
just being.*

Janet found her considerable skills were much in demand in Australia and she quickly found work which paid a lot more than she would have received in Britain. Since making the move they have travelled quite a bit in eastern Australia and made long visits to the USA and Britain as well as the decision-making journey in India. They have developed friendships with a number of kindred spirits and a few months ago they moved into their own home in an inner-city suburb. Here Janet has spent the long hot nights, when she has found it impossible to get comfortable, working in the tiny gardens. 'A tropical one in front and an Australian bush one in the back. I have also knitted heaps of baby clothes and read. Usually I collapse into bed about 4.30 am.'

As self-aware as ever, she has kept a diary throughout her pregnancy. 'I won't read back through it until after the birth. Then I plan to keep a weekly diary of all that happens, including a photograph with each entry. Pregnancy has made me feel not more female but more feminine. More aware of how vulnerable we are to male power. I have felt a decrease in my own power. That's been hard to cope with on occasions. I remember one day when I was about seven months, I had this list of things I wanted to do which involved spending three hours in a hot car with my belly pushed against the steering wheel. Quite suddenly I realised I just couldn't do it all. The idea of not being able to do what I wanted to do and, worse than that, the recognition that this is how it will be on occasions from now on, more or less, for probably about twenty years was just so overpowering I sat down outside the greengrocer's and had a big cry. The poor greengrocer came out and gave me a peach and tried to calm me down but that only made it worse!

'But feelings like that have been rare, mostly it's been a great experience. I have become quite fascinated with other pregnant women and suddenly the world seems to be full of them. I can spot a pregnant woman a mile off and I will dawdle and wait for her to go by so that I can examine her. Often we exchange looks of intimate understanding. I think a pregnant woman is very voluptuous and sensual, not sexy, but immensely attractive. There's a group of women, all of us pregnant and all of us in our thirties who go to our local pool to swim. We all take our cozzies off in the shower and it's great. All those bodies ripe and ready to go. Also I find I notice little babies and I stand and stare at them and notice their perfect little fingernails and the fragile bloom on their skin and try to imagine all that growing inside me.

'I am really looking forward to it. We are going to classes together which are held at the Active Birth Centre at the Royal Women's Hospital. Last week the class was for the mothers only and we all took off our clothes and listened to each other's baby and everyone said how strong my baby's heart sounded and that made me feel very proud. Silly really! As if I was personally responsible for this strong heart, though in some ways I suppose I am.'

Janet's partner and two close women friends will be with her at the birth. 'Neither of the women have children of their own but one is very practical and the other is very spiritual so that between the three of them I think they will create the atmosphere I want my baby to be born into. I chose not to have a home birth because I have seen too many results of a difficult birth to be willing to take that risk. It's comforting to know that medical help is available if I should need it, though I don't anticipate that I will and I want to have as natural a delivery as I can.

'I recently saw slides of a birth at the class which in a way I wish I hadn't because it was staggering to see how much a woman's body opens up and for a few days I worried a lot about whether my body would be able to do that, but then I looked at all the women in the street with babies and I thought, well, if they survived so can I. I am expecting it to be painful, but not unbearably so. The centre allows a woman to give birth in the position in which she feels most comfortable and I think I shall have my baby squatting. It's how it feels most natural. It's how I work in the garden and having babies and digging in the soil, they seem interlinked.

'I think I shall be a good mother, of course I do. I have no fears about that. I realise I might be rather dominating but I think all my other interests and my work will make sure that I keep motherhood in perspective.' The baby's father is planning to give up full-time work and organise his professional life as a city planner on a job-sharing basis. 'That's so he can maximise his involvement with our baby. He is forty-nine and has been married and had children but not lived with them; the reasons for not doing this are complicated and far removed from our story together. He is very excited about the child in our life and sees it as the beginning of another experience together, and we've shared many.

'I realise that becoming a mother will have a big effect on the choices I can make, but at this stage I feel I can do anything and everything. So I am planning to do my Masters in Linguistics, which should take a year because it involves research for my thesis. And at the same time I'll work one day at the clinic as a special educator for handicapped children. We also have plans to travel around Australia in the near future and by the end of next year we would like to go and work in China, possibly in educational research.

'But I know through my work that kids are great modifiers and although we have a lot of plans we don't know yet how having a baby will affect them. Then of course there is the future decision about whether to have more children. I don't like the idea of single children. I'd have to decide within the next two years because I would want them close together in age so they would go through the various stages at the same time. But I am not thinking about all that just yet. I see a person's thirties as a pretty important time in their lives, a time of important decisions.

'Perhaps the only thing I am not looking forward to with much relish is this little thing in here being a teenager. I once shared a house with a couple who had a teenage son and daughter and it was horrendous. But that's a long way off and perhaps Jo will leave home at sixteen!'

Jo is their name for the imminent person. 'That's how it's been referred to all along, that way it can be girl or boy, Josephine or Joseph. We have more or less decided that if it is a girl we shall call her Hannah and if its a boy, Owen. A girl would take my family name and a boy would take his father's. We discovered this is the way it's done in China and it seemed like as good a solution as any. I have no preference for a boy or a girl, neither of us has.'

Janet is looking tired. She had another sleepless night last night. Because she is tiny the baby seems to be huge, to the extent that she is almost swallowed up by her belly. Her fingers are puffy, swollen and uncomfortable. 'The only time they go down is when I swim. I am still doing sixteen laps a day, that's as much as I can manage. I have kept very healthy. I'm a vegetarian and conscious of eating good, nutritious food. I shan't raise the baby as a vegetarian. That would be an imposition of my values. I won't cook meat but I'll have pre-cooked meat in the house and what is eaten elsewhere will be a personal decision.'

With only a very short time to go Janet is looking forward to it happening and being able to get back to her former good shape. 'I have always been sensitive to any underlying tensions or atmospheres and my pregnancy has intensified those perceptions. Also, being pregnant has made me quieter and more self-aware. For the first time in my life I can really love being on my own and just sitting, perhaps thinking, perhaps just being. But what I am really looking forward to is to be able to do the ironing without getting burn marks across my belly!'

Julie Agius

Julie sits curled up in a big chair. She is six and a half months pregnant, a little anxious that it doesn't show more, and radiates joy.

North Shore made me pregnant.' Julie Agius makes this bizarre statement, adding, 'Without GIFT I would still be a thirty-three-year-old infertile woman, cause unknown, longing to be a mother.'

North Shore is every Sydney-sider's familiar diminutive for the city's biggest and best known medical treatment centre, the Royal North Shore Hospital. GIFT is the acronym for Gamete Intra-Fallopian Transfer. This is a procedure by which human eggs are removed from the follicles during a laparoscopy. During the same operation these eggs are then transferred to the Fallopian tubes along with previously prepared sperm. This means that fertilisation takes place within the body.

It's a lateral development from the IVF procedure in which conjunction of the human egg and sperm takes place in a laboratory dish (in vitro) and the fertilised egg is then placed back in the woman's body. It's an interference with the natural process of procreation and as such poses a number of complex emotional, moral and legal questions. But for Julie none of them matter because, as she puts it, 'It's the gift of life.'

Outside it's a grey, wet, wintry day. Inside the home which Julie and her husband have lovingly renovated she sits curled up in a big chair near the slow combustion fire and caresses her two tiny chihuahau dogs, Chachi and Fonzie. She is six and a half months pregnant, a little anxious that it doesn't show more, and radiates joy. 'My husband tells me he thinks I look great, that pregnancy suits me. Before I became pregnant he used to say it didn't worry him, that he married me because he loved me and my not being able to have children didn't affect that. But I used to think, how can he love me, I'm not a full woman, if he'd married some other woman he'd have six children by now. All our friends and relatives had children and I was so jealous I didn't even want to visit them. My husband would come home and tell me about another friend, or perhaps one of his brothers who'd had a baby and I'd see the excitement on his face and hate it. Being infertile can make you very bitter. I'm fairly easygoing but during the years we were trying to have a baby I must have been a horrible person to live with. Now I'm just so happy and am longing for it to be born.'

For Julie not to be a mother or not to be married had been unimaginable ever since she was a teenager. 'I started a glory box when I was only fourteen! By then I was going out with a boy a year or so older than me. We went steady for five years. Mum and Dad didn't like it, they thought I should play the field, but it was more or less accepted that one day we would get married. In the end we both decided that we were too young. But during those years I put together a collection of pots and pans, tablecloths, napkins and tizzy negligees. When I went through them, years later, I couldn't believe how outrageous the negligees were, all pompoms and yuk!'

Julie left school at fifteen and went to work as a dressmaker for a large manufacturer of women's clothing. She spent one day a week at technical college studying design. 'I enjoyed the work, I've always loved sewing, but after three years at it I'd had enough of being stuck inside and I had finished my tech course so I went to work in one of the Jeans Junction outlets. I stayed with them for five years, ending up as a manager. During that time I broke up with my first boyfriend and within eighteen months I was married.'

Her husband worked in a menswear shop near the shop Julie managed. 'He was a really nice guy but as my dad always said, he was not really the marrying kind, more of a bachelor. Perhaps I wouldn't have married him if I hadn't gone overseas on holiday with my dad for three months when I was still madly in love with him. I missed him so much I could hardly wait to get back home and get married. It would have been better if we had lived together and I could have got him out of my system, but that's more than ten years ago and it wasn't so acceptable then. Mum and Dad wouldn't have approved. Mind you, my younger sister lives with her boyfriend now. In a way older brothers and sisters clear the path for the younger ones.

'I really knew after only a few months that I had made a mistake. He didn't want children and I did. He didn't think of marriage in the same way I did. He only wanted us to go out and have a good time and I saw marriage as something far more serious and important than that. We were just very different from each other. But I hung in there for a couple of years before I admitted first to myself, then to him and then to other people that it wasn't any good. I felt I owed it to other people to make it work, especially my parents and his parents. I thought of all the money my dad had spent on the wedding.'

When the break finally came Julie moved back home for a year. 'I felt as though I had failed. I've always had a bit of a problem with confidence. Probably because of my hand.' Julie's left arm finishes in a neat stump rather than a hand. But it's not in the least visually offensive, and to the suggestion that perhaps it was just as well she had one slight physical defect because being so attractive she might otherwise bring down the wrath of the gods for being too perfect she says that's just the sort of remark her mother would make. 'But then Mum is biased!' she adds, smiling.

'I suppose I am attractive. I know I try. But still when people look at me I can't stop myself wondering whether they are thinking, she looks attractive, or poor thing. And I can't bear the idea of people feeling sorry for me. I don't feel in the least sorry for myself.' Though she does have some distressing memories.

'One time in particular that I remember vividly was when I was at primary school. There was an end-of-term concert coming up and one of the Sisters wanted me to be the main fairy, who was called the Shamrock Fairy. You can imagine how delighted I was! She came around to see Mum and told her, "We would like Julie to be the Shamrock Fairy, because she is so pretty with her blonde curly hair, but we have to work out some way to hide her hand." Mum was livid. She told the Sister, "if that's what you want then my daughter won't be your Shamrock Fairy." I had wanted to be that fairy so badly, it broke my heart. I was still in the play, but only as one of the ordinary fairies and that wasn't the same. Things like that are important at that age.

'Mum and Dad discussed the idea of me having an artificial hand but they were told that couldn't be done until I had stopped growing and by then I didn't want it. If people don't like me the way I am I really don't care. Mum was always worried that I would have trouble meeting boys but I didn't. I always had a boyfriend and then later on a husband. In fact I've always needed that. Unless I am with someone I feel really isolated. I think this is part of the insecurity thing and that it comes from my hand being like this. But none of it matters because I don't regret anything and I know I'm a stronger person for it.'

Julie met her second husband at the beach. 'A friend introduced us. It took him a month to get up the courage to ask me out, but I knew that he would. Women know that sort of thing, don't you think? We started living together, by then my parents had adjusted to the idea, and I began to think about having children. I'd been on the pill for about eight years and though I had always taken regular breaks I didn't feel happy about staying on it. I'd never really liked it. I know it's the safest, easiest contraceptive but I don't think it can be all that good for you. Also I think I felt the time was right, for me anyway, to start a family.'

Julie told her partner, 'I'm not going to take the pill any more. I want to become pregnant. But this is my choice and if I do have a baby then you don't have to stay around if you don't want to. Mind you, I have to admit that I knew he would stay. He has too many morals to leave a woman in the lurch. And I wanted him to stay. But having a baby was my first priority.

'I don't know whether every woman feels like this but in the back of my mind I had always wondered whether or not I would be able to have a baby.' After nine months Julie was doing more than just wondering. 'In the beginning I wasn't particularly concerned, we were just having a good time. And there was no reason for me to be anxious because I'd always had regular periods and no gynaecological problems.' But when after nine months she still hadn't fallen pregnant that vague notion she'd always had started to become more insistent.

What finally drove Julie to her family doctor was that she developed a persistent discharge. 'The pap smear he sent off to the pathology lab showed pre-cancerous cells. It was panic stations. I had to go to North Shore for further tests. Mum couldn't come with me, she gets too upset, so Dad came. I wasn't yet married again. In the end I was given the all-clear, which was an enormous relief, but for some reason the scare made me even more determined to have a baby and when I told them that I had been trying for almost a year they suggested I have some further examinations and tests. That was the beginning of a five-year horror stretch. Even now I can sometimes hardly believe it's over. I wake up with a start thinking, I must get to the hospital for my blood test. My body ceased to belong to me. It belonged to the hospital and to all the doctors. I visited that many doctors I have lost count.'

The first procedure Julie had to follow was to keep accurate daily recordings of her vaginal temperature. 'It was essential that this was taken first thing in the morning, as soon as I woke up. I couldn't talk or move or hardly breathe before taking my temperature for three minutes.' It was also necessary for Julie's partner to have a sperm test. 'I think all men get a bit funny about this. For a man to be infertile is just as bad as it is for a woman. Your fertility has to do with your sexuality. The two things are bound together in your head. To be infertile is to be worthless, really it's as bad as that. You feel worthless and alone. He was great about taking the test and I was as delighted as he was when it came back positive. Funny thing is I felt that if one of us was going to be infertile it was better that it was me. Perhaps because I had some idea about what I would have to go through if I wanted to go on and try to have a baby and I can't imagine any man doing that, can you ? So I said to him, "You're lucky, that's all you've got to do." But of course that's not quite true, and through it all he has been very, very supportive. He never once complained.'

So supportive that even though her partner now knew that Julie was infertile, he proposed to her. 'Because my first marriage had not been in a church but in front of a celebrant, we were able to be married in the church where my parents were married and that was terrific. Perhaps it was some small consolation to my husband's family. They never said anything, but I know they didn't approve. Not only do I have a hand missing, but I had been married before and worst of all I was infertile. His family are Maltese and Catholic. He is the youngest of seven brothers and sisters, all of whom have families. Right from the start of our

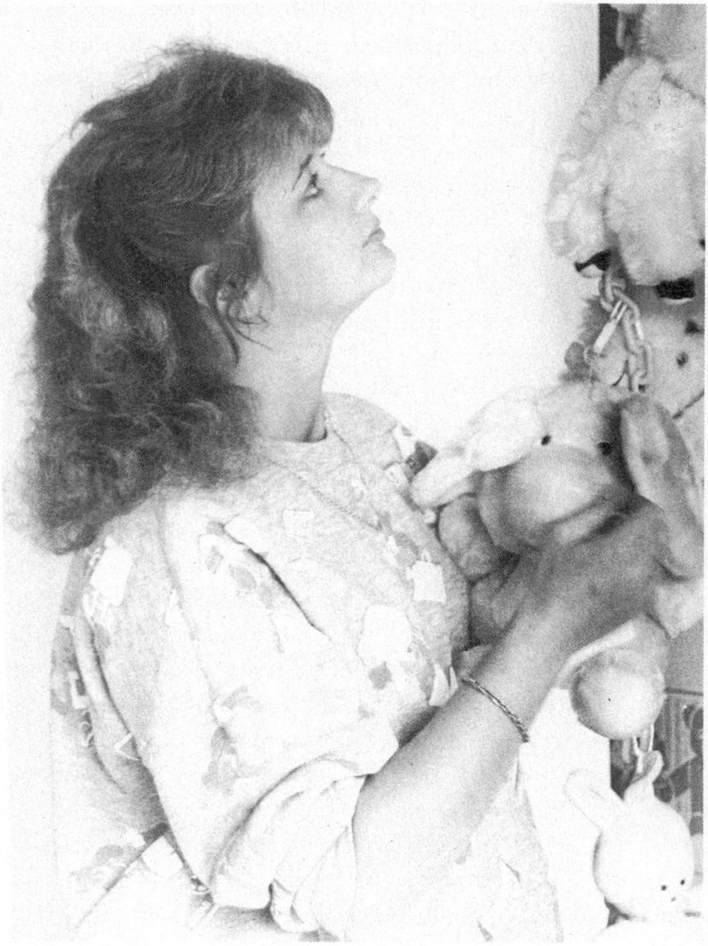

I'll never forget what she said: 'Mrs Agius, you're pregnant.' And between my tears I kept asking her over and over again, 'Are you sure?'

married life he told me that he had married me because he loved me and that my not being able to have children didn't make him love me less. But also right from the start I was determined we would have children.'

The next test was to find out whether the sperm, once deposited in Julie's vagina, were able to swim up into the uterus, or whether her secretions killed them off before they had the chance of fertilising an egg. 'We had to have intercourse at 4.00 in the morning. That meant setting the alarm clock and then making love no matter how we felt. Even when you love someone it's very off-putting *having* to make love. Then, without having a shower, that was the worst part, I had to go into the hospital at 8.00 in the morning to have an internal examination. I had a woman doctor at this time. You would think that she would have some understanding of what it was like to be continually poked and prodded but she was rougher than all the men. She told me the sperm were getting through all right but still nothing was happening, so she suggested that I try a course of fertility drugs. She also said that because there didn't seem to be anything physically wrong with me, my tubes weren't blocked, my ovaries were functioning normally, that she was sure that with the pills I would be pregnant within a couple of months.

'Of course I was delighted. I gave up my full-time job because visiting the hospital took up so much time, an hour each way. And I wanted to concentrate on getting this baby under way. I felt that it was important to be fit and not to be tired. This was all more important than work. I've never had any trouble finding work. I don't believe people who say they can't get work. There's plenty of work for people who really want it. I've only ever once not been accepted for a job and I've never forgotten it.

'Whenever I went for a job interview I didn't let them see that I have only one hand. You get very good at being able to disguise and hide the fact. Then when they would ring and tell me I had been accepted I would say, "Well, there is just one small thing I didn't tell you at the interview," and tell them about my hand. It never made any difference except on this one occasion. I had applied for a job at a big jewellers and they told me I had the job and then when I told them about my hand they came up with all these excuses about why it wouldn't be possible for me to do the work. Really what they were saying was that they thought customers would be put off. I was terribly upset. But it was the only time.'

Julie took a casual job as a receptionist in a squash centre and while continuing with the constant blood and urine tests, the ultrasounds and the internal examinations, as well as keeping a daily temperature record, she began the course of fertility drugs. These had no side effects but she was told that she might have a multiple birth. 'That didn't worry me at all. I was prepared for anything! All that mattered was having a baby. Other women have said to me that they wouldn't be willing to go through what I went through in order to become pregnant. But every woman who has ever said that to me already has children and it's easy to say that when you've never been faced with the prospect of being childless.'

This prospect loomed larger and larger when even on the fertility drug Julie still failed to become pregnant. 'It was then that I heard about another doctor who might be able to help. The sister of the woman who made my wedding dress had been trying for twelve years before she became pregnant. She gave me the name of the doctor who had done it for her. He had a clinic in the city so I travelled in there every morning for more tests and examinations. This doctor ran an AIH program. AIH stands for Artificial Insemination by Husband. It's another spin-off from the IVF procedure, and involves the husband's sperm being deposited, artificially, directly into the uterus.

'I'll never forget the very first time I underwent the AIH procedure. It has to be timed to coincide very, very accurately with ovulation, so I had to keep extremely accurate temperature charts as well as give daily blood samples. We had to ring up every afternoon at 4.00 pm to check from the tests they had made on my blood where I was exactly in my menstrual cycle and my husband had to be ready, wherever he was, to drop everything and race in to give sperm. He is a contract driver with a courier company and it was just as well that he had a two-way radio in the truck! He was in constant communication with his base and a couple of the girls there knew what we were trying to do and were very supportive.

'The first time they told me I was just about to ovulate and should come in immediately, I got on the phone to him and he rushed over to the hospital and gave his sperm ready for the big party! All the staff, the nurses in particular, were wonderful. I can't say enough about how wonderful they were. They said things like, "Your husband's specimen is great. They are just jumping off the dish they are so ready to go!" My husband sat there beside me and they injected the sperm up into my uterus, not very comfortable, and I had an instantaneous bad reaction. I felt as though I was going to vomit or have diarrhoea or do both at the same time. They kept telling me, "You have to lie still for at least twenty minutes." But it wasn't possible. I had to get up. Needless to say that one didn't work and that meant waiting another month for the next ovulation to occur before we could try again. But before then they decided that they would treat my husband's sperm even more thoroughly before injecting them into me, hoping that this would stop my violent reaction, which thankfully it did.

'Occasionally all this does have its funny side. I remember one time going in there with my husband and lying on my back with my legs up. While the doctor did the procedure he chatted away about his weekend on his boat and when he finished he said, "All right, you can get up now," and he went on chatting to my husband. But I couldn't get up. I still had that metal clamp up inside me. I lay there, too embarrassed to say anything, while he chatted on. He looked down at me again and repeated, "You can get up now." I managed to say, "No I can't," and gestured to my insides. He looked a bit puzzled for a moment, then he realised and said, "Oh sorry," and took the thing out. Afterwards it's funny but at the time it's embarrassing.

'It was this doctor who sent me for the worst test I've ever had. Even if it meant not having a baby I would never have that test again. It was so painful. Fortunately my husband was with me. That morning when he said he was coming I said, "No I'll be all right on my own." Every time he took time off work to come with me it meant he lost money. But I was very glad he came with me this time. He told me later that he had some idea of how bad it was going to be because the wife of one of his workmates had been through it. That was why he decided to come.

'The test was done at a clinic and involved injecting dye into my Fallopian tubes, which made it possible to view them on an X-ray and confirm that there was no blockage. I wasn't given anything to ease the pain or make me relax a little. I was told the test would take fifteen minutes but it took an hour. They said it would feel like a small period cramp. Well, my god. I could feel the perspiration rolling off me. When they told me to hold my breath while they took the X-rays I thought I would scream. And when it was all over and I sat up I nearly passed out. My husband was waiting in the car. He took one look at me and didn't say a word. I just burst into tears.

'I don't consider myself a chicken when it comes to pain but that was something I'll remember for the rest of my life. When I went back to the doctor for the results he said something like, "Not a very pleasant test is it?" and I thought, how would you know? He told me the X-ray showed a possible blockage and I went in for my third laparoscopy. The laparoscopy could find no blockage and the doctor then told me, "We can't find any reason for your infertility. You are what we describe as Cause Unknown. Fertilisation occurs because of a chain of events. If one link in that chain is broken then fertilisation cannot occur. In your case we don't know which link is broken, so we can't mend it." That is the worst part, the not knowing. Every time I had a test or underwent a procedure I would try to think positively and tell myself, "This is it, this time we'll crack it." But we never did and I remain to this day Cause Unknown.

'The doctor finally told me, "We've done everything we can do, tried everything we can. All I can suggest is that you try to get on an IVF program." So I went along to the North Shore.' Here Julie was told that the demand for IVF was so great (at that time Royal North Shore was the only hospital in New South Wales with such a program) that there was a two- to three-year waiting list.

'I didn't want to wait that long before starting a family so at the same time as my name went on the IVF list I began to think about adoption. My husband's first reaction to that was, "No way. If we can't have our own we won't have any." But I think my older brother, who already had a daughter of his own, took him aside and said, "You may not want to adopt but have you thought about what Julie wants and what she has already been through?" Gradually he accepted the idea. He took time off work to come to adoption seminars and we put our name into Youth and Community Services' — usually called YACS.

'Luckily by this time we were in our own home. You have to be in your own home before YACS will consider you as adoptive parents. We wanted to adopt from overseas, because that is quicker, even though we were told it might still take up to two years. We became particularly interested in getting a baby from Chile. I thought a baby from Sri Lanka would also be nice. But we talked about the problems of having a dark-skinned child. I think it would be more difficult for them to get a fair go. Though I have always stuck up for myself and hopefully I'll teach my child to do the same. We were also a bit worried about what our relatives and friends would think. YACS came and did their home study to see whether we would make suitable parents. That was more than six months ago and we still haven't heard from them!'

Fortunately, while she waited for YACS to come good she received a letter from the IVF clinic at the Royal North Shore

Hospital. 'Because I had no apparent problems with either my uterus or my tubes they told me I was a candidate for GIFT, and because by then other hospitals in Sydney had started their own IVF programs the waiting list was shortened to six months. So I started on the old daily routine of blood samples and temperature taking. Then they phoned to say the list was down to three months and that I should be ready to come in at a moment's notice. I gave in my notice at the video and TV sales and hire place where I was working. They wanted me to stay on but I wanted to put all my energy where it was needed. I couldn't help getting very excited again. This up and down of your emotions is very exhausting. You live in a constant state of nervous tension.

'A week before Christmas they told me there was room for me in the next intake just as long as I ovulated on time. I thought, wow, what a Christmas present! But it wasn't to be. I ovulated later than expected, perhaps it was all the excitement, on the twenty-second, the day they shut down for the Christmas holiday. All we could do was wait for my next ovulation.'

But meantime, more good fortune, Julie and her husband went along to his company's Christmas party and won first prize in a raffle — a week's holiday for two, all expenses paid, on Queensland's Gold Coast. 'We couldn't take it then of course, because we had to keep running in and out to the hospital with blood and temperature charts!'

The next month came around and just prior to her expected ovulation Julie was given a series of injections of a fertility drug. 'Timing was so vital that the last injection was given at 12.00 midnight the morning before my ovulation.' Everything ran smoothly. An ultrasound was taken which showed that Julie's follicles contained five eggs. '"Nice eggs" is how the doctor described them. He said they were all two millimetres big and he seemed pleased with that.' Her husband produced his sperm. D-day or perhaps more accurately B-day had arrived. Julie went into surgery and here the doctor, in a procedure which rivals normal conception in its miraculousness, performed a laparoscopy during which he moved Julie's eggs into her Fallopian tubes and then introduced her husband's sperm into the same receptive environment.

'When I came round from the anaesthetic the doctor told me that he had placed four eggs in position, two on each side and that he was very hopeful that they would be fertilised. He was as excited as us. The operation took place on the twenty-first of January. By the eighth of February, when my next period was due, I would know whether or not the operation was successful. All we could do was wait, so we decided to take the holiday we had won.

'It wasn't exactly a second honeymoon! We were told not to make love and not to lie in the sun, so all we could do was eat! We'd wander around the shops and stop for a snack. The worst thing was that the day before we went away my budgie, Ralf, died, and it was my fault. I hadn't wanted to leave him in the house by himself. I thought he would be lonely. So I insisted on driving him across to my sister's place. It was one of those terrible hot January days and travelling in the car the heat killed him. I was that upset. I'd had him since he was an egg. He was only a little over a year old but I had taught him to speak and he was so gentle and intelligent.'

Julie paused in memory of her bird. Her two dogs, which had remained asleep on her lap throughout our conversation, dreamed on. 'If anything happened to them I don't know what I'd do. Fonzie is nine and Chachi is seven and they have been through everything with me. People tell me that they have heard of dogs being so jealous when a baby is born that they have savaged the child. My dogs wouldn't do that and won't get the opportunity anyway.'

The time for Julie's period came and went. 'We tried not to get too excited but after a couple of days we went to the chemist and bought one of those predictor kits, which showed up positive. Straight away my husband was on the phone to our families and friends telling them I was pregnant! We decided that even though we hadn't had our full holiday we would go back home so we could visit the hospital. The very first thing I did when we arrived home was to phone the hospital and tell them I had used a predictor kit and that it had showed positive. The nurse said, "They aren't 100 per cent reliable, so you come in and have a test tomorrow."

'I went in, had the test and the nurse said, "We'll phone you at home with the results at 4.00 this afternoon, will you be there?" Would I be there! I went straight home and waited and waited and waited for the phone to ring and when it did I'll never forget what she said: "Mrs Agius, you're pregnant." And between my tears I kept asking her over and over again, "Are you sure?" She said, "Yes, I'm sure," and finally I believed her. Then I rang my husband's office and asked the telephonist to pass on this message to my husband: 'the test is positive". She told all the girls in the office and I could hear them all calling out, "Congratulations Julie!" My husband came home as soon as he got the message and, well, if you could have seen his face; it might well be true that he would have gone on loving me whether or not I had our baby but it's for sure that he loves me now I'm having it!

'I still can hardly believe it even though I can feel him kicking. I feel I am having a boy even though I would prefer a girl just in case I can only have one. And I think my father would like a grandson too. But really I am so thankful that I am having one at all that I don't mind which it is as long as it is healthy. I've been very well all through. I had a bit of morning sickness, except it came in the afternoon, but other than that, nothing. And I feel very well. In the beginning I was careful with myself. There is a higher rate of miscarriage among IVF and GIFT babies and at eight weeks I had my first ultrasound to make sure the baby was properly attached to the uterus wall and that it was developing normally. That was when they told me that I was having just one baby. That was a relief, although I would have been happy to have more, just as long as I had a baby.'

And what about the fifth egg she had produced, what has

happened to that? 'That's gone into the freezer! It will stay there until I decide what I want to do with it. Once a year I have to tell them to go on keeping it for me. I shall probably do that because it's good to know it's there as a backup should something go wrong. When you have been through what I have you want to keep as many options open as possible. If I haven't used it in ten years they will throw it out.' Another bizarre concept and perhaps a worry to a Catholic couple?

'Not at all. I know there are people who object to IVF and therefore to AIH and GIFT on religious grounds. But I disagree with the Pope's ruling on this and I don't feel this makes me less than a good Catholic. How can he condemn us when all we are trying to do is to create a life? We are two people who love each other and want a child together, so how can that be wrong? I don't have the slightest feeling of guilt and I shall tell my child how he was conceived and will bring him up in the Catholic Church. I have been told that one of the reasons why the Pope objects to this form of conception is that it obviously involves masturbation. Well, I don't think it's what you do it's why you do it that you should be judged by. It's not as though my husband was masturbating over pornographic movies or pictures. He did it so that we could have a baby.

'Yes, there have been times when I have thought God has not done the right thing by me. Everyone feels sorry for themselves, sometime, don't you think? At times I have thought, first of all you only give me one hand and then you make it impossible for me to have a baby without going through all this. You've taken away my womanhood. That's how being infertile makes you feel. After all, a woman's purpose is to bear children. That's what we are put here on this earth for.

'I think if you didn't have children then when you got older you'd be pretty lonely, and although we would eventually have been able to adopt a baby I wanted the experience of being pregnant.

'I've had to struggle to regain what almost all women are born with. I have struggled and I've come through and I am glad, very glad, and I don't feel I have done anything wrong. Not at all. I've told Him that. I suppose I must believe in a personal god otherwise I wouldn't have these conversations with Him. I also believe that there is a heaven and when I die I shall probably go there because I haven't been too bad!

'Perhaps it was just my turn to have these difficulties. It has been good in a way because if things are a little bit harder you have to work a bit more to make them come good, don't you think? I certainly have. At the beginning of this marriage things were pretty rocky. Partly because I thought I had failed before and partly because I was frightened of getting too close in case I failed again. Well, all that we have been through has really cemented our relationship. So it's had its good side. We have had to fight for a lot of what we have, including this baby, and it has made us appreciate everything a whole lot more.'

Julie and her husband are preparing for the new arrival. 'Now when I go shopping I don't have to steer clear of the baby departments and I think, where do I begin! I am sewing all the time. I've never sewn so much. We go to birth classes together and my husband is as excited as I am when we see our baby on the ultrasound or feel it kick. A friend is having a baby and when my husband asked the father what doctor his wife was under he didn't even know. My husband was amazed at that and said, "He doesn't know what he's missing." He comes to all the consultations and wants to be present at the birth. I am going to have as natural a delivery as possible. We have heard from other couples that once the head is out the doctor allows the husband to take over the delivery. I asked him whether he would like to do that and my husband said, "You bet."'

Julie is not planning on going back to work. 'Not unless I need to make ends meet. My mum never worked, she was always there when I came home from school. Other kids' mothers weren't and I always felt sorry for them and glad that my mum was. I am reading everything I can find about pregnancy and birth and new babies and breastfeeding and nutrition and exercise and the whole thing. It's so exciting. Do you want to see his room?'

On the way out we stop off in the nursery. Already it's full of the clutter of early motherhood. There's a cot and toys and nappies and tiny clothes (can a human being ever be that small?). The wall is decorated with a coloured frieze of teddy bears and I comment on a bright green ceramic bear which stands as a lamp base. 'I made that. I do a lot of ceramics. So does my husband. He did this elephant.' White with gold-coloured tusks and upraised trunk it stood, half a metre tall, silently trumpeting in the corner of the sitting room.

Whether Julie's baby is a boy, to be called either Jacob or Lucas, or a girl, to be called Carlie ('a combination of mine and my husband's names'), it's more than likely that it will be creative, determined and attractive. It's absolutely certain that it will be wanted and loved. What greater heritage could a human being have, no matter how it was conceived?

Jenny Giannikouris

I think of the baby as a boy. I don't know why. But I shall love him whichever he is and the most important thing is that he is healthy.

Jenny Giannikouris appears much older than she really is, but this is not surprising, because for a young woman of only just twenty she has packed in a great deal of experience. Right now she is living in a hostel for unmarried pregnant women and is in the final anxious countdown — only four days to go!

'I'm not really frightened. Well, I suppose I am a bit, that I won't be able to handle the pain. I don't want it to go on for hours and hours. I tell myself other women do it so I can too, it's just that I haven't done it before so that's what's scary.' Odd to be scared of that when she has survived so much that would terrify most of us! (This is something I have often noticed before in women, that they are unaware of what they have sustained, endured or created until it is pointed out to them, and then they say, 'Oh yes but . . .' minimising, almost trivialising their abilities.)

Jenny has taken firm control of the situation, directing me through the killer traffic on Parramatta Road, via short-cut back streets to a parking station, and then through the equally daunting human traffic in the gigantic Westfield Shopping Centre to a coffee house with harsh lights and horrendous musak. I need a coffee to help me recover from it all but Jenny, urban chick that she is, is totally at ease, sitting well back on a hard chair and pressing down on her baby, who is kicking uncomfortably up against her breasts.

I ask her how long she has been staying in the hostel. 'Three months. My aunty's a social worker and she got me in there. It's good because Mum's place is only a couple of streets away so I can go and see her during the day when he's at work.' He? 'Her husband.' You don't get on? 'You could say that. Actually, I can't stand him. And he can't stand me. He's the reason I left home when I was seventeen. He chucked me out.'

Jenny's father was killed in a car accident when she was eight. 'I still miss him. Sometimes I even cry for him. He and Mum came here together from Greece when they were both in their early twenties. I was born in Sydney and my little sister was born seven years later, so she was only a baby when Dad died. He had worked as a cleaner and Mum worked as a kichenhand in a big hospital.

'Mum married again when I was eleven. He's also Greek. He works as a printer. He and I never liked each other. You know what I hate the most? It's when he tries. That just turns me up. Mostly he treated me like some sort of slave, "Fetch this, fetch that" — an ashtray or a drink, or change the channels. Too lazy to do it himself. Has to show he's the man and he's in charge. I couldn't stand it. So I didn't listen to him and we were always fighting.

'I left school at the end of Year 10, when I was sixteen, and I did a secretarial course. But all that sitting on your bottom, I couldn't stand it. I like to be moving about. So when I quit that was the reason for another fight and he said I should leave. Mum couldn't say anything, how could she? The man's the boss of the house, even though she owns the place.

'I was seventeen. I didn't have anywhere to go. I went and stayed with this man I'd been going with for six months. One night he took me to a strip show up the Cross and I thought, I wouldn't mind doing this. So I went and talked to the boss and got the job. I enjoyed the work. It was a fantasy of mine, taking my clothes off in front of a lot of men. There wasn't any more to it than that. I had plenty of offers to have sex with men but I didn't want to take the risk and anyway I was making enough money stripping.

'I told Mum what I was doing. She wasn't too worried about the stripping, more about the drug scene up there. But I never got involved in that either. I could see what it did to all those who were on it. I could always tell when they were on something. I'd rush upstairs to change between shows and find girls with needles sticking out of their arms. It made me feel sick. Yes, sure it was a tough life but I learnt a lot about men. It put me off them a bit. Some of them who came into the shows I'd see during the day with their wives and I'd think, they're married, why are they coming to see me take my clothes off? Dirty old men. And I'd wonder if their wives knew. But mostly it's just young men who come in with their mates for a bit of a laugh and a good time. The girls who were doing stuff, they never had any money, they spent it all on drugs. But I did it for the money, to save it and get out of there. I lived on top of the club, which was cheap, and I did four shows a night, six nights a week and saved a lot. The boss was Greek. Even though he drove around in a big flash car and had plenty of money he never behaved like he was any different from us. He was very good with the girls, especially those on drugs, he'd talk to them and even loan them money. I worked there for a bit over a year and in that time I saved enough money to buy some really good furniture so I took a lease on a place on my own in Coogee and then I found work there in an ice-cream parlour.'

Jenny worked at the parlour for a year, during which time she started dating a young man who worked as a DJ. 'I told him about my past but he just said to put all that behind me. We were talking about getting married and had even become engaged when I found I was pregnant. I've never really used contraception properly. I tried the pill but I kept forgetting to take it. I've had quite a lot of pelvic infection, which has probably stopped me getting pregnant before, but the longer I went on without getting pregnant the more slack I got about taking the pill. And then it happened. I didn't mind at all. I definitely didn't want an abortion. But my boyfriend freaked out. He's twenty-two and I think it was the idea of all that responsibility he couldn't handle. So he left me when I was three months gone. My lease ran out on the flat, I knew I wouldn't be able to go on working right till the baby was born so I moved back in with Mum.

'She was fine about the baby. She said if I was happy then it was okay with her. She's great, Mum. We're like sisters, or good mates, more than mother and daughter. She's only forty-three. She has fights with her husband, but nothing too bad, they sort of get along. She's been through a lot and I know it hasn't been easy for her. Two years ago she had cancer and had a leg amputated. I think it was probably brought on by all the upset when Dad died and then me leaving home and all that. But she's fine now. She has an artificial leg and it's so good she wears skirts and stockings and people don't even notice it.

'But of course he wasn't too pleased, her husband. Oh boy. I couldn't stay with them, the atmosphere was too bad, so I moved about a lot sleeping at friend's places and then my aunty found me the hostel just around the corner from Mum's and I moved in there. It's okay. There are about a dozen girls, all pregnant and unmarried. The youngest is fourteen. We don't talk to each other about our past or what we plan to do in the future. That's what the nuns are there for, the girls talk to them. I suppose some of the girls will put their babies up for adoption. But that was never something I thought about.

'I've always wanted to have a baby. When I thought about it I always imagined I would be married before I had a baby but that isn't the way it worked out. Life is like that. The unexpected happens. When I was first pregnant and my boyfriend was so against it and wanted me to have an abortion I went so far as to make an appointment at a hospital to have one but I didn't go along, because I knew I wanted to keep it.

'Then he left me and I went through a stage of worrying about whether I could support myself and a baby without the father. I decided I can. I know I can. That's what I want to do and I thought I would be better off without him if it wasn't what he wanted. I love little kids. Look at that one there!' Jenny points out a toddler in an orange jumpsuit with "Hot Tod" written in large letters on the back. She smiles with delight. 'Isn't he just great! Since I've been pregnant I've noticed how many babies there are around. It's as if the world is full of them. I love going into baby clothes shops. Recently I bought a pram for him. It was great fun. I brought it back on the train, all collapsed up, but when I got off the train this end it was too heavy to carry like that so I unfolded it and pushed it home. I saw quite a few of my friends on the way and they all rushed up to look inside because they thought I'd had him already!

'I think of the baby as a boy. I have ever since I knew I was pregnant. I don't know why. He just feels like he's a boy. I hope he is because I prefer boys. You can take them to the park and play ball with them, not sit inside dressing dollies. I've never been one for staying indoors. But I shall love him whichever he is and the most important thing is that he is healthy.'

A month ago Jenny's boyfriend reappeared. 'He apologised for leaving me. He said he wanted us to have the baby together and we had a long, serious talk about our future, the three of us. I understand why he panicked and left and I think it took a lot of

I've always wanted to have a baby. When I thought about it I always imagined I would be married before I had a baby but that isn't the way it worked out. Life is like that. The unexpected happens.

courage to come back. I never stopped loving him but I put it on the line what I would expect from him if he wanted to be the baby's father. At first I was worried he might just have come back to use me for sex but we have talked honestly with one another and I feel good about us. He wants to be there when the baby is born and then we'll find a place together. We're going to take it all one step at a time. We're not going to rush into things like getting married. There will be time for that later when everything settles down. I know he loves me but he is scared about how he will feel as a parent. He hasn't told his parents yet. They are separated. His father is Greek and his mother is Australian and she doesn't like me because she knows I've worked up the

Cross. We've decided that if he is a boy we'll call him Theo and if he is a girl then my boyfriend gets to choose the name. He would prefer a girl. I like the name Vanessa but it will be up to him. I want something unusual, not a common name.'

Jenny has been well all through her pregnancy. 'I gave up smoking at three months and I've only just started again in this last fortnight. I think it's nerves. I want to have it as naturally as possible with maybe just a whiff of gas but definitely no epidural. I've been to classes at the hospital where I am going for the delivery. My boyfriend hasn't been able to come because of the hours he works. My little sister is really happy about it. She surprised me the other day when she suddenly said, "Did you know your cervix is going to open up ten centimetres!" It must have been something she learnt about in PD at school.'

We order some sandwiches and more drinks and Jenny talks to the waitress in Greek. 'I worked here for a couple of months when I moved back to Mum's. Everyone here is Greek. It helps when you are looking for work if you speak the language. We grew up talking Greek at home and I still speak it all the time with Mum and my sister. My boyfriend doesn't speak it but I'd like my baby to learn it. I'd also like him to learn good manners, to be kind and polite and to have what I didn't have. I want him to be happy and feel loved and secure.

'I want to do a correspondence course while the baby is young. When he goes to kindy I want to go into catering and restaurant management. That's the business I enjoy the most. I like meeting people. I'd like to run a place like this.' The cafe is full of shoppers resting between forays into the crowded shops. 'I also want to work to keep my independence. My boyfriend and I are going to try to make a go of it. We're happy together and we want to go for it. But if it doesn't last and I have to manage on my own, well, I feel I could do that too. After all, Mum did it for years.

'I certainly don't want another baby for some time. I'd like to be married before I have another one. And I know my boyfriend doesn't want any more just yet either. He says he is going to make sure I take the pill by giving it to me himself every day at breakfast! Right now all I want is for it to happen so I can get back into my tight, size ten jeans!'

STARTING OUT

Trish

Pamela Wright

Georgene Hughes

Brenda

Trish

'Mum, how old was I when you started back at work?' Zara asked a few years ago. We were heavily embroiled in the horrors of the teenage years. She was wagging school for the day, on the pretence of having what she called a heavy cold and, still unwashed, uncombed and in her pyjamas, she had spent the morning slumped in front of the television.

A discussion about the merits and otherwise of mothers working outside the home had come up on *The Donahue Show*. It irritated the hell out of me that she could be so slack as not to go to school just because she had what I dismissed as a slight sniffle. I was trying to write and had shut the door to my office, but it had been impossible to soundproof myself from slick television journalese and its superficial treatment of questions that most women can barely face answering in their own hearts, let alone before a man, a large audience and array of cameras.

All this had made me ratty. So without looking up I said, 'Let me think; you were born at 2.10 in the afternoon and that evening I was on the phone to set up a couple of interviews for the BBC. So I guess you would have been about five hours old'. I glanced up at her and was gratified to see that my reply had given her the shock which was intended! She scowled and slobbed off to listen to the less threatening replies given by the frighteningly glossy mothers of America. And I tried, guiltily, to return to my writing.

What I had told her was true. I also made several other phone calls during the three days I was in hospital, setting up interviews and tracking down research material. So in a way I never 'went back to work' because I never left it. 'My work' is not work, it's a way of life. I had made a conscious decision to avoid a career structure. Although I may appear superficially gregarious I realised early on that I'm a loner by instinct and would not be happy toiling away for long periods inside a large corporate structure. Instead I've always been self-employed and paid for doing what I enjoy.

We welcomed Zara to our tiny apartment decorated for her homecoming by her father with homemade flags of the United States, Britain and Australia, to denote her triple heritage. He thought of himself as her father. That's how I felt too. She grew up with him as her father, although she always knew about her very beginnings. Oddly it was others, even family and friends, outside our trio who found that concept hard to grasp.

He had found a discarded cot left out on the sidewalk (it's possible to furnish your entire life with what New Yorkers throw out!) and we painted it up for her. Babies break down barriers. My parents sent a couple of white knitted jumpsuits, which showed every speck of the filth which falls on Manhattan. A friend from Hong Kong sent a Chinese-style sling in which we carried her, almost smothered in a blanket, through the snowy streets and on subways to meetings with an enormous range of interviewees.

I vividly recall the first time I went out on my own without her. I left her with her dad, who was editing away, while I went down the street to the supermarket on Columbus to buy some provisions. It felt very, very weird to be without her. After almost a year of having her either tucked up in my womb or slung from my shoulder I felt curiously empty-handed, naked even. And I also felt as though I should have some mark on me to let other people know, perhaps a badge which read I AM A MOTHER, or some other outward sign of an inward feeling. I thought people should be made aware of my contribution! I was no longer just me, I was something of far greater value, a mother!

But no one in the shop seemed in the least impressed! Not even our local nutter (every city block in Manhattan has at the very least one resident nutter), who even in the bitter depths of winter wore only a pair of thin trousers, sandals and a shirt open to the waist and with the sleeves rolled up. Instead of enjoying my first little taste of freedom I hurriedly picked what I needed from the shelves and almost ran back home to the security of my role, to where I was needed.

When Zara was only six weeks old her dad graduated from his production course and we celebrated by fleeing the rigours of a New York winter and heading south in a car which we drove down for its owner, who had flown ahead to Miami. From there we headed out to Cat Island in the Bahamas. We spent a month on the edge of an empty fine-sand beach in a house with no running water or electricity which cost us $5 a week! Zara slept on her blanket in the shade while we soaked up the sun. My husband visited us — a difficult reunion. But better to grapple with these emotions than to push them aside and hope they will go away.

We travelled on to South America and then returned to New York, where we were busy keeping up with requests for radio interviews from broadcasting networks in Britain, Australia, New Zealand and Canada.

Financially we turned the corner and could even afford to make a brief visit to my sister Erika and brother Robert, both of whom had emigrated to Toronto. I remember the visit because it was the first time I had seen them since I left England four years before and more or less the first thing I did was haemorrhage on Erika's kitchen floor and get carted off to the local emergency outpatients, where they took out an IUD I'd had fitted the month before.

I had not wanted to become pregnant while I was still breastfeeding. Was there enough of me to produce food for one and at the same time grow another? But she was now four months old, so we decided to make love to make a baby. I remember it so well. Of course almost every doctor would pooh-pooh the idea but I am certain that I realised the split second of conception. It occurred in my head and my heart and my loins at the same time, and with every one of my five senses. I saw it, heard it, smelt it, felt it and could even taste it. I was it and it was me. It was a yogic experience, and it was wonderful.

The interviews continued: Steve McQueen, Sammy Davis Jnr, Harpo Marx, Eartha Kitt, Johnny Mathis, Dionne Warwick, Clint Walker. Zara met them all and many more besides. Often I would breastfeed her during these interviews and we would get home to edit and find contented suckings and burpings on the tape! The BBC's correspondent in New York was a radio man who didn't care to do television interviews, so he invariably passed these on to us. The first one was Cassius Clay, later Mohamed Ali. Next came the opening of the stupendous Lincoln Center, and all the while we continued to track down radio interviewees at first nights and openings, which are so much a part of New York life. The Vietnam Moratorium was in full swing, so there were street demos with singers like Pete Seeger and then there were the famous concerts in the park, the best of which was Barbra Streisand. We took Zara to all of them in her sling or bassinette.

Occasionally we left her to be babysat by Wilson, the black would-be actor who lived in the apartment above us. But when one of his former lovers moved back in and Wilson found him passed out on the lavatory, the needle with which he had just shot a fix of heroin into his vein still hanging from his arm, we decided it was safer to take her with us.

Summer came and just before the sweltering heat trapped in the city finally got to us we were asked to cover Jock Sturrock's America's Cup challenge in *Dame Pattie* at Newport, Rhode Island. We took an apartment and began to commute between there and Manhattan. Zara loved the train rides. For the first time since London I met bulk Australians again. Once more they appeared larger than life. In the evenings they would congregate in the Black Pearl and sing 'Waltzing Matilda'. It made him homesick and he began to talk about going back to Australia. One of the ringleaders, who seemed even louder and larger than the rest, was a man called Derryn Hinch. He made me wonder if I wanted to go to Australia!

By the time of the races I was great with child and pushing Zara in a stroller. Australia lost of course, but the party which followed was my first instruction in how different we (Poms) are from them (Australians).

It was a big bash, held in one of the huge mansions built right on the cliff edge at the turn of the century for the immensely wealthy Vanderbilts. The Australians gave it a welcome dose of democracy. The women had brown leathery skins and clutched Oroton handbags. The men were even browner and consumed an amazing amount of booze. They all had a great time. It was more like a celebration for a win than a wake for a defeat. If this had been a British do there would have been a great deal more restraint and by comparison even the Americans appeared desperately polite to the point of being plastic. There was an infectious vitality and energy about the Australians.

It was therefore natural that when we returned to New York and met the then general manager of the ABC, Talbot Duckmanton, who told him that if we came back to Australia there would be a job for him on a new nightly current affairs program, we took up the offer.

He wanted to see his son. He wanted to smell the gum trees and see the red soil, the Southern Cross and the vast blue skies. I was nervous. He drew a map of Sydney and told me it was fifty miles from one side to the other. He said this with such pride, how could I tell him I preferred places less than five miles wide! He also drew a map of what he called the Peninsula north of Sydney and pointed out an almost semicircular beach called Bilgola, which he said was where we would live. I believed him and he kept his promise.

It was not much of a wrench to leave New York. We'd arrived as two, broke and friendless. We left as three and three-quarters, able to pay our own way to Australia, with money in the bank and friends. We had made a go of things in a place which is considered very tough. And even though a lot of that is American hype and bullshit we felt good about having done what we'd done.

I didn't know it then but leaving New York was a big emotional turning point for me as a mother. Having Zara had made very little difference to my lifestyle. Sure, I had lain awake in those first few weeks after her birth anxiously waiting for her to make a little movement or noise to reassure me she was still breathing. And I certainly felt more complete, more rounded as a woman and a human being. But one child is a snap! And we had continued to live like a young madly-in-love couple with very little thought for the future. We had no ties, just ourselves, and no restraints. Even now when I go to New York to work and to visit friends I experience the same lift, the feeling of freedom. Everyone knows about its down side but despite that New York, or at least Manhattan, remains an exciting, stimulating place for affluent, single, childless professional men and women. For those reasons it's the epitome of a twenty-first-century city.

After a month's transcontinental vacation by car across the United States we flew to England, where we survived the first meeting since our amalgamation with two sisters and a brother and met up again with my husband. We then flew down to the Canary Islands, where Dad and Ingrid had retired, for another refined interrogation, exquisitely done as only parents know how.

I don't think it's just because I love him that I think people easily warm to my partner. But they did. Zara helped. My dad bought her first pair of sandals and when, within less than two days, she was staggering up and down the patio of their apartment, he felt justified in announcing that she would never have walked if he hadn't been wise enough to see she needed shoes! Going through his papers after he died I found a water colour he had done of that patio. It's framed now and hangs on a wall by our dining table, so I can see it often. I like it very much. The perspective and angles are like those in a child's painting. There's the couch he sat on, leaning forward, the ever present cigarette in a holder dangling between his fingers, encouraging my daughter to walk. I loved him very much and miss him still.

The visit was a success and it was hard to leave. Having a father who was considerably older than the norm — he was almost fifty when I was born — is just one of the many reasons why I think people should get on with parenting in their twenties. Every time I said goodbye to my old man, I thought perhaps it was the last time, because of his age, that I might see him.

Zara took to long flights with panache, adopting the technique she has employed ever since on lengthy journeys, whether by air or land, of slipping into an alpha state. We stopped over in Istanbul, to take the ferry across the Bosphoros, and in Singapore, to lap up Asia once more, and flew on to Australia, arriving in Darwin in the middle of the night. Even though I was eight months pregnant, not married to the father of my baby-to-be, travelling with a daughter who did not have the same name as her father, and was a foreigner with no visa, no job, no home to go to and very little money, I was welcomed with a 'g'day' and no questions asked. Two weeks later I voted in a referendum! Coming from a background of over-regulated Europe, I experienced a delicious sense of freedom.

Across this vast land we flew. Why is it that although America is the same size as Australia, travellers from LA to New York do not experience the same feeling of covering immense distances? Nor is there the same electric atmosphere of excitement when you land in New York after a transcontinental flight as there still is when you touch down in Sydney. Passengers do not spontaneously burst into applause at Kennedy as they so frequently do at Kingsford Smith and as they did, to my complete astonishment, on that late December morning in 1967.

At 8.00 am the temperature was already in the thirties. Was that the reason why everyone seemed so underdressed? I had never seen so much bare flesh! A friend of his met us and told us he had found a 'unit' for us overlooking the beach near Manly. A unit of what? I didn't dare ask! But I was relieved when it turned out to be a unit of living space — in other words an apartment, a flat.

Within a week we celebrated the arrival of the New Year at a 'L'il Abner and Daisy Mae' party held at the Manly Surf Club. Quite an introduction to Australia — sawdust on the floor, vast quantities of beer and hundreds of suntanned, very attractive, sexually extrovert, skimpily dressed women and even more skimpily dressed men. It was confronting and exciting in a quite different way than New York. It was going to take some adjusting to, but I thought I was going to like it. Three weeks later our son was born.

Again I had arrived in a place about to pop and not knowing any doctors. So it was pot luck that I found Doctor, now Sir, William McBride, the man who discovered the link between the drug thalidomide and malformations in newborn infants. He was not at all keen on having fathers present at births, but our son came into the world in the same manner in which he intended to live his life, in a rush of enthusiasm, so there was no time to hustle his father away.

Again I enjoyed the whole experience, the drug-like pain building to a crescendo and just when I felt, what the hell am I doing this for without any help? a sudden burst and out he came. Not a pretty sight, except to his ecstatic parents! This was no beautiful, silken, smooth-skinned creature! He was covered in gore, which I can only imagine was from the placenta because I was not damaged. And he was wrinkled and squashed. We have enlargements of the photographs their father took of both of them at their birth. Zara's would make *Life* magazine. When I took the negatives of her brother in to order an enlargement the horrified chemist thought that he had been battered or burned!

It was already forty degrees when he came zooming into the world at 8.05 in the morning. The delivery cubicle in the Crown Street Women's Hospital had no air-conditioning. It was just as well the photographs were in black and white, because I was so red-faced and sweaty with the effort.

I had arrived at the hospital with an outrageous dose of tonsillitis, pustules coating both sides of my throat. Four hours later, with my new baby at my breast, to my complete astonishment, I realised the tonsillitis, pustules, aches and pains, the lot, had gone. All I can assume is that for the birth my body produced enough positive energy to rid itself of such irritation. I've often thought that there is a marketable product there somewhere, just waiting to be isolated.

We were transported across town to a nursing home on the banks of the harbour, where I unwrapped my baby to make sure he was in working order and was reprimanded by a ferret-faced sister. He had a very deep dimple at the base of his spine. So deep I couldn't see the bottom of it. Visions of unfinished spinal cords and spina bifida filled my imagination. I panicked and demanded to know from Dr McBride what was wrong. 'Nothing. It's very common and it will close over within a few months.' It took almost two years.

By now, what other people, family or friends, thought of the situation in which we chose to live mattered so little that it made no impact on our choice of names. We called him Sean, the Irish eqivalent of his father's name, Allan, after my dad, and Adams, his mother's maiden name. He took his father's surname.

I breastfed him as we took him home on the ferry and received some pretty odd looks. Each breast was bigger than his head. We bathed him in the kitchen sink and now the first flush of wonder and excitement was over I did begin to wonder if he was always going to be this shrivelled and ugly. We introduced him to his sister and she looked as though the same thought crossed her mind! Slowly over the next couple of months he began to unfold like a blossom opening, growing into his skin. And slowly I began to realise that my life had changed. And not for the better!

I had never wanted to own a house. I was still enough of a communist to not believe in private ownership of property. So this positive mania Australians have about their triple-fronted brick veneers was something to which I could not relate. But my partner is third generation Australian, and the desire to legitimise his claim upon this most ancient of lands in bricks and mortar, or at least fibro and wood, was not to be resisted.

By the time Zara was twenty-two months and Sean was eight months we had bought a house overlooking that beach he had told me about back in New York. It was the second house we looked at and we so fell in love with its privacy and energy that we didn't even care that we couldn't get inside to have a look before we bought it. I use the word bought in its loosest sense. More accurate to say we had put ourselves into debt for what seemed then to be a huge, huge amount of money. It took us six months to raise the finance for it.

We moved in with two suitcases, two second-hand cots which their father painted, one red, one blue, and a highchair which for some extraordinary reason I painted lilac. Every morning I would go out onto the balcony and wave him goodbye and watch as the car wound its way around the coastal road towards the city. Then I would stand there, staring down at the ocean, at the khaki green of the hillsides around me, and at the other houses sprinkled across this beautiful landscape, no doubt many of them containing women feeling as trapped by their freedom as I did.

I would stand on that balcony with tears in my eyes, experiencing a tremulous mix of bleak loneliness, homesickness (for where?), alienation, and anger at myself that I could have so much and yet be so bloody spoilt as to be discontented. Many, many times I wanted to scream, 'Help . . . is there anyone out there who understands?'

Bilgola is beautiful. But it is still a suburb. I had never lived in a suburb. I didn't like suburbs. They filled me with dread and reminded me of Surrey and the stockbroker belt and people whose values are very distant from mine. In all this space I felt more trapped than ever before in my life. Marooned. Unable to drive and unable to afford a car even if I could drive. Unable to afford a car because I was unable to work because I had two children under two. Worst of all I had no idea how to go about putting all this right. I couldn't remember ever talking to a woman who was in the position I was in now. So I had no one I could relate to. No history of experience to fall back on. I knew no one at all in Australia, apart from my children and their father. I had a telephone, but who could I call?

It was winter. I'd had the usual image Europeans have of Australia as the land of perpetual sunshine and this made the relatively cool weather seem unexpectedly bleak. The effort involved in going out and at least seeing, if not actually speaking, to other people was daunting. I was still breastfeeding so jaunts had to be taken between feeds. I'd get the two of them into clean nappies and warm clothes and strap them into their shared stroller, with Sean reluctantly half lying down and Zara in a little dicky-seat on the front. Then I'd cling onto the handle so the whole thing wouldn't get away from me down the steep hill to the shopping centre. There was very little time to look around before my breasts and Sean's yells would tell me it was feeding time again. So I'd begin the wearying trudge back up, pushing the dead weight of the two of them plus any groceries which I had bought. Inevitably one or other would get the grizzles and I'd arrive back at the house frantic and exhausted. I was more tired than I had ever been and yet I was doing far less, or anyway that was how I saw it. Every night I'd fall into bed totally exhausted and tense because I knew I would not get a full night's sleep.

It started with Zara. This is not one word of exaggeration. She woke every night, at least once but more often twice or even three times and cried out. I'd never been a light sleeper but I became one. My heart would leap with her cry and I'd get up and stagger into her room quite often finding that she had already fallen deeply asleep. Sometimes she just needed a cuddle to be reassured that we were there and then she'd drop off again. I understand exactly why women hit their children. Every mother understands. It's less understandable why they don't hit them more often! If, when I got in there, she had fallen asleep again I had a mad urge to shake her awake and demand, 'What do you want?' Commonsense and a desire to get back into my own bed prevailed.

But what was most amazing about all this was that Zara kept up this routine for six months. And — wait for this — the very first night she slept through, Sean started! For another six months he did exactly the same, waking us with a yell once, twice or even three times a night. We took it in turns to go in to them but even if it wasn't my turn, I always woke and couldn't drop off again until he came back to bed.

I thought that it was just as well I wasn't working because my brain was constantly befuddled from lack of real sleep. But I was so accustomed to working that I didn't feel comfortable sitting around during the day reading and playing with the children. Doing that made me feel guilty. After all he was out there working his butt off, so I should do my bit, pull my weight, and so on. All I could see my bit being was keeping the house spotless. So that's what I did. I approached maintaining a clean home with all the vigour I had previously put into my work. One room a day I cleaned. And I mean *cleaned*! The walls, the ceiling, the windows, the few bits of furniture we had picked up at the tip or had been left by the previous owners. I became a fanatical house cleaner. Not quite as crazy as the woman I heard about a few years later who went on what she called a 'tidy walk' through her house every hour on the hour, keeping everything shipshape. But very nearly as crazy.

Crazy enough to seriously consider pissing on the carpet, which had also been left by the previous owner. True. I remember one day sponging down yet another pissy patch left by one or other of the children or perhaps by the puppy or the kitten which we had also taken on. (You can't be a real family unless you have pets was one of the ideas which had been programmed into me during my own childhood.) I found myself thinking, I may even have spoken the thought aloud, a tendency which I began to display with frightening frequency during this period of madness, 'Zara has pissed on this carpet, Sean has pissed on this carpet, Moby (the dog) has pissed on this carpet and Kiko (the cat) has also pissed on this carpet. I am the only abstemious one. And as I am the one who has to clean up why don't I do the same!'

Perhaps it was this thought, and the realisation that it foreshadowed insanity, that made me grab a hold of my mind. Or maybe it was the day I poured a glass of beer over his head at the high point of a fight we were having because I didn't want visitors on the weekends. I was desperate to spend time with just him, to regain the closeness we had shared when we hadn't owned a bloody house and had two bloody kids.

More than two because now there was his ten-year-old son, Guy, who stayed most weekends with us. This despite the fact that during their divorce, which his wife had organised almost immediately we arrived in Sydney, the judge had said that Guy should not visit his father until he regularised his relationship. Fortunately Guy's mother realised it was far more important that her son spend time with his father than we take heed of such a harsh judgement. It was not easy to accommodate the needs of children of such disparate ages, and in the very beginning, partly because ten-year-olds were a foreign country to me, I think Guy missed out.

All these adjustments and self-inflicted torments meant that I was not an easy person to live with. It wasn't his fault. He had to get on and earn the money to meet the mortgage repayments. And that meant him going off to work which meant me staying at home. Trapped. I took my frustration out on him for the simple reason there was no one else to take it out on.

The turning point came with the visit of an old friend from Hong Kong, a woman who had become my husband's lover, helping him through the bad patch when I left Hong Kong for the second time. She had four children, but she came to visit on her own just at the time when I realised I had better shape up. Her scorn at my inability to drive a car spurred me into lessons. Her collection of wildly erotic poetry, which she wanted to have published in Australia, put me in touch with publishers, so that by the time she left I was working again. I was editing those excrutiatingly dreadful nurse romance novelettes. I have kept one as a souvenir, *Nurse Lambert's Conflict*. Open it at random, and there are sentences and sentiments to make you puke. I graduated to cowboy dramas. Another souvenir, *Larry and Streak* — flick through and come across, 'Big Al hunkered down as the leaden messengers of death winged atop his boulder stake-out'. Yes. Well. I spent a fortnight on each book and became so entranced that I really felt by the end that I had created 'Literature'!

I stopped caring about the piss on the carpet, unseen corners remained uncleaned, summer came and the children, relieved of the responsibility of living up to my expectations, stopped waking up in the night and during the day played contentedly with each other on the back patio. Zara played with dolls and Sean played with trucks (except he couldn't manage the hard 't', which instead came out as an embarrassing 'f'; I could never get him to switch to calling them lorries).

If I didn't have children I would no doubt say they played with stereotypical toys because those were the options with which they were presented. But for Zara and Sean that wasn't true. And watching one female and one male develop from birth has convinced me that there are natural differences. It has also made me worry less about them. Worrying about boys playing with trucks and girls with dolls is rather like being rude to a man who opens doors or stands up at the table for a woman. It is more important to ensure a child's values and goals are not influenced by society's sexual definitions. Sean now uses skin conditioners and talks about having children and Zara displays those attributes which in men are seen as positive and in women are dismissed as unfeminine and aggressive.

She began practising this art of getting up people's noses very early on, trying it out for starters on her family and in particular on her brothers. Sean would waddle, his nappy worn with the same casual elan with which he now wears numbers by Jean Paul Gaultier, towards a chair and his sister would scream, 'Don't sit there!' He would stop, mid-movement. She would yell, 'Can't you see Jenny is sitting there?' He would scrutinise the chair, see nobody, but sense that retreat was the only sensible way to go, and back off. Jenny was Zara's totally invisible and correspondingly dictatorial friend. We all lived in dread of doing the wrong thing by Jenny. Years later Guy told of being bossed about by a three-year-old Zara who would stand at the end of her cot, when he was babysitting her and her brother, and issue orders. Such memories die hard.

I passed my driving test and a couple of times a week I would drive him in to work, have the car all day for myself and then pick him up. I began looking outside my nuclear family for friendship and stimulation and joined a WEA discussion group. We met once a week in one or other of the members' homes, to discuss the set book we had read during the week. We took it in turns to keep notes and send a report in to the university lecturer assigned to us, and once a term this lecturer would make the long trek out from the city to visit us. The group of women and men who met in this manner, of different ages, backgrounds, interests and beliefs, has remained the core of friendship on which I have built a wider circle of acquaintances.

On reading all this through, I can see what I have always known about myself, and yet found difficult to accept and even more difficult to reconcile — that I need to work outside the family and to be financially independent. Otherwise my sense of self is eroded to a point where I take it out on myself, and on everyone else. Being a mother is a deep, deep need and my commitment to them is vital but — and it's a big but — my commitment to myself is even greater!

My workload increased, which meant that I earned more and could afford to put the children into part-time care. I had stopped breastfeeding Sean only after the occasion when I was sitting on the garden step with him suckling away while holding a barbecued hot dog in his hand. 'I think you have to wean him,' his father said, and I burst into tears because I knew he was right and because I knew I would never breastfeed again. We had decided three children between us were as many as we wanted.

I have a photograph of Sean on the front step, clutching his little suitcase containing his sandwich, an expression of total confidence on his face. It was taken on his first day at preschool. He was eighteen months — I can just hear the howls of outrage! The woman who ran the little group asked how old he was (she didn't take children until they were two) and if he was toilet trained. I lied about both! He was big for eighteen months and small for almost two. And he only wet his pants for the first few days.

Along with starting to come to terms with myself, I began to come to terms with my new country. It's difficult for those born in Australia to understand how emotionally traumatic it is to shift such deep historical allegiances, and with all the emphasis about discrimination towards migrants being focused on non-Anglo newcomers, it's easy to overlook the fact that while it may not be as difficult for the Poms as it is for them, it's still no small task to fall in love all over again with an alien culture. British newcomers make the same mistake as Australian-born people, assuming that because we have the same historical roots we automatically have a great deal in common. This is rather like assuming that because two people have the same mother and father they have similar beliefs and emotional responses. Far from true. It was because I had made those assumptions that it was many years before I felt at ease here.

It was partly to escape this unease and partly because we had such happy memories of Asia and wanted to go back there that after living in Australia for just on two years we moved to Singapore. My partner had been offered the post as ABC correspondent based in the Republic. For me the chance to return to a part of the world where I felt so immediately at ease and where I would be able to have full-time help in the home was a joyful opportunity.

Instead of flying direct to Singapore we chose to drive overland to Darwin and fly from there. It was another great journey. Across western Queensland and straight up the middle. No agoraphobia this time.

Perhaps I was too busy with two small children to have time for my own problems. What an amazing country! Longreach, Cloncurry, Mount Isa, Katherine, Tennant Creek and finally Darwin. Despite the heat, the condition of the dirt roads and the innumerable punctures, or perhaps because of them, I got an inkling of what it would be like to be committed to this vast land.

Singapore was all that I had anticipated and much more. The colours, light, smells, and the vibrancy of Asia. Oh, how I had missed it! The tropical heat increased every sensation. A terrific Malay woman called Maria took over the running of our domestic lives. She had an enviably lackadaisical attitude towards housework. Only I noticed that things were not kept quite as overpolished and well presented as they appeared on the surface and I remember thinking, what the hell have I been worrying about all this time? He doesn't even notice if a smidgin of dust lurks in the corner of the bookshelves or if the bottles on the spice rack are not arrayed precisely in diminishing size order! But just to very slightly alleviate my guilt at not running the house, once every month or so I would say, 'Right, Maria, today's the day.' And she would roll her eyes and puff and pant as I insisted on helping her roll up the carpets to wash the tiles underneath.

I recently asked Zara if she remembered Maria. Her eyes lit up. 'Oh yes. She used to take us to her kampong to visit her son, who was about my age, her mother and her sister. We'd eat sticky rice with our fingers and on the way back in the bus Sean would fall asleep in her lap and she would roll up the bus tickets and stick them up his nose so they looked like little horns and he never woke up even though we laughed so loudly!'

The children went full time to a Chinese kindergarten. They were expected to go to the school the children of all the other expatriates attended. But why be in a new culture and only learn about the old? I didn't realise then, but they had begun their schooling in the irregular manner in which it was to continue. They were much larger than all their classmates. Sean looked like a little blond thug. Zara like a little blonde angel. At one of the school concerts she commandeered centre stage and sang a traditional nursery song in Chinese.

School meant the onslaught of the usual run of childhood diseases, including bouts of the common cold. For a couple of weeks that is what I thought Zara's perpetually runny nose was, though it seemed odd that the mucous was coming from only one nostril. The doctor put her on a course of antibiotics and when her nostril continued to ooze he put her on a longer, stronger dosage. When even this made no impact and he obviously had run out of his store of knowledge I insisted we visit a specialist. This chap took one look at Zara, said, 'Ah yes,' tipped her head back, put forceps up her nostril and pulled out a germinating rambutan seed with at least an inch of greenery sprouting from it!

Sean's visit to a different specialist was due to his mother's anxiety over the fact that he did not seem to be able to get one chubby little leg past the other without hitting and bruising it. Knock knees, I panicked. The doctor looked at me and sighed. 'Nothing of the sort. Just sturdy legs which will glide normally past each other when they grow. He's going to be tall.' For once a doctor was right. But you never know, do you, and that's why a boy has a mother!

With the children we visited Chinese temples for their New Year and Hindu temples for the festival of Thaipusan. We swam with members of the faded British Raj in the pool of the Tanglin Club and with the multi-racial new elite at the Singapore Club. We made new friends, one of them an eccentric Englishwoman who ran art and pottery classes which the children loved to attend because they were encouraged to get covered in clay and paint. Zara began ballet classes and on weekends we drove up the Malaysian coast and camped on the beaches, where we could swim naked and watch the Sultan's Arab racehorses gallop with their trainers through the shallows. Sometimes fishermen dropped us off on a small totally isolated, offshore island and we played Robinson Crusoe for a few days. And when the monsoon rains filled the stormwater drains at the very bottom of our large garden the four of us would ride them like a water-slide, screaming with pleasure under the anxious scrutiny of Maria waiting to whisk the children away from their mad parents and into a hot bath.

Children and house cared for, I was able to leap full pelt into my chosen work. I began writing feature articles for the *New Nation*, a bright, afternoon tabloid which had recently been started up as a part of the Straits Times group. I wrote on a very wide cross-section of social issues, from kampong resettlements to sex change operations, in both of which areas Singapore was on the leading edge! Because of my connection with the paper, I was able to arrange 'contra' flights to other parts of Asia, which meant that I often accompanied my partner on his journalistic expeditions and wrote stories about them for my paper.

I travelled to the Philippines, through Indonesia and then India, Bangladesh, Laos, Cambodia, Thailand and of course Vietnam. It was great to be back working together, even though he was collecting television and radio material and I was looking out stories for my newspaper. We work well together. Both of us are able to view each other's work with professional detachment and honesty. ('What's this then, Trish,' he winces when I get a bit carried away, 'literature with a capital L?')

I didn't always travel with him and on one occasion when he was away and I was working at home on a radio documentary something happened which made me realise how much being a mother had affected my life.

The phone rang and it was a new friend we had both met, a fascinating American in his sixties, Simon Casady. A retired newspaper proprietor, who had been brought to Singapore as an adviser on how to run a newspaper, Simon was a well-read, well-travelled, cultured and charming rebel. He had been vociferous in his attacks on the US government policy in Vietnam. His wife, Virginia, was equal to him in all respects, they had a great marriage and five grown-up sons. They gave wonderful dinner parties at which you inevitably met fascinating and quite often outrageous people. These evenings were an island of prickly veracity in the swamp of Singapore's nervously cultivated calm. Simon had called with an invitation to such an event. I said how much I would like to come but that my partner was away. 'Well that's too bad,' Simon roared California-style down the phone, 'but you'll come won't you?'

'Me? By myself? Well. Yes of course.' I put down the phone and let out such a whoop that Maria came running in and found me leaping up and down the stairs yelling at the top of my voice, '*Me*! They want *me* to come to dinner. By *myself*. Just *me*!' She joined in my maniacal laughter even though she didn't have a clue what I was laughing about. What was I laughing about? I was laughing because for the first time in what seemed like a lifetime, though it was really only six years (but then so much had happened in that span it was a lifetime), I had been invited to a social gathering on my own merit. Not as someone's partner, or as Sean or Zara's mum, but as myself. Until that moment I hadn't realised how very much I had missed being more than a mere appendage!

I let the discovery, that despite being a wife and mother I was still an individual and even attractive to some men, rather go to my head for a while. Nothing too serious. After all I knew I wanted to spend the rest of my life with the father of my children. And perhaps the little splurge was necessary as a boost to my battered ego. It's well nigh impossible to realise yourself as an intellectually stimulating, sexually attractive person when you spend the greater percentage of your time cleaning up shit and vomit! Anyway, we were as totally honest over this as we have always been about everything, encompassing it within the ever-expandable boundaries of our own relationship, and definitely more good than bad came from it all.

For both of us honesty is an essential ingredient to keep our marriage going. (Yes, we think of it as a marriage even though we have no bits of paper.) Just as important is to share our experiences. So by this time we had made the joint decision that when it came to a choice between travelling and working together or being more sensible and not spending that money on an airfare but putting it in the bank, we'd opt for being together. It's so easy to grow apart through having separate everyday living experiences. (How can he relate to what it's been like to spend the day with three children under the age of five, any more than she can understand what it's been like for him to make immediate and tough decisions on which may depend thousands of dollars or the jobs of fifty other people?)

One such experience happened to us during this time. It was an experience which changed our lives. Not in a dramatic, outwardly visible way, but much more importantly it made us re-examine our values and cross-examine our consciences. In 1971 we went to cover the refugee crisis which had developed in West Bengal. Ten million people had crossed the border from East Pakistan, what was soon to become Bangladesh, seeking refuge from the brutality of the East Pakistan army.

Nothing I had ever read or seen or heard could have prepared me for the sight of 30,000 people crammed into an area the size of a football field — just one of the hundreds of refugee camps. Because their half-dozen makeshift latrines were overflowing with effluent and crawling with huge maggots, people were shitting anywhere they could find a space, often perilously close to their own water supply. Many of them were already close to death from exhaustion and starvation when they arrived at the camps. Some of them had walked for more than 100 kilometres from their homes in East Pakistan, where they had left everything behind.

West Bengal, which already had six million unemployed people of its own to feed, had this sudden influx of homeless hungry refugees to care for. All the camps had uncontrollable outbreaks of cholera and typhoid. I saw scenes which were like mediaeval illustrations of hell. Not surprisingly it was the dying and dead children, the clichéd innocent victims, which made the greatest impact. Was it possible this was happening on the same planet on which I lived in a large house and had two healthy children and domestic help? Was it happening on the same planet on which two million dollars a minute was spent on arms and on which there were mountains of stockpiled food? Questions like this seem simplistic when asked in the abstract. Asked in proximity to a mother holding a dead child to her shrivelled breast the answers are an obscenity.

For the weeks we were in those camps we hardly spoke to each other. What was there to say? When we arrived back in Singapore it was almost Christmas and the first thing the children wanted was to decorate a tree and tell us what they wanted Father Christmas to bring them. An understandable reaction would have been to tell them, 'No Christmas this year. Not while children your age are dying of cholera and starvation'. Instead I wanted them to have the most wonderful Christmas ever; to love them up and hold them tight, to do for them what I couldn't do for the children we had left behind. Mind you, I also wanted them to know how extremely fortunate they were and I told them then what I have told them repeatedly ever since: 'You are so very fortunate, but with that good fortune comes responsibility, the responsibility to expand on that opportunity and to do so with care and love'. I honestly believe that if I never did anything else for my children, the fact that they are Australian is gift enough. If, with that as a starting point, they can't get off their butts and live a happy, creative, successful life, then they are undeserving of their fortune, and it would have been better for the world if someone else had been blessed with their inheritance. Tough.

What we had seen in those camps made us even more certain that our decision not to have more children was the right one and not just for us. So when I became pregnant shortly afterwards I had an abortion. Sure, we talked about the pros and cons, not the moral ones because I've always thought that it is a woman's right to give or withhold life to her foetus. And I don't try to tap dance out of the moral dilemma. Yes, abortion is murder. The same way euthanasia and, in a sense, suicide are murder. But they can be justified by the circumstances. I was taking the contraceptive pill when I became pregnant. Not good. Because you are not as mentally prepared for that possibility as you are if you are jiggering around with the less safe methods. Deciding to have an abortion was not easy. We loved each other. We could afford another child. In the end the factors which tipped the scales were that he had been responsible for children since he was twenty-one and three was enough.

Thankfully in Singapore terminations are legal and encouraged. But when I became pregnant again, within six weeks of the first termination, when I hadn't even stopped taking the pill, it was anger that persuaded me to abort that too. Anger at myself for believing doctors when they told me that the pill was all but 100 per cent safe. And anger that after all this time it's still women who bear the major responsibility for the choice whether or not to have a baby. I consoled myself with the belief that by the time my daughter was my age things would be different. Fool!

The terminations were very distressing for him too. He said he wanted to have a vasectomy and I agreed. I was fed up with sticking things up me and in me. Pills, foaming creams, jellies, diaphragms, IUDs. And I was fed up with having male doctors probe around my insides with their hands, their instruments and their ignorance. To hell with the whole bloody lot of them! I flushed four months' supply of contraceptive tablets down the loo and felt a wave of relief. Within the next few weeks, and I don't give a damn what male doctors say (what the hell do they bloody well know?), I registered a very noticeable improvement in my sense of hearing, smell and taste. I felt like a woman released; look out world!

In the new year we took off up the east coast of Malaysia to camp out on the beautiful empty beaches and try to get our minds and hearts in order again. Guy had joined us on his second visit to Singapore and now that his sister and brother were past the muling, puking stage we could all of us enjoy one another more.

Now there were other problems. Guy had grown into a teenager with hair, as was the fashion, down to his shoulders. When we tried to cross the border back into Singapore he and his father were ordered, under brand new regulations, to get their hair cut. His father handles authority in a different way than I. He smiles a lot and feeds their egos. But Lee Kwan Yew's immigration officers are made of stern stuff and he had to go to the ludicrous lengths of phoning the Australian High Commission before they were persuaded that as foreign residents of Singapore the same stringent rules need not apply. The following day he returned to the border, with a camera crew, and shot a story for the ABC, showing immigration officials giving would-be visitors pudding basin haircuts.

We shall never know the exact reasons for us getting the flick from Singapore. Perhaps it was the haircutting incident. Perhaps it was because after our visit to the refugee camps we became heavily involved in raising funds, over a half million dollars, to send as aid. At the time we did this, pragmatic Singapore, surrounded on all sides by Muslim neighbours, had still not officially sided with either Hindu India or Muslim Pakistan, but was waiting to see which side won the war that followed as a result of the refugee crisis. Another reason for us getting the shove could have been the government shutdown of the *Singapore Herald* newspaper. In a very visual demonstration against this action, I painted 'Save the Herald' in metre-high letters on the side of our elderly campervan and drove it all around Singapore.

It was in this van (minus its exhortations) that we took off for a holiday around Europe, visiting my family and ex-husband in England. The ABC had wanted him to return to Sydney, but we weren't ready for that yet so he had lined up a number of broadcasting companies who were happy to have him as freelance stringer. Unfortunately we were only back in Singapore for a month before we were peremptorily informed by the Department of Information that our work visa was no longer valid and that we should leave the Republic immediately.

He was offered a full posting by the American Westinghouse Broadcasting Corporation in Beirut. At the time the Lebanon was only simmering away, the boil-over came soon after. I was so glad we decided against it. I had been close enough to one war to do me for a lifetime. It's difficult if you spend a lot of time in war zones not to become addicted to that way of life. I have seen it happen to friends. So we plumped for a return to Australia.

Maria and her family and our other friends came to see us off on the ship in which we were to sail away. Goodbyes were still very difficult for me because I had yet to realise they are just another form of hello.

Pamela Wright

I am happy just to be by myself with him. Often I find the day has gone before I have done anything more important than just be with him.

What never ceases to amaze people other than mothers is the intensity and the totally basic nature of the emotions which motherhood dredges up from some unknown and unfathomable source: fear, joy, and of course love. If women knew, really knew, what motherhood would demand, would they still choose to have children? Yes, though maybe choose is not the correct word. Like it or not, we would be driven by the same imperatives which have forever driven women to perpetuate the species. It would be encouraging to think of ourselves as intelligent beings making independent choices, but more honest to recognise we are doing little more than fulfilling a role.

All of us go into a first pregnancy knowing only in abstract what to expect. But if that pregnancy meant months of lying motionless in a hospital bed for fear of losing the baby, suffering an unpleasant birth to produce premature twins and then going through the unspeakable torment of seeing one of those babies slowly die, would we be willing to put ourselves at risk of all that happening again? For Pamela Wright the unhesitating answer is yes.

'I want to have a family and one child is not enough of a family for me. I would also like a daughter, though of course that's not something you can control.' And what if, in order to have another child, she had to go through what she went through the first time? There is only a minimal pause and then, 'I'd still do it. Perhaps I only remember the good things, lying down for four months is not such a bad thing you know! I learnt how to knit and I read books friends gave me that I would never have chosen myself. There were plenty of women in hospital at the same time as me who had a far worse time and, well, just look at him, he's worth it all.'

Thirteen-month-old Jeremy, immediately aware from her tone of voice that his mother is talking about him, looks up from the floor where he is surrounded by bright toys, and indulges us both with a wraparound grin. His mother goes soft at the edges. 'But often now when I look at him I think, where's your little brother, mate? Eh? Something is missing and he needs a playmate to be a family.'

Pamela herself had a happy early family life, '. . . and perhaps that's why I think it's important for Jeremy to have a brother or sister. I had two brothers and two sisters, three older and one younger. They're all married and have kids. I was the last to do both. They're spread around Australia, in Perth, Melbourne and in Adelaide, where we grew up. We had a shack on the beach and there were always loads of people around.

'Mum made a career out of raising her family. There's twenty years between the oldest and the youngest. I am very close to her. She has a good sense of humour, comes out with funny, spontaneous one-liners. I loved my dad but we weren't as matey as Mum and I. He died of cancer of the lungs when he was sixty-nine. That was six years ago when I was thirty. He had been a heavy smoker, but he'd given it up and they say the lungs regenerate. Don't mention that I smoke. I don't smoke in front of Jeremy.'

Pamela finished high school in Adelaide and spent a year in the newsroom of Channel Nine 'as a sort of dogsbody and runner for everyone.' Then she went off to England. 'I'd always wanted to travel. I don't know why. Just curious to see new places and people. And in London I found work with one of those borderline travel companies who ran charter air services across the Atlantic. Nothing illegal, but the sort of deal offered was a cheapie flight, London to New York, which omitted to point out that you had to fly to Toronto and take the overnight bus down to New York; that sort of thing.'

After a couple of years travelling as well as working in the travel business in Europe and a year or so in Los Angeles, Pamela returned to Australia because her father was ill. 'During those years having children just hadn't been an issue. I certainly always assumed I would have them, one day. But I hadn't met anyone I wanted to have children with. I was just rolling along enjoying life.'

It was hard to adjust to Adelaide after Los Angeles, so when three of the girls she had flatted with in London suggested that she join them in Sydney she took up the offer and began working again in a similar, slightly suss travel company. 'Somebody from ABC TV came in to buy a dodgy airline ticket and we started talking, and he said there was a job going at the ABC and if I was interested I should apply. I did and I got the job.

'I spent the first six months typing but within a year I had done a training course as a production assistant and was on *Checkerboard*.' It was while she was working on this program that she met the man to whom she is now married and who is a television executive. He was separated, in the process of a divorce and had two young sons who lived with their mother. 'We couldn't leap into marriage, because of his situation, and we probably wouldn't have done so even if we could have. It's not in either of our natures. The fact that he had a family already did away with any immediate need on his part and that was okay with me too because I was happy to pursue my career. Not that I really think of myself as having a career. It's something which seems to have happened without me trying too hard.'

In 1978, after a few years in television, a colleague suggested that Pamela should give radio a go, '"Because you have a nice voice," is what he said. I think because it's fairly low for a woman. So I put together a sort of squashed version of *City Extra*, interviews with Larry Pickering and David Coombe, hosted by Steve Cosser, and presented it as my audition tape. On the strength of that I was employed as a radio producer and was finally given the job of producing *Sunday*, a weekly magazine radio program hosted by Mike Jeffreys.

'I enjoyed doing that for a while and then I began to get itchy feet and wonder how I could combine my need to travel with my job and to think what I could do that would please me rather than working to please everyone else's ego, and I came up with the concept of a travel program. Simple really. Obvious.'

By then Pamela's love affair had grown into a live-in shared life. 'At some time or other I remember having a fantasy about sharing an instant family and putting that together with children of our own. I would have enjoyed that. But then his ex-wife remarried and went to live in the USA, and the travel thing took off so the need to have children retreated. By the time his children came back into our lives they were teenagers. So I buried myself in my work, which I enjoyed a lot.'

Pamela's program, *Traveller's Tales*, was one of the ABC's great success stories. It first went to air on a Saturday morning in February 1981 and it ran in the same weekly timeslot for five years with Jeff Watson as the amiable and dry-witted host chatting with numerous people about their travel experiences. There was a spin-off in the form of a book and a number of the interviews have been aired on Qantas's in-flight sound programs.

'I'd turned thirty, my dad had died, both things which made the idea of having a family bubble to the surface more often. We got married, partly to finalise things, as a cementing, and partly because we were going to India on a camel trip in the desert and we thought it would be simpler if we were. It also was fun to have such an unusual honeymoon. A couple of times he also mentioned having a child, but we never seemed to coincide, I mean we never seemed to both want children at the same time.

'Later we had his oldest son living with us, which was not all that fabulous, but still the urge to have children came up more and more often. I'd had a bit of gynaecological trouble, some pre-cancerous tissue removed from my cervix. I was told it wouldn't affect me having children, but I stopped taking the pill. I was getting about a lot for the program; I went to Kashmir, China and Zimbabwe and when I did get pregnant it didn't occur to me that I would have to stop travelling.'

Pamela was almost five months pregnant when she miscarried. 'I was very upset, naturally. But once again I don't think I was worried for one moment about not being able to fall pregnant again or there being any problems if I did. I was told that one in seven pregnancies end in spontaneous abortion or miscarriage and I sort of felt there was a definite reason the baby didn't go full term and because of this it was just as well. I got pregnant again more or less straight away because I wanted a baby and there didn't seem any reason not to any more.'

At thirteen weeks Pamela was told that she was having twins. 'I wasn't really surprised. My sister has twins and they say it runs in families. I had no worries at all. Twins seemed like a good thing to have, especially if they turned out to be a girl and a boy.'

At eighteen weeks Pamela began to bleed heavily and she was hospitalised. 'I stayed there for the rest of my pregnancy. The first week was the worst, until I adjusted to the idea of having to just lie there. They didn't have to tell me, because of course I realised, the longer I could hold on to them the more chance my babies would have. A couple of times things became a bit difficult and I was very quickly shot down to the acute care ward and put on a drip to stop the premature labour, but for the rest of the time it was just a matter of lying there and willing them into staying put.'

Pamela settled into hospital routine. Her husband visited every evening. 'He would bring food, Italian, Chinese, Indian, and wheel me out into the balcony. With our backs to the ward, we would eat overlooking the city, so it was like having our own townhouse! The nights were hot, there was no air-conditioning and perhaps I wouldn't have liked it if there had been. Every morning, at 3.00 am, I would hear the long-distance trucks start out on their journey to Melbourne. Then I would doze till tea came and the daily routine started.

'I had plenty of visits from friends and we'd laugh a lot. I didn't really get to know any of the other women in the ward because we were all bedridden and couldn't get up to visit each other. There were women who had been there for almost their entire pregnancy. You learn to not feel sorry for yourself because there is always someone who is much worse off than you are. One woman who had been lying there for six months, pregnant with her second child, woke us all with her screams one night and in the morning we were told that she had lost the baby.

'In an old way my head became separate from my body. My head went on being me while my body became just this baby-nurturing place. I knew that twenty-four weeks is about the minimum age at which a foetus will survive if it is born. I didn't care how long I had to lie immobile like that, as long as I didn't lose the babies. What I learnt about myself was how strong my urge was to be a mother.'

Pamela hung in there for eight weeks. After six her husband was due to go on an overseas business trip. 'The night before he was leaving I told him, "Don't", and he stayed. I don't know why but I just knew he would miss the birth if he went. As it turned out the boys were born the night before he would have been due to get home.

'I started into labour and even though they tried there was nothing that the medical staff could do to hold it back. They let me go for two hours and then the doctor told me that he was going to give me an anaesthetic because it seemed likely that in order to save the babies I would need a caesarian. When I woke up the first thing he told me was that I hadn't had a caesarian and the second thing he told me was that I had two little boys. Firstly I felt elated that they'd been born alive and then I felt a tiny twinge of disappointment that I hadn't had a girl and a boy. Then he showed me the babies and I remember thinking that I had imagined they would be bigger, but the staff all behaved as though their size was perfectly natural, so I accepted it as that.'

But it was not perfectly natural. Born at twenty-eight weeks the twins were two pounds (990 grams) and one pound four ounces (660 grams). Right from the start it was a fight for survival, and for Julian, the smaller twin, a fight he had little hope of winning.

Pamela spent the next three months more or less living between the intensive care wards of two hospitals. 'For only two weeks Julian and Jeremy lay side by side in their separate humidicribs in the same hospital ward. It was at this stage that I thought they both would make it. Then Julian developed a heart problem and was moved to the Children's Hospital. He also developed the biggest hernia the doctor had ever seen and during the time he was struggling to live he had twenty-seven blood transfusions.

'I coped because there was no alternative. No choice. That's what I learnt; that when you have to, you can cope with anything. I couldn't go under because they needed me. When I first got out of bed after they were born I couldn't stand up because my muscles were so wasted. But I couldn't say, 'I don't feel like going to the hospital today, I am too tired', or, 'I don't want to face it any more'. I don't think it's made me a better person, just that I understand myself more. I didn't have time to be scared or sorry for myself.

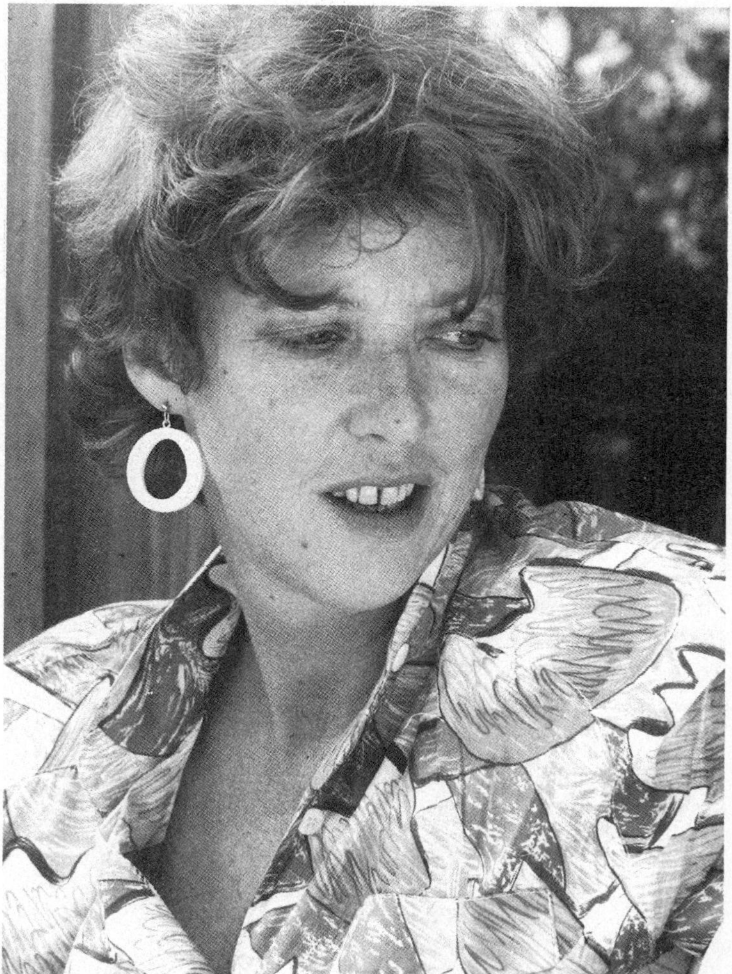

Every part of me, my brain,
my heart, my whole being
was set around one thing,
the babies surviving.
Nothing else even existed.

'Every part of me, my brain, my heart, my whole being was set around that one thing, them surviving. Nothing else even existed. It was like living on another planet away from the rest of the world. In some ways it was a state of insanity. I didn't ever cry. There wasn't time. Or perhaps I realised that once I started I wouldn't stop and then I wouldn't be any use. And I never thought, why me? After all, why not me? But I didn't think that at the time either. All my effort was concentrated on getting through this day and into the next. I knew that the stronger they seemed the greater their chances.

'We both felt the same way, though of course it is different for the woman, the mother. We talked about it but that became repetitive. All either of us could do was hope. He had to get on with his own professional life and my life was centred on them. I kept a daily diary. Perhaps that helped as an outlet. I kept it until two weeks before Julian died and then I just stopped. I didn't read back through it until two months after he had died and then I realised that although at the time I told myself and other people that he was going to live, everything in the diary was telling myself that he was not going to make it. That is what is so amazing about the human mind, that it can play tricks like that on itself, as self-protection. I'll keep that diary, along with the photographs I took, so that when his brother is older he can read it as well as see what his twin looked like. I think that's important.

'The hospital staff, both the doctors and nurses, were just fantastic. They worked around the clock. You could go in there at any time of the day or night and they would be there watching and caring. They would sit there for four, five or six hours simply holding these little things in their arms, trying to fill them with the will to live. I'm sorry, even now it makes me cry to think about it.'

We leave the sanctuary of the balcony to walk about as a way of accommodating the emotion. Jeremy watches from startlingly large blue eyes, his gaze unwavering, even when she tousles his fine blond hair. 'How could anyone regret going through that when this one has turned out so brilliantly.' She fairly glows with that enviable joy so special to first-time mothers, and which makes my arms ache with emptiness.

'Jeremy came home the day he had been due to be born. By then he weighed three kilograms, still only six and a half pounds. The doctor told me to keep remembering that he was three months younger than his birth certificate shows. I think they tell you that so you won't panic when you compare him with other children. They say that after three or four years there won't be any difference but at the moment he is thirteen months, though only ten, and I can't help wanting him to get up and walk like other thirteen-month-olds! He gets very frustrated as I'm sure his head says he can do it but his body doesn't follow.

'I am conscious of the need to stimulate him a lot because he has started off a bit behind others, but I don't have any great plans for his future. I do want him to go to a good school, a coeducational one, and naturally I want him to do something more than be a builder's mate. But that's all a long way down the track. For now I am glad he's been a placid, healthy baby. No awful night-time feeds, no problems at all, so it's been easy to do what the doctors said and treat him like a normal baby. He has weak lungs still and they said in the hospital that I should be prepared for him to be prone to bronchitis. He hasn't had it yet, though he has had a few little colds. I haven't been overprotective. Well, I don't think I have, but of course I don't have anything to compare with. The love I feel for him is incredible. I expect I am a bit overboard about him, in his mind, but not in mine!'

It was two weeks after Jeremy came home that Julian died. 'The truth is that it was a relief really. He'd had three and a half months of struggle. He had never been without pain, though the hospital told me he didn't hurt too much. Of course he did, he just didn't know any different. He never smiled. That's sad. But it also made his death easier for me because I knew he wasn't happy. I had just reached the point when I was almost frightened that he wasn't going to die naturally and that I would be faced with making awful decisions. So I was strangely relieved for him.

'But the next couple of months was the hardest period. It made us feel closer to each other, even though we were helpless to help each other. I think I became a stronger person, even if only for that particular time. The strength has faded now, except that I suppose I realise in an intellectual sense that as I could call on it then I could call on it again, though I hope I never have to in the same way.'

It was also then that Pam gained great strength from other women. 'My mother came up from Adelaide and was absolutely wonderful. My sister Helen, who was still living in Sydney then, was also a terrific help. I don't know how I would have coped without them and a few friends, in particular my good friend Susan. We had been friends for some time but this made us really close friends. Susan has two children, so she understood and we didn't have to talk about it. She visited a lot and we would just laugh and joke. It was great.'

Pam has gone back to work at the ABC doing a weekly night-time travel program with Bob Hudson on 2BL. When Jeremy was seven months she went to Finland for ten days for the program. 'His father was here, and told me later that he loved having time on his own with him. We had a full-time live-in nanny so I was relaxed about the kind of care he was getting, but I still phoned every day, just to make sure he had woken up, that he was alive.'

Three months after Julian died Pam went back to the hospital for Jeremy's first checkup and to thank the staff for all they had done. 'The sister asked me if I could face going back into the nursery ward, because there was a woman there who had a very premature baby and she thought it would give her courage to see how Jeremy had developed into a normal, healthy baby. She said, "You don't have to do it but if you could I am sure it would help," so of course I said, "Yes."

'Well, it came as such a shock. All these tiny little creatures, like dolls, in humidicribs. This woman's baby was thirty grams bigger than Jeremy had been at birth and yet he was so minute. It just shows how your mind adapts to be able to cope. When my boys were born I just took it all in my stride and lived from day to day.

'I suppose that's what we do all the time anyway. Right now I know that I don't want to work full time and within the next couple of months I have to make up my mind about how I see my commitment to work. I know the danger is that I shall lose my professional confidence unless I keep working in some way or other, it's really surprising how quickly that happens. Although I've worked hard and enjoyed my work I need deadlines to keep me up to the mark otherwise I slack off.

'And anyway, I am very happy just being with Jeremy. He's a great kid. And then there is this thing about having another one. Although we never talked about it I had always assumed I would have at least two. Before I became a mother, children and families were not part of my world. I never really envied family life. I just never thought about it. Now I see families on picnics in parks and think, that's nice.

'I've not exactly lost any friends, but I do tend to see more of the ones who have children and less of the ones with grown children or no children. And I have struck up new friendships with women in the same situation as myself. The other thing which has changed is that I am happy to be just by myself with him. Often I find the day has gone before I have done anything more important than just be with him. Which of course is the most important thing. I guess you could say I am more content.'

Georgene Hughes

There will be plenty of time for me later on. Right now they are what is important.

'Well, I gave it my best shot', is how thirty-three-year-old Georgene Hughes describes her eight-year battle with infertility. It's a phrase she used several times during our conversation, which she squeezed in between dropping one of her children at school, a second one at kindy, and yet another visit to her doctor. It's a phrase which summarises Georgene's attitude to life and in particular to mothering. Yet it's too brief and dismissive to pay real tribute to what she must have endured in order to get her family.

Georgene and her husband have adopted three children, all of them from Chile. 'When people say, "What wonderful people you are to have rescued those children from all that poverty. How lucky they are that you have taken them in," I tell them straight. I never considered that. And I see it as me being lucky to get them. I did it for myself. For selfish reasons. I wanted children and couldn't have my own. So I adopted.' But of course it wasn't as simple as that.

Georgene and her husband, who works in the computer department of an airline, have been married for fifteen years. 'We started on the fertility trail only six months after the wedding, though we didn't realise at first that this was what it was. The initial indication that there was a problem was that my periods stopped. I'd had trouble with an IUD. Dreadful bleeding. They told me, "You have to give it a chance to settle down," so I tried hanging in there but after three months, when I was bleeding so heavily I passed out at work, I thought, that's it, and had it taken out. But I think that by then the damage had been done. It had set up an infection. In fact we are suing the manufacturers.'

Georgene had always imagined that she would one day be a mother. 'Like every young girl, I suppose. I remember the woman next door had a new baby when I was about eight or so and I was always going round there to ask if I could feed it or take it out and push it around in its stroller.' Georgene has a younger brother who is married and has children. 'I left school at sixteen and took a secretarial course, because I didn't have a clue what I wanted to do. And then I went to work, mostly for stockbrokers and merchant bankers and for my dad's advertising agency.'

Just before she was eighteen her mother died. 'She had a heart condition brought on by alcoholism. She was forty-four. She and Dad had never got along so I don't have many happy childhood memories. Perhaps that's one of the reasons why I was so determined to have a family of my own.' Within six months of her mother's death Georgene was married and in less than a year had discovered that a family of her own might not be as easy to achieve as she had assumed it would be. 'Even now I can't tell you for sure what it was that made me so determined. I do have this stubborn streak. Just ask my husband! So I think it was partly that the more difficult it grew the more determined I became. Perhaps I wanted it because it was something I couldn't have! It was a challenge!'

Over the next eight years Georgene had two children, both stillborn at seven months, and three miscarriages. The sorrow and heartache behind that bland sentence is proof of the inadequacy of words.

'Perhaps if it had been possible to know in advance what I was going to go through I wouldn't have done it. But fortunately you can't see ahead like that. I wanted a family and my husband did too. I remember him once saying that if you weren't going to have children there wasn't any reason to get married. But he was adamantly against adopting. Like most men he wanted to sire his own. There was never any conflict between us over this. He just said, perhaps a couple of times, that he wouldn't ever consider adopting children, and that was enough for me to accept that was how he felt. I could understand, even though I didn't feel that way myself. So the only thing was for me to go on a fertility program and to give it my best shot.'

From the very beginning it was a nightmare that only the very determined could have endured. 'After a laparoscopy and numerous other examinations and tests established that my Fallopian tubes were not blocked I was diagnosed as having secondary amenorrhoea. I underwent psychological testing to make sure there was no underlying mental reason for the failure of my periods. Then I was put on to a drug which stimulates egg release. It was very, very expensive. This was ten years ago and even then it cost $45 for only fifteen tablets. It also made me suicidally depressed.

'I managed to keep working, on and off. But it was difficult because I had to visit the fertility clinic virtually every day; either to give wee or blood, or to perform some test or be examined. Then I went onto a follicle-stimulating hormone and as a side effect developed extremely painful ovarian cysts. So painful that a couple of times I was hospitalised.

'But then I was one of the very few lucky ones. I became pregnant on the first course of injections. Happy? We were ecstatic! Even when after the first ultrasound I was told it was triplets! From the start I had accepted the risk of a multiple birth. We called them Huey, Louey and Dewey, and thought, well at least it will be over with in one hit! No more injections. Two months later the ultrasound showed just one baby. I think the original operator had been a bit overkeen! That was a relief really.

'I can't say I have ever enjoyed being pregnant. I just wanted the end result. But I was healthy and well and there were no problems at all. I started knitting little things and preparing myself mentally. I was very happy. We both were. My husband had been very supportive all through. He had even run into the clinic on several occasions with my two litre bottles of wee so as to save me the trip. I remember the day the *QE2* was in and there was such a jam on the Harbour Bridge, everybody stopping to have a look at her, that he could see he wasn't going to get to the pathology lab on time. It was imperative to give twenty-four-hour urine samples and all the bottles had to go into the machine for testing in one batch at 8.30 am. And there he was sweating in a traffic jam with this accusing bottle jiggling away on the seat beside him! He finally reached the lab at 9.00 am only to find that everyone else had been delayed by the massive traffic jam so they held the bottles till 9.30 am.'

Georgene laughs at the memory. She is petite and deceptively frail-looking. We talk on the balcony of the new home which the Hughes are building. It has spectacular views of water through the treetops and she has taken me on a tour of the various empty rooms describing the fittings and furniture they plan to have. There is a strong emphasis on it being a family home. Each of the children will have their own room. There is a large play area and even the garage has been planned so that when they have grown into raucous teenagers they will have a space of their own in which to have parties. Her two-year-old daughter is content to play imaginings with a collection of dolls and miniature furniture. Already honing her mothering instincts.

It's only by sheer willpower and the determination to go forward that the distress of the past has been replaced by the content of today. 'I knew my baby had died. I felt it die inside me. One evening I had a big, big pain. A searing pain that doubled me up. I phoned the hospital and they said to sit down and relax and if it wasn't any better in half an hour to phone again. I willed myself into feeling better. But that was it. From then on it moved slowly and eventually stopped. I couldn't tell my husband. I didn't want to upset him unnecessarily and I still clung to the hope that it was all right. But I asked him to take the day off and come to the hospital with me.

'My doctor examined me and told us, "There's no heartbeat. It's died." I remember it being very hot in that little room and the doctor putting an arm around each of us and all of us crying. He knew what we had been through. I had been going to him since before I was married. He booked me in to the hospital for early the next week for tests and all being well for an induction. There was nothing else to do about it so we went out to the brickpits and ordered a thousand bricks for a brick path my husband was laying.

'Two days later I went into spontaneous labour. The contractions were only three minutes apart but before I would let my husband drive me to hospital I washed my hair, like all good women do! Once I was in the hospital the pains slowed down to coming every hour and from then on things were not so crash hot. I was in labour altogether for seventeen hours. When she was finally born my husband hit the floor, collapsed. They were so busy attending to him they didn't have much time for me! I remember the physical details but all the feelings I experienced I've blotted out of my mind. I only remember that I was all right until we had to arrange for the funeral. You can either have a full funeral or for $40 the hospital arranges the whole thing. I remember walking across to the office in another block of the hospital to discuss details and there I became hysterical and they had to get me back to the ward and give me valium to quieten me down.

'I won't pretend it was easy. I would cry and cry and cry. I'd be washing the floors and crying. Friends were very supportive but in the end you have to snap out of it. You can't go on feeling sorry for yourself. People say,' 'Oh you poor thing', but I don't feel like a poor thing. Everybody said we should take a holiday and we did. We went to the Philippines, I've no idea why, and it was a disaster. I was still bleeding. And we were both still upset. We should have waited until we were more able to enjoy a break away together.

'When we came back I waited a few months and went back on the fertility program. I didn't hesitate. I wanted a baby and this was what had to be done in order to have one. More injections. More tests. More blood. More wee. More daily hospital visits. It became a way of life. This time I wasn't as lucky. I became pregnant three times. Two of them, which were described as biochemical pregnancies, miscarried under three months. The one that went three months required a D and C to clean me out.

'My fifth pregnancy was unstable from the beginning. The placenta kept coming away from the wall and several times I went into premature labour. But I hung in there for seven months and felt very positive about making it to full term. Then exactly two years and two days after our first daughter was born I had a second girl, also stillborn. She had died inside me but this time there was no spontaneous labour and I had to have an induction.

'This second death was much easier to handle. Perhaps because the morning after her birth, when my husband came to take me home, we had a long discussion and came up with two alternatives; either get out and travel the world or adopt a family. Adoption won out. I've never asked him but perhaps it was just that he couldn't go through all that again.

'I have no regrets at all about doing any of what I have done.

I've been lucky enough to be pregnant. A lot of women haven't had that experience. I've had a delivery and an induction. And now I have three children. So I've not missed out on anything. And apart from that IUD I've never had to mess around with birth control; the side effects and the decisions about staying on the pill or having my tubes tied that my girlfriends have had to make. So you see it has its up side! And once we had decided to adopt I shifted the whole focus of my energy in that direction.'

The Department of Youth and Community Services (YACS) must have felt that 'focus of energy' as if they had been hit by a particle beam accelerator! 'When they told me it would take at least seven years for us to get an Australian child I was stunned. Nowadays it can take ten to fifteen years. And the paperwork and never-ending bureaucracy. It's unbelievable. My life changed from like being inside an episode of *Young Doctors* to being inside an episode of *Yes Minister*! The kindest thing you can say about YACS is that perhaps they do it to try to weed out the ones who aren't keen enough.' But there was no way Georgene was going to be weeded out! 'Dealing with YACS is good training for dealing with small children; you need limitless patience!'

During the YACS home study visit Georgene and her husband made it clear that they did not want to adopt an Aboriginal child. 'The YACS people were at the time encouraging prospective parents to adopt Aboriginal children. Nowadays that attitude has changed and it's almost impossible for white Australians to adopt Aboriginal children. We thought the general prejudice against them would have been too hard for us to handle. If we were adopting in England then yes. And in Australia it would perhaps be easier to handle the problems of adopting a West Indian baby than it would be in England. We didn't want to make martyrs of ourselves. After all you are looking at a lifetime commitment. I admit that this was in part a racist response and we have completely changed our attitude now, but that was how we were in the beginning. That attitude went against us in our home study and YACS told us that, but we honestly believed that a child of Anglo-Saxon appearance would assimilate more easily.

'At that time there were few countries open for overseas adoption. Korea had just closed its books for the time being, which I was sorry about because I would have dearly loved a South-East Asian baby. The only options were Colombia, Sri Lanka and maybe India. Taking what we saw as the easier way out we decided on Colombia.'

The home study visit was not a pleasant experience. 'It makes you feel invaded. They ask very personal questions and you feel that all your values are being tested. Which they are. It's ludicrous really when you look at the way the majority of people go into parenting. It's very rare for people to question their own worth or their ability to be a good parent; whether they can afford to have separate rooms for their children or what sort of bathroom facilities they have. But all these things are looked into, along with your health, your financial status, your marriage, your police record and your religion. The only thing they don't ask is which party you vote for, though you can sense they try to assess that too. And of course the final touch is that all these questions are usually asked by young, unmarried women, with no children of their own. Luckily I am very good at playing these games, keeping my mouth shut when necessary and trotting out the right responses. Especially when something I really want is in the balance.'

After all this Georgene's babies came through a private source. 'It's still necessary to be approved by YACS and even though I was on the Colombian list I kept putting out feelers in other areas. It's a small world, the adopting world, you quickly work out that they all know each other. I had begun by talking to the various religious groups which are involved, mostly the Anglicans and the Catholics.'

Georgene is herself a Catholic. 'I don't go overboard and my husband isn't, but we're converting him, the children and I! We were married in a Church of England because my local parish priest wouldn't marry us unless my husband converted and I wasn't going to ask that of him. After all he fell in love with me not with a particular religion. But I have found that over the years my faith has become more important to me. My husband has seen how much a belief in God helped me through those difficult times. Being able to pray and talk about my hidden fears to someone I felt cared about me. Mind you there were times when I wondered if God really did care then why was all this happening to me; perhaps I'd done something wrong . . . I found comfort in going to church and I was happy when one Sunday recently my husband asked if I would like him to come too. Mind you, he would soon jack up if I was to insist on going every Sunday, but he can see how important it is for children to have religious beliefs.'

Georgene's faith had no bearing on her decision to try to adopt a baby from the strongly Catholic country of Chile. Her reasons were far more pragmatic. 'I just hoped I'd be able to get a baby faster from there. We were given the name of a solicitor in Chile who handled adoptions. I phoned and asked him to put us on his list and then I sent him all the paperwork from YACS, priority paid! I expect I drove him crazy because I kept phoning to pester him, just so he wouldn't forget us.

'There's plenty of competition for Chilean babies. Many of them go to homes in the USA and in Europe. The Swedes adopt so many that they have set up a Swedish Adoption Agency funded by the Swedish government in the capital, Santiago, to deal with the paperwork. I really admire what the Swedes do. They allow people to adopt children with physical difficulties whereas the government here will only permit babies with completely clear health records. That's awful. I think they don't want to take in anyone who may be a burden on the health care system. That sort of attitude is morally indefensible.

'We were incredibly lucky because six months after my initial approach we had a phone call in the middle of the night saying that our baby had just been born. I remember my husband doing a little dance at the bottom of the bed! We were so excited that we stayed up for the rest of night, drinking numerous cups of tea, talking, making plans and throwing a few things into a suitcase. The next day we were on our way to Chile to pick up Petene.

'We left with no money, because the call had come in the small hours of a Saturday morning so of course there were no banks open. But when I spoke to my dad he said, "You go, I'll send some money over to you by telegraphic transfer." He had been through everything with us, right from the start; the stillbirths and miscarriages as well as the adoption plans. He had been incredibly supportive, even to the extent of giving us money when we needed it for some additional unexpected expenses. Adopting from overseas is not cheap; not by the time you pay the phone bill, the airfares and accommodation, the legal fees and in the case of Petene the private hospital bill. Not that we ever thought of her in those terms of course. We did eventually manage to get the money in Santiago, but only after spending four frustrating hours in a Chilean bank trying to explain in our non-existent Spanish what it was we wanted!'

The man who had called with the news from Santiago was the solicitor Georgene had spoken to several times during the previous months. 'Carlos met us at our hotel and took us straight to the private clinic where Petene had been born. Chile is a very different country from Australia. From the moment we knew that we would be getting our baby from there we had read everything about the country that we could lay our hands on: fiction, non-fiction, political, historical, the lot. It's surprisingly difficult in Australia to find out much about Chile. We discovered *The South American Handbook*, which is a sort of bible for travellers on that continent, and that was more informative than anything else.

'Their society is far more divided than ours. About 5 per cent of the people are immensely wealthy, the rest are dirt poor. There's almost no middle class. The majority of the babies who come up for adoption are from poor families and they are given away simply because the mother cannot afford to keep them. It's very sad for them. I cannot begin to imagine how awful it must be to have to give your child away.

'If a girl from the wealthy classes has an unwanted pregnancy she is simply sent away, ostensibly on a skiing holiday or something like that, for six months. That was the background we assume Petene came from. Both her parents were only fifteen. And that was as much as we were officially told. Unofficially we learnt a lot more. But first of all there was Petene.

'We had decided that if our baby was a girl that was what she would be called. It's a combination of my name and my husband's. As you can imagine, we really wanted a little girl because of losing our two daughters. It wouldn't have mattered if she had been a boy but we were extra delighted when she was a girl.

'Can I remember what I felt the first time I saw her? Can I ever! I thought, what have I done! She was the ugliest baby I had ever seen! She looked like a little gorilla: thick black sidelevers, a black moustache and eyebrows that met in the middle! And to top it all off, so to speak, they had shaved her head so the white skull stood out in sharp contrast to all this black hair. I found out later that all highborn Chilean babies' heads are shaved at birth. But I can tell you that the way she looked was such a shock that I was lost for words. Afterwards in the taxi my husband told me that he had assumed I was so overjoyed I couldn't speak. He said, "It's rare for you to be lost for words," and then I told him that what I had been thinking was, can I give her back?

'I think it was partly that I wasn't adequately prepared, how can you be? But it was also a fact that she was specially hairy. She still is a bit. We have told Petene all this. I don't believe in pretending or keeping things from your children. Now we can all laugh about it. And I tell her, thick eyebrows are all the go, look at Brooke Shields, and by the time you are a young woman that fashion will have gone out and come back again, like all fashions!'

Just before leaving Chile the Hughes were invited to dinner at the home of a wealthy friend of Carlos the solicitor. There were several other guests, including the doctor who had delivered Petene. 'The children of our hosts were all present, barring their fifteen-year-old daughter. We started to put two and two together, especially after a conversation with one of the other daughters, who also had a baby which she was breastfeeding.

'When I knew that our baby was imminent I had started taking an anti-nauseant which had the side effect of encouraging my milk to come in. I wanted to do the whole bit. As it turned out I didn't manage to keep my milk. But at least I'd tried. Given it my best shot. They made me salivate like mad, so I was constantly drooling! To help the milk come in I was advised to massage my breasts. At the time I had a dress shop on the North Shore and I'd be driving home with one hand on the wheel and giving myself a massage with other. God knows what all the people I drove past in buses thought of me! Anyway the day we picked up Petene my husband was shaving and I was standing behind him trying to get a look in the mirror and I gave the old boob a squirt and out it came all over him and the mirror and I was delighted!

'While this other daughter and I were upstairs feeding, looking over each other's babies, like new mothers do, I said, "I wonder whether Petene's eyes will change colour as she gets older?" and the daughter said, "Oh no, they'll be dark." I thought, uh-huh, and dropped a few other queries, like how tall would she grow and whether her hair would be curly or straight. It was obvious from her definite replies that she knew the mother of the child. All this is assumption but we're pretty sure we were being given the once over. We have sent Carlos photographs of Petene and suggested he send them on to "the couple we had dinner with and who showed such an interest in Petene". But we have never had any response. And I think that is as well because I don't think I would ever like to meet my children's natural mothers.'

Back in Australia Georgene became an instant working mum,

taking Petene with her in a bassinette to her dress shop. Within six months the Hughes applied for another baby. 'I had always known I wanted more than one child. One isn't a family. we didn't stipulate whether we wanted a boy or a girl, after all you can't do that if you have your own. Again we went through Carlos and again we were very lucky and just snuck in there and only had to wait seventeen months, which was a perfect gap between the two of them.'

The Hughes's second baby was a boy, Lloyd, who is now four years old. 'He came from a very different background. His twenty-four-year-old mother was poor, unmarried and already had a little girl who was looked after by her grandmother so that the mother could go to work. At least she had a job. But the grandmother said she couldn't manage to look after a second child, so Lloyd came up for adoption.

Again the reality was not what Georgene or her husband anticipated. 'He wasn't born in a private clinic. He was a week old when we picked him up from an old nurse in the suburbs and he was almost smothered in clothes, poor thing. I unwrapped him and the first thing I saw was his nose. He had a big nose. A very big nose. We immediately called him Snozzle! This time in the cab it was my husband who was quiet and when I asked him what he was thinking he said, "I'm thinking that if we put away a dollar a week from now until he's eighteen perhaps we'll be able to afford for him to have a nose job then!" But of course his face has grown and his nose shrunk in proportion; and now his nose is nothing more than just a big nose!'

Lloyd also suffered from very poor health. 'I knew that something was wrong. He was so very different from how Petene had been at the start. He didn't thrive. He was a slow feeder and I felt he was too docile. He didn't improve and finally I took him to a paediatrician who put him into hospital immediately. I remember hearing him talking on the phone to the hospital and saying, "This baby is very important to this woman!" They discovered a urinary tract infection and then diagnosed salmonella. Never again will I listen to old wives' tales such as, boys' urine smells more than girls, or, boys are quieter and do wee more than girls. My advice to any mother is to follow your own instincts.

'Once he was diagnosed we tried everything. Everything. Changed formulas. Different drugs. You name it, we tried it. In the end they said, 'Look, there is nothing more to try. He has an immature and irritable gut and you just have to wait till he grows out of it.' All right for them to say that. They didn't have to live with it every day!

'For three years Lloyd had diarrhoea, poor little bugger. And when I say diarrhoea I mean *diarrhoea*! Like fifteen times a day, running down his legs like water. And every time he had a spasm I had to disinfect the entire room to get rid of the stench. At nine months he was almost back down to his birthweight. He'd try to crawl and he'd collapse. It was heartbreaking and it was also exhausting. He developed a whine, which he still has and although it is quite understandable it really gets to me. Then he began to have tantrums. I got so desperate I'd be in tears myself just with the tiredness and stress and a couple of times it got so bad I put him in hospital for a day or so just to get a break from it and have someone else clean up after him.'

It didn't help that during this time Georgene had financial troubles with her shop and sold up. Or that she was also caring for her dying father. 'Dad died of retirement and that's the truth. After Mum died he really only lived for me. We were very close and he was a wonderful man. He was all for us adopting and was a really positive force behind us. But when he retired he just faded away. He had no other interests. He was only sixty-eight when he died. Lloyd was only six months. It was a big blow to me. I am really sorry that he never saw our third baby and didn't live long enough to enjoy being a grandfather.'

During this time Georgene was also putting a lot of effort into running a support group for prospective adopting parents and in particular for those who were interested in adopting from Chile.

Raising a family is hard, physical work. But my tiredness is made up for many times over by what they give me. Love and happiness and great pleasure.

'They would come to the house and look at our two and we would tell them about our experiences. It's very comforting to meet people who have experienced both the emotional and physical traumas involved. In a way I felt it was my responsibility to share this with others, to give encouragement; a way of saying thank you for our good fortune if you like.'

One of the things which this support group did was to meet new parents and their babies off the flights from Chile. 'It's then that you need a boost because you feel, help, what have I taken on here? My husband particularly enjoyed this official welcoming party role. And it was at one of these gatherings, when Petene was two and a half and Lloyd was fourteen months that we heard that Lloyd's natural mother was pregnant again. Well! I caught my husband's eye and he immediately shook his head and said, "No, George! You can't cope with two," which was true, "how could you possibly manage with three?" Well, sometimes I'm rash and sometimes I wait half an hour! This time I had to hound the old boy for two weeks! But in the meantime I had approached YACS and asked them to cut corners and at that stage they couldn't see any problems.

'If my husband had been dead set against it of course I wouldn't have gone through with it. But I knew he'd come round. As he always says, there isn't room in this relationship for two generals! In the end he said, "You always get what you want, George, so go for it!"'

So go for it she did, no doubt leaving YACS whimpering in the corner! 'They weren't at all helpful. In fact they were obstructionist. At one stage we were told that approval would only be allowed if there was proof of the same mother and father. Mum was easy; Dad impossible. Final approval came through at almost the same time as Chile closed its overseas adoptions. I knew I had to move fast or I'd lose her.

'The day the YACS approval came through was a Friday and I got all the paperwork done in four hours, which I am sure is a record! Prospective parents are not allowed to touch the paperwork so we had this ludicrous situation of following a courier car around from government office to government office to make sure our papers were shuffled by the right people and received the right stamps. I was way out in the far western suburbs of Sydney at 4.50 getting the last bit of approval when the woman behind the desk said, in a nasty tone, "You won't be able to get back into town in ten minutes to get the telex sent to the Australian Embassy in Santiago asking for the baby's re-entry visa, will you? And you can't fly out without that." I didn't bother to reply.'

The woman should have known better than to think that a mere piece of paper would unseat Georgene. 'The next day we were on the flight to Chile and I just arranged to have a friend go into the Department of Immigration and arrange things. All these rules and reglations are made to be manipulated. I tell you I have learnt a great deal about the public service and the people who work for it and about government and politicians. And almost none of it is good!

'But I had succeeded in my biggest wish; I had my new baby home in time for Christmas. That's a very family orientated time for us and we didn't want to be away from the other two.'

Georgene found, like many women before her, that whereas two small children are manageable, just, with three the problems are magnified not to the power of three but to the power of ten! 'I very quickly came to the decision that with three it was a physical impossibility to walk out of the door looking like a fashion plate. Not when you have vomit on your shoulder and Vegemite down your trouser leg! I had always been very fussy about the way I looked. The hair, the nails, the full bit. Now it's a quick shampoo and shower, and if I'm lucky a quick zip over the legs with the razor, because they want something to eat, or they have to be run somewhere, or they need something fixed or perhaps they just need you to be there. There's simply no time left for me any more. It was much better once I just gave up and accepted that. I don't resent it.

'There will be plenty of time for me later on. Right now they are what is important. The time of full-time mothering goes very quickly. Petene is already at school and Lloyd goes to kindy twice a week. I cried like a sook the night before her first day at school and I was dreading taking her there. But she just skipped in with her friend without even so much as a backward glance! I wouldn't go out to work when the children are this small. I have toyed with the idea but there's no way my husband would let me. And I think those first four years are a very important time for bonding. After that, well I haven't looked that far ahead yet. I'm busy with them and the new house and we are still very involved with the Chilean Support Group as well as raising money for an orphanage in Chile which houses children who are unable to be adopted.

'I look forward to the holidays when we can all go off to the pantomime or to the beach or zoo and have a generally good time without having to rush. One of the things you don't think about before is that raising a family is hard, physical work. Most evenings I am so tired that by 6.00 I can hardly wait to open the fridge to have a glass of wine. I never have one before but quite often I am really only just hanging in there waiting for the hands to reach the magic hour!

'But this tiredness — it's more like continuous exhaustion really — is made up for many, many times over by all the things they give me. Love and happiness and great pleasure. I enjoy them so much. I don't have any great plans for their future. I just want them to be happy and feel loved. They all know they are adopted and that they come from Chile. We don't sit them down and say, 'You are adopted,' it has just come out in the natural course of events. Sometime in the future we would like to take them all on a holiday to Chile. And I have to face the fact that it's pretty much an odds-on certainty that one of the three of them will want to meet their natural mother. I don't know how I'll handle that if and when that time comes. Right now it's not something I relish. But I'll worry about that if it happens.

'I have other things to worry about at the moment, like how to handle the ignorance and prejudice we sometimes cop. Oh yes. I've learnt that we're an ignorant lot, us Australians. Petene had only been at the school two weeks before she came home and said a couple of the children were calling her Brownee. Little kids don't think those sorts of words up by themselves. That has to come from their parents. I was down the school quick as a flash and told the Sister in charge and that put a stop to that.

'But almost every time I go out with the kids, down the street, in the supermarket, or wherever, a woman will come up to me and say, "What lovely hair your children have," or "What lovely eyes." What they are really asking is, "Where did you get them from?" The more blatant ones say, "My, your children are dark, is their father Australian?" and when I say yes, they go even further and ask, "And are you Australian?" Sometimes I just say yes and leave it at that. It depends on my mood. I suppose they are just being inquisitive but I get the feeling they are prying and that it's none of their business. I just want my children to be accepted for what they are, good kids. After all by the time they are adults the Anglo-Saxons in Australia will more than likely be far outnumbered by the rest. It's a worldwide trend. The future is theirs.

'Each of them have very different personalities. Even Lloyd and Teghan are dissimilar, though they are half-brother and sister. I have always believed that how a person develops is influenced 95 per cent by environment and only 5 per cent by heredity. We have noticed with adopting families that gregarious parents have gregarious children. Quiet parents have quiet children.

'I have discussed with my husband the possibility of adopting another child, an older one, because I don't think I could go through that baby stage again and we have realised that older children are the ones in need. But right now it's a financial impossibility. Also right now I'm two months pregnant! This is the first time I've fallen pregnant without stimulation. I'm not getting too excited just yet. If there are difficulties like I've had before they would be very much magnified by the fact that I have three small children to look after. But we'll take it one step at a time. When I first found out I was pretty stunned. My husband was too. Our first reaction was we can't go through it again. I worried about how I would cope, but over last weekend I bled a little and had a lot of pain so I thought I was going to lose it and I found that I didn't want to. It's part of me now. I rested, which was something we had decided I wouldn't do because the three we have are more important than this possible one, but those hormones have started working! This afternoon I am going for an ultrasound and after that, well, I'll give it my best shot.'

Brenda

'I decided the moment I had the result of the test and it showed positively that I was pregnant, that I was going to have the baby. I didn't have to make up my mind. It was already made up. I had always wanted a child. I was thirty-four and financially secure. Now was the time.

'Everyone has their own priorities. Some people wait until they have established their career, or they've been overseas, or they have a house, or whatever. The fact is if you waited for the ideal situation before having a baby you'd wait forever. I thought, if I don't have this baby what am I going to want in order to have one? Enough things were right. The fact that the father would not be around was insufficient reason not to have the baby.'

For most women having the father around is the initial priority. They fall in love, marry and have children. Far more frequently than is admitted they fall in love, become pregnant and then get married and have children. A little less commonly they fall in love, live together for a while and when they decide to have children they then get married. But the common denominator in all these real life dramas is a man. At least in the first act. But for Brenda the man was only around for scene one of act one, and after that she made the unusual decision to perform the rest of the play single-handed.

This decision makes Brenda appear extraordinary only if viewed out of context. Almost immediately on meeting her it seemed quite in keeping with her whole life; and after just a few hours of conversation it appeared more or less inevitable. What seemed more difficult to reconcile with her highly individualistic views is the fact that she is a doctor, which is the reason why her surname is not given.

To meet a medico who doesn't automatically assume you realise and respect the fact that she sits at the Creator's left hand and therefore has total dominion over other mere humans, is a pleasure to be savoured. When she said that in becoming a mother she felt she had become a better doctor, was it just my imagination or did I hear an hrumphh! of displeasure resounding from hallowed halls on high? Perhaps it's no mere coincidence that the two things Brenda has always most wanted to be were a doctor and a mother.

'Within the family it was more or less taken for granted that I would be a doctor. My father was a coalminer's son who wanted to be a doctor but trained as a psychiatric nurse because that was the closest option. So as a child it was assumed that I should study medicine. He was a remarkable man. He left Glasgow as a seventeen-year-old coalminer and came to Australia to seek new opportunities, to make something of his life. He certainly did that and along the way he became the first communist trade union secretary in the health field. Even though he died when I was only three I inherited the strength of his political convictions and perhaps also the confidence to live life by my own values and not to be swayed too much by what others might think.

'When he died my mother was left with three children, all under five years of age. I come from a family of psychologically very strong, self-reliant women. My grandmother was left during the Depression with two children whom she brought up by herself. I think that both these women, what they endured, what they created and what they achieved, had a very significant impact on me.

'I have always felt that it is women who have babies and who are ultimately responsible for them. It is great to have the father around but women shouldn't go into motherhood feeling that there will always be a man to take care of them and the children. You only have to see the number of women who are divorced, separated or widowed to realise it's an unrealistic expectation. This is not a put-down of men. It's an acceptance of the facts of life. I couldn't have continued with my pregnancy if I had needed to be dependent on someone else. I would not have had my baby unless I was sure that I could manage on my own.

'As a child I took it for granted that one day I would have a baby. I guess a lot of that was also upbringing but as well there were all those stereotyped images in magazines and on television of happy families with mothers in aprons baking cakes. What little girl can avoid them? I didn't feel complete until I had James. It's really as simple as that!'

At high school Brenda was an above average student, '. . . probably because I loved it. I found it easy so that meant it was enjoyable. But that also meant university came as a shock because it wasn't enjoyable. It wasn't so much that I needed to make an extra effort, it was that I didn't fit in with the other medical students.

'They came from privileged backgrounds. Almost all of them were still living sheltered lives at home. They'd drive to uni in their mothers' cars and they didn't become involved in the mainstream of university life. They gave the impression of thinking they were above all that. University for them was an information factory, not a place to develop your ideas.

'I came from a very different background. I left home when I was nineteen. For a year I lived in a room in my grandmother's little inner-city flat, which was near enough to the university for me to get there by public transport. After that I moved into a communal house set-up, sharing with a bunch of other students, none of them from the medical faculty. Those were the days of the Vietnam Moratorium and I became very politically active, which was another reason why my studies suffered.

'What I was learning was interesting enough, but I found the other medical students uncongenial and there were plenty of times when I felt like totally changing my direction and joining the arts faculty. But people kept assuring me it would all be much better once we were into clinical studies, so I hung in there only to find that clinical studies were even worse!

'I remember the occasion that made me decide to give it all away. A woman had come in with lumps in her breasts. She had only found them herself the day before and had gone straight to her own doctor who had immediately sent her in to the hospital for a further examination. It had all happened so quickly she was still in a state of shock. The doctor asked her if she would mind being examined by medical students and when she objected because as she said most of them were young men the same age as her own sons and she felt embarrassed, the doctor simply ignored her request and this poor women found herself suddenly surrounded by a crowd of males, all of them trying to feel her breasts. I was devastated for her and I thought, no, no, this is not what I want to do with my life. I want to work somewhere where they care for women, where they see them as more than just lumps and numbers.'

That place was Preterm, a family planning and abortion clinic where Brenda had been working as a counsellor on a part-time basis since it opened. 'Those were exciting times. We were fighting for women's rights. As I see it a woman's choice to control her own fertility and to say, "Yes I want this baby," or "No I don't," is an absolutely fundamental human right. I don't try to play moral games. I accept that a foetus is a life right from the moment of conception. It is the start of a continuous line which if left to develop would in nine months be a baby and in seventy years an elderly person. But I feel that the mother has the right to intervene with this natural course of events when it is as nebulous a life as it is at six or eight weeks. Every termination is a sad event and in all the years I have worked for Preterm I have never met a woman who took the decision lightly. I accept that sometimes it's necessary to make that sad and difficult decision.'

During her early student days Brenda had the usual run of boyfriends. 'There were a couple who lasted six or twelve months. In my mid-twenties there was also a relationship which lasted several years and which was very important to me. In fact it was probably more important than any other relationship has ever been, even to this day. He was a doctor but we didn't meet through work. There was no question of us marrying and when I became pregnant I had a termination and that more or less sealed the end of the affair.'

Satisfying though her work as a counsellor was, after a couple of years '. . . it became a dead end. I could see that. There was nowhere else to go, no place to spread out a bit, unless I took a degree. If I wanted to go counselling outside of Preterm, in the VD clinic, or in the drug rehabilitation area, or any government job, I required a degree. I was already halfway through my medical degree so it seemed sensible to go back and finish it. I had now met plenty of positive role models, dedicated women doctors who gained satisfaction from their work, and who encouraged me to go back to medicine, so I gritted my teeth and re-enrolled, fully prepared to hate every minute of it. Instead, I loved it!

'One of the reasons for this was because instead of returning to the large, impersonal, supposedly elite city hospital where I was before, I went to a small, friendly suburban hospital where all the staff knew us by name and where we were treated like members of a large family. The work was a pleasure and I had no problems at all finishing my degree.'

By this time Brenda was thirty. 'I felt happy with the direction my career was taking but in the back of my mind I was beginning to feel that I really wanted a baby. I still had plenty of casual boyfriends and lovers but nothing serious.' One of these lovers was a man in his late thirties, a country man who ran a cattle property in Queensland and visited the city only occasionally. 'He was a cowboy really. I had met him when I was still making up my mind about going back to medicine and was working as a waitress at Noosa Heads on the south Queensland coast. Later we always got together when I went to Noosa or he came to Sydney on business. It was a good sexual relationship and I always looked forward to seeing him.'

But there was no one who looked like sharing Brenda's life and being a father to the baby she wanted. 'Sometimes I can't help wondering whether there isn't something wrong with me. Other women don't seem to have any problem forming a relationship. Perhaps I'm just too particular. Though I did manage to become engaged! He was an Englishman whom I met here. I even went to England, met his family and spent three months with him. He was gentle and polite and sent me roses once a week. It's awful but the truth is that in the end he bored me stupid! Also he'd had a vasectomy. Reversal is often possible but the chance of becoming pregnant is somewhat reduced. When the relationship ended it was almost a relief.'

The urge to become a mother was growing stronger and stronger. 'I don't think I would have just selected a man to be the father of my child and then purposely set out to become pregnant. But who knows what I would have done eventually if it hadn't happened the way it did.' Brenda's cowboy came to town. 'We hadn't seen each other for three years but we'd been trying to get together for six months or so. I'd even flown up to Queensland for Easter to be with him but then he'd been delayed and I'd had to come back to work without seeing him. So when he phoned one morning to say he'd be in town overnight I was delighted.

'By the time we met I was all a-tremble. He always had that effect on me! We had dinner and spent a great night together. It was early in my menstrual cycle and I used a diaphragm and the morning-after pill. The next day he flew off to the Northern Territory and I went back to work.'

Shortly after this visit Brenda took a job as a locum in a country town. 'It was winter and it became pretty cold out there and I remember saying to someone, "My god, it's so cold my nipples ache!" But when the aching went on and my periods were a few days late, I thought, ah-ha, this is more than just the cold. I didn't think that as the unmarried locum in a small town I should send in my own urine sample for testing so I bought a predictor kit from the chemist and tested myself. And of course it showed positive.

'Whether or not I was going to have the baby was never really an issue at all. It wasn't a difficult decision to make. I was pregnant and I was going to have the baby. I was delighted. I never had any doubts that having a baby was the right thing for me to do. And as there was no man looming on the horizon nor any history of such men, well, it looked as though I would be having the baby on my own.

'Once the pregnancy was confirmed I did phone the father. I was certain he was the father because I hadn't had sex with anyone else for weeks before his fleeting visit. I just put it to him straight. I said, "I'm pregnant and I'm going to have the baby. I'm not asking for any support from you, financial or otherwise, and I realise this is as much of a shock to you as it was to me, so I don't want you to say anything at all now but if you want you could phone back." He never did.

'Yes, that did upset me. Not from the point of view of being a sole parent. That was something I was quite happy to accept. But what did upset me was that it was such an ungenerous response. I didn't expect or even want him to make any offers. After all I have my life here and my career and that wouldn't fit in with his, travelling around Australia and living in the outback. But I would have liked him to phone back. Perhaps to say, "Look Brenda, I'm not interested in being a father but let's stay friends." Or even if he had just said, "Goodluck and goodbye." But not to say anything, that made me question my judgement of men. It made me feel a little insecure about myself and wonder why I had such poor judgement.

'However, I was busy getting my own life sorted out and preparing for motherhood so I didn't have much time to waste on useless speculation. I knew that I would want to take six months off work after the baby was born, and in order to earn enough money to be able to do that I needed to work flat out.'

Brenda took on an extra job which entailed her leaving after Saturday morning surgery and driving for a couple of hours to begin a weekend shift at a country hospital. 'I was on duty through the entire weekend. Sometimes it was so busy I'd get no sleep at all and other times it was slower and I'd manage to catch a couple of hours. At 9.00 on Monday morning I was back at my other job. I could only keep that pace up for the first five months; after that I worked less regularly as a casual locum on weekends. I was lucky that I stayed healthy most of the time.'

But not all of the time. 'I had two bouts of acute back pain. Each time it was so bad I was forced to stay in bed for ten days or I hobbled around bent double on a walking stick. It's not uncommon during pregnancy for the change in hormones to soften the ligaments. That's what happened to me. On the first occasion, when I was eight weeks pregnant, I just sneezed and put my back out! The second time it happened was when I was seven months. Both times were extremely painful and both times I found myself worrying about how I would cope with such things when I had a baby to care for and no one to care for me.

'I was very lucky with the obstetrician I had. He knew what my situation was and he asked me, "Have you heard from the bloke?" I told him no and he said, "Now because you are doing this on your own I am giving you my home telephone number and I want you to phone me any time you have a problem or you just want to talk. Other women, when they wake up in the middle of the night and feel worried, have a man beside them whom they can wake up and talk it over with. But you don't and that can be pretty scary. So you feel free to phone me. Even at 2.00 in the morning." When he said that I just burst into tears!'

Brenda also had the total support of her mother, stepfather, sisters and brother. 'We're a strong unit and a close family. Whatever I choose to do I can rely on their support. They don't question my decisions. They mightn't agree and perhaps they think that sometimes I pick up too heavy a burden but they are always right there behind me, 100 per cent.

'When I became pregnant I was renting an inner-city house which belonged to my parents. It was good to know that if there had been any problem and I hadn't been able to work there would have been no hassle about paying rent. Since then, with family assistance, I have been able to buy my own, larger, house and moved in here when James was a baby.'

The house has large airy rooms and a feeling of space and light despite being close to the city. We sat and talked in the kitchen at a bench top littered with maps of the mid-west of the state and a souvenir brochure from the Western Plains Zoo which Brenda and James, who is now two and a half, had visited the previous week. 'He loved it. I get such pleasure from his pleasure. We had a great time together. It's on occasions like this I find myself thinking it would be even better if I could share his pleasure with another adult, a man, if not his father. But it's not something which comes to mind very often.'

Although Brenda's pregnancy continued normally she was told that the baby would more than likely be born as a breech delivery. 'He moved, but he never at any stage turned completely. He was always head up, bum down. I also knew from the results of an ultrasound done at thirty weeks that I was having a boy. I am glad I knew that because I really wanted a girl. Partly I think because of the strong female line in my family and partly because I thought it would be easier to raise a girl on my own. A boy is more in need of a male role model. Knowing in advance that I was having a boy gave me time to adjust.

'What worried me more than anything else was that the baby would be in some way abnormal. Perhaps I was even more anxious about this than other women because being a doctor meant that I had seen many sad cases. There's a far higher chance of a breech baby having some form of abnormality and as students we were always told, never trust a breech.

'It's safer with a breech delivery to have a caesarian section, safer for the child and the mother. Only a very small percentage of babies are breech and they are often delivered by caesarian but my obstetrician had taken measurements of my pelvis and seemed sure that I could manage a normal birth. He also assured me that it was always possible right to the last minute to change my mind and have a caesarian. Even so I couldn't prevent myself being worried, and then James was ten days late, which didn't make me feel any better because that can pose other problems. I guess it was a matter of knowing too much for my own peace of mind!'

During her twelve-hour labour Brenda's mother and a close female friend kept her company. 'I had wanted to have a natural delivery. The doctor who delivered him was someone I had worked with and had great trust in. What I hadn't anticipated was feeling so out of control. Everybody else took over. When I asked for an epidural block the sister refused, saying it was too early on and would slow the labour. As a doctor, I would have said, "Do it anyway." As a patient I had no control. I had to do what I was told.

'Because it was an unusual delivery it attracted a roomful of people. All the nursing sisters stopped by to have a look! But really I didn't mind because I'd been an observer in similar cases often enough. What I recall most vividly was reaching down and feeling his balls like two tense grapes at my vulva and calling out, "It's him! I can feel him!" I knew from the ultrasound I was having a boy. But to actually feel his maleness there as part of my body and about to become a separate human being, that was an experience I'll never forget. It's beyond words to express.'

From the hospital Brenda went home with her son. 'The first

three or four days were a nightmare! I couldn't stop crying. A complete lack of emotional control. I'd never experienced anything like it. It was awful. Awful. My sister was staying with me and was a great support but I really felt the lack of a partner. One morning I woke up and said to myself, "That's enough." And I stopped crying.

'Another thing I hadn't anticipated at all was how tired I felt. Utterly exhausted. He was a wakeful baby. He'd want to be fed every two and a half hours, day and night. The worst thing was I was so exhausted that once I had got him to sleep I would lie down myself and then be wide awake again in dread of him waking up! I'd lie there thinking, oh my God, I won't even get to sleep before he wants feeding again. And I'd feel my heart speed up and my pulse begin to race with anxiety.

'After a while we settled down together but those first few months I wouldn't want to go through again. At the time I worried I just wasn't as competent as those mothers I'd read about who breezed through it all, tucking their baby under their arm to go off climbing mountains or under the desk at work. I certainly wouldn't have been able to do that. I don't think I was less competent. It was just that they had different babies!

'I can say that the whole experience has made me a better doctor. At least a more tolerant and understanding human being and that has to rub off on my doctoring. Before I had James if a woman came in to the surgery and sat there complaining that her baby wouldn't stop crying I'd examine it and usually find nothing wrong. Then I'd tell her, "Babies cry. It's natural. You have to expect it." Now I sit her down and talk to her and say, "I know how hard it is and I sympathise with what you are going through." More often than not this is what she needs, to talk to someone who really listens and who understands.'

Now Brenda also understands how extremely difficult it is for a mother who works outside the home to find good care for her child. 'I stayed at home with James for six months and then I went back to work at Preterm for three days a week.

I remember when I was eight months pregnant and I saw an X-ray of him in my womb. I thought, my body made all that. It was a great feeling. And I look at him now and feel the same emotion. I have no regrets.

That was like going home. There is a great sense of sisterhood, commitment, involvement and caring there. So that was good but what wasn't so good was finding a place to leave James. I tried through my local council because I had been told that social workers screened the child-carers who worked under their supervision and I wanted James to go to someone who was trustworthy and competent.

'Instead of waiting until the very last moment, just as I started work, I began by leaving him with the woman for one morning a week for six weeks before I went back. It all seemed to be working well until the very day I started and when I went to pick him up after work the woman said she couldn't take him any more because he cried too much!

'The last thing you can be as a single parent is unreliable because the very first time you let someone down they will say, "Aah, she can't cope," and you'll lose the job. So I had to find someone else quickly. As it happened I found a woman privately to mind him and it worked very well. Since then I have used private carers, advertising in the local papers, insisting on checking references. He has had an excellent carer for the last eighteen months, a Greek woman who lives locally. It is expensive, however, and I couldn't afford it for full-time care. More recently he has spent some time at a child-care centre. In fact I should go and pick him up from there now.'

In her car, a decidedly non-medico status symbol, a rather battered older model full of the clutter of early motherhood (learning-to-read books, model cars and finger paintings), Brenda talked about the reasons for her decision to return to full-time doctoring. 'I felt my career needed some new direction. I enjoy working at the clinic because of the atmosphere and because the women I see are healthy, fit people. Becoming a mother certainly hasn't changed my attitude towards abortion. I still see it as a woman's right. But I wanted to move on to something else.

'Being a single parent certainly limits my options. I can't be on call weekends or nights because it would mean strapping James in the car and taking him along with me, which is hardly practical! So although I've worked regularly for a local GP I can't work full time for him. I don't think I would like to anyway because it's very lonely being a solo GP with no colleagues to discuss your work with, and that can lead to losing skills. That leaves 9.00 to 5.00 hospital jobs and there aren't too many of them, so I am fortunate to have been offered a post at a large hospital as a full-time resident specialising in geriatrics. I have always loved working with old people and this will be just the challenge I want. My career is very important to me. Perhaps it's become increasingly important since I hardly have any social life.

'No I don't feel any resentment towards James over the fact that I have major social restrictions. It's not his fault. It was my choice. Perhaps I didn't realise quite how isolated you become with a child. I spend a lot of time alone, especially at night. I'm even thinking of renting the third bedroom just for the company.

'When I was pregnant my friends said to me, "Oh, you won't be fun any more once you have a baby and you know you'll never get married now." Perhaps they're right. I know I give off different vibes now when I meet a man. I've just had one brief relationship since I had James and I would like to have a man in my life if only because it's sexually frustrating not to have one! It's also lonely. And I'd like sometimes to be able to say, "Oh you take over, I've had it and I'm going for a walk for half an hour!" I get cranky when I hear someone giving advice on the radio saying things like, "Well the best thing to do in this circumstance is to let the father take over," because there is never that option for me. I always have to be there for him.

'But I'm not complaining and I don't see any of this as crucial. I certainly am no more likely than I was before I had James to settle for less than I want or to make compromises in a relationship. I'd be happy to meet a man who wanted to mix his life with mine but I certainly don't want to accommodate his life and career to the extent of making major adjustments to my own.

'I've not met with any negative reactions to my being a single mother. Living in the house next door there's a widow and her unmarried sister, both in their seventies. When I moved in the unmarried one commented on James being a lovely baby and asked about his father and I said, "I'm not married," and the way she accepted that it was obvious there was no condemnation. In fact I sensed a wistfulness, perhaps she wished times had been different when she was young.

'People who don't know me well just take it for granted that I have a partner and if they ask about my husband I tell them I am not married and that is that. Perhaps it embarrasses them into retreating. But more often than not people are happy to see that you are happy and pleased enough to accept you as you see yourself.'

At the child-care centre Brenda zeroed in on her son and carried him back to the car along with yet more finger paintings. He eyed me with the same wide-set clear-eyed gaze his mother has and when I commented on how like her he looks she laughed. 'I can't see it myself but everyone says the same thing. I have to occasionally remind myself that he does have another half to him. There again perhaps he doesn't and I was so keen to have a baby I did it all myself!'

In the quickly gathering dusk the rush-hour traffic kept us from doing more than inching slowly back to the house. James didn't mind at all. Sat up like Jackie in his sheepskin-lined baby seat he surveyed the snarl of vehicles and announced, 'Dinosaurs!'

'No James,' his mother prosaically corrected him, 'there are no dinosaurs here. He discovers a new word and uses it constantly. A while ago he started calling every man Daddy. I suppose he had heard other children call their father that. I felt sorry for him then that he doesn't have someone to call Daddy. But I can't start to let myself feel guilty about that, after all it happens frequently that children grow up separated from their fathers by death or divorce.

'Our relationship has become a great deal easier as he has become older and is better company. But I do worry that because he is all I have I might hold him too close to me and that I might warp him by not being able to let go. I lie awake and worry about him having a motorbike accident or becoming a heroin addict. And I am pretty sure that when he is fourteen or fifteen he will want to go off to track down his father. I worry that he will be hurt but I would never expect to stop him. I worry that he will feel his father rejected him but all I can do is tell him the truth, that his father never knew him, so that it wasn't him he rejected. I shall tell him what I've told you and I shall do my very best, that's all I can do, and hope that it's enough to make him feel loved and wanted.'

James can hardly fail to see that he was very much wanted. A woman would have to want a child very much in order to make the choices Brenda has made. 'I remember when I was eight months pregnant and I saw an X-ray of him in my womb. I could see his little bones and I thought, my body made all that. It was a great feeling. And I look at him now and feel the same emotion. I have no regrets. None at all. I was just thinking about all this the other night sitting at home alone with no man in my life and realising I have never been as content as I am now.'

'Dinosaurs,' said James as he waved goodbye.

THE GOOD TIMES

Trish

Jan Cristaudo

Dianne Willcocks

Marelle Thornton

Trish

It was about the time we scuttled back to Australia and the children started at primary school that the emphasis of my anxiety for them changed from being focused on their physical wants to their intellectual, spiritual and emotional needs.

The next seven or eight years was the time I enjoyed them the most because this was the period when they struck their own happiest balance between being independent of me and yet still liking to know I was around. Because they were at ease and secure in themselves they were relaxed enough for it to be a pleasure to mix my life with theirs.

They were old enough to be able to go on a scramble around the rocks without getting tired and needing to be carried but also without me being in constant dread that they were going to slip and fall. Even though they were always pressing to be given more freedoms, by the time they were seven they had persuaded me it was okay for them to run down to the beach on their own; this was done without the aggro and hostility which came later.

We still all enjoyed each other's company. They wanted to come to the movies, art galleries and concerts with me. And I loved taking them because their spontaneity added an extra dimension to my own view of the world. They were so innocent, so wide-eyed and enthusiastic, both emotionally and physically, that every day was an adventure for both of them. And if they did have a problem then at least they could tell me about it. I no longer had to guess what was making them scream with pain as I had before they were able to talk.

It was a relief to be able to find out, by cross-questioning him, that when Sean doubled over with a pain in the gut I need no longer assume that he would die within twenty-four hours of an undiagnosed cancer but that it was more than likely caused by his not giving himself time to have a good shit for a few days. Because there was always so much he wanted to do, wasting time on imperative physical functions was something Sean had difficulty accepting! Even now if he mentions that he has a headache or a stomach ache I cannot restrain the motherly instinct to ask, 'When was the last time you went to the lavatory?' And I'm almost always right!

It wasn't just the physical pain they could now communicate. They could also ask those searching questions to which there are no simple answers. What happens when you die? Is there a God? Why? How? It would have been terrific to have all the answers, to have a religious belief which gave form to the myriad versions of the very basic human need to feel there has to be some pattern, some reason for why we get up every morning and function all the days of our lives, as if driven by some irresistible force. But as I myself was still grappling with this conundrum, the best I could manage was to be honest and tell them I knew of no certainties.

Perhaps this non-answer was the turning point at which they realised I was just a mere mortal who was fumbling her way through life along with the rest of the mob. This happens at some time during this stretch of childhood. They find their god has feet of clay. It's inevitable and it's a relief, at least I found it was. Being omniscient is not a role I enjoy.

I do have one slight regret about their religious, as distinct from their spiritual, education. I think they missed out by not having conventional lessons in Christianity. There were scripture classes at all the primary and high schools they attended but our society was going through a phase of not wanting to brainwash children and instead was keen to open their minds to a wider perspective. So scripture meant comparative religion and philosophy rather than taking a close look at the Christian ethic and story. This is not a complaint against teachers, they can only ever reflect what society wants and at that stage there was a very definite swing away from teaching Christianity in schools.

I was part of that swing and because I also never took my children to church except on extremely rare occasions and then only as a cultural experience, to admire the architecture or the singing, rather than for religious practice, they are definitely culturally poorer for it. There are so many literary and musical as well as historical references to Christianity which just float by them unrecognised. Of course they don't feel the deprivation, you can't miss what you've never had, but it's because of a failure on my part that they will never find the Evensong solace of beauty: 'Lord now lettest Thou Thy servant depart in peace'; nor will their hearts leap with shared sister and brotherhood for the writer who 2000 years ago penned the ultimate expression of our oh-so-fragile immortality: 'To every thing there is a season, and a time to every purpose under heaven. A time to be born and a time to die.' For them it's a pop song and the almost title of a James Bond movie.

Nor, until they read about it for themselves as adults, will they fully grasp the historical and therefore the political impact of Christianity and how this affects the way nations interrelate. Why we react in such an avid manner towards the Arabs (because they are our spiritual kin and there is no feud like a family feud) or why we seem inured to the starvation and poverty in India (Hindus believe in elephant gods and reincarnation so what can you expect), and why in the end communism will fail (people have a spiritual need to believe in something or someone larger and more meaningful than the State).

But while they were not learning these things they were learning plenty of others. For a start they were learning that there were schools where theirs were not the only white faces.

On our return to Australia from Singapore by ship we sailed into Sydney Harbour, through the heads, with a full rainbow arcing from one side to the other. (True! Perhaps it was turned on by the Department of Immigration for the scores of British migrants on board!) We had decided not to go back and live in our own house immediately. There were two reasons for this. Firstly we were so broke we couldn't afford to keep up the mortgage repayments, so it was better to leave the tenants in it and to rent another, cheaper, place for ourselves. Secondly I wanted to live closer to the centre of Sydney. To offset my anxiety about returning to Australian suburbia my game plan was to Get On Top of Sydney.

We rented a house in Northbridge on the north side of the harbour from friends. My partner took a job with ABC radio, hosting the morning current affairs program *AM*; cycling to work on a borrowed bike across the bridge because we couldn't afford to buy a car. We lived close enough for the children to be able to walk to their primary school. And I set about Sydney. I made a list of magazines and newspapers I wanted to write for and then I approached them with story ideas. Top of the list was the newly published *Cleo*, edited by a pre-celibate Ita Buttrose. She was the best person for whom I have ever worked. I would give her a list of story suggestions, she would go through them saying, 'Yes, no, no, yes.' We'd discuss the approach. She was very clear about what she wanted. I'd write the story, take it in and get a cheque within a week. Good stuff. None of the faffing around which so often plagues freelancers. It's one reason why her professional life has been so successful.

We started to pick up with Guy's life again. Zara and Sean were delighted to have a brother who was not old enough to be adult and therefore boring. He was deep into the horrors of the teenage years, no doubt driving his mother loony while all we got was the good stuff! Although occasionally we were fielded a doozey. The most memorable was a phone call from the parents of his current girlfriend summoning us to an immediate meeting at their house.

We were so sure that it was all grief, we didn't even change out of gardening jeans and boots and throughout the meeting I couldn't help being anxious about the mess we were undoubtedly leaving on their wall-to-wall electric blue nylon carpet. The mother behaved like the sort of person who would care about such things. She kept pulling down on the bottom edge of her sweater. She did all the talking. Her husband said not a word. According to her, Guy had been intimate with their daughter, and they found that distressing. But seeing as the daughter was eighteen, two years older than Guy, it seemed that if anyone should complain it might have been us! I found it difficult to feel outrage, except at the colour of her carpet, so I left it to Guy's father to trot out solicitous phrases.

In the middle of all this Guy and their daughter arrived home, she was sent to her room (a woman of eighteen!) and Guy was brought in and cross-examined. He did what he often does when he's put on the mat — he went silent, dark, broody. It was all excruciatingly embarrassing. I can't remember how we got out of there. All I do know is that the relationship didn't last long after that. Less than a year later their daughter married a policeman, had two children in rapid succession and was divorced.

It took a year before I felt able to move up the coast to our own house. We bought two Minis for $300 each (it costs almost that much to have a car serviced now!), I kept writing, he kept radio-ing and I leapt into mothering with a vengeance.

I joined the Mothers' Club at the school, but I only went to two meetings. On both occasions almost the entire time was taken up with a discussion about the school uniform. The relative merits of various materials and designs were appraised. Lobby groups tried to influence decisions. It was all taken with an astounding degree of seriousness. After two hours of earnest and sometimes heated debate, a resolution was passed that the present uniform should be kept. I decided my time could be better spent.

Sean joined the local soccer team and I became the team's manager. This involved keeping the parents of team members aware of when and where the practice and the Saturday games were taking place and arranging a roster of mothers to bring a couple of plates of cut oranges for the boys to suck on at half-time. It also involved taking home a bagful of eleven sweaty, muddy uniforms to wash and return for the next match. I quickly learnt what anyone who has ever been involved with school or social groups knows: that only a minute percentage of people become involved in the running and organisation required. The manager's job which I found the most fun was writing up a report on each match for the *Soccer News*, being careful that every member of the team was mentioned by name at least once during the season.

Naturally we had to go to their matches every Saturday, stand rugged up on the sidelines and cheer on our team. It was an education. Fathers, mature (well sort of) men, would yell at their little darlings, 'Gawahn,'it 'im. Kick 'im where it bloody 'urts!' They showed not the least sign of embarrassment or restraint in what they suggested their seven-year-old sons should do to members of the opposing team!

Zara continued the ballet classes which she had started in Singapore, only now it became the real thing, with examiners from the Royal School of Ballet coming out from London once a year to put the girls through their paces. The benefit for me was that watching these beginners training under the pernickety eye and strident voice of Miss Rosalie made me even more appreciative of an art form I had always greatly admired. The deficit was another chunk of time out of Saturday mornings.

In fact Saturdays were now so fraught that I began to dread them, even to the point of finding it difficult to sleep on a Friday night in anticipation of the rush and trauma of Saturday! In between the soccer match and the ballet lesson, I cleaned the house and also bought the fruit and veg and did the Franklins rush, throwing the cans, bottles and boxes of sensible stuff which I chose into the trolley and throwing the cans, bottles and boxes of junk which Sean and Zara chose back onto the shelves. Fighting the 'no you can't have that topping, those biscuits, that soft drink, they are full of sugar' war against all children's natural instincts to eat rubbish. Giving in on at least one point because they had so worn me down it was easier to say yes and feel guilty than to continue to say no and still feel guilty! Trying to do all this in super-quick time so as not to be late for matches and classes. All this so that I could have a clear run on Sunday to work on the house which we were renovating.

Such a weekly scenario was a certain recipe for disaster. Eventually it happened. I loused up.I confused the venue for the soccer match. Crammed into a Mini, Sean in his soccer clothes, Zara in her ballet outfit, me balancing a couple of trays of cut oranges on my knees, their father driving like a hoon because we were late, none of us speaking except our dog who was barking at every animal we passed, we finally arrived at the park where I thought the match was to be played. No one. The four of us stared at the empty pitch. I developed an instant headache.

He didn't say anything, just kept the engine running, his hands on the wheel and his gaze straight ahead. 'Well, if it isn't here it must be at Hitchcock Park,' I said. That was ten kilometres back up the road. In silence he swung the car around and hurled it back out into the congested traffic. 'If I am late we'll forfeit the match,' Sean said. 'I feel sick,' Zara announced. The dog barked. I rummaged desperately through my brain, trying to visualise the list of soccer venues, most unsure that Hitchcock was the place. Then I tried a different tack. I willed, with all my will, that Hitchcock *be* the right place.

It was. As we skidded to a halt on the gravel entrance we could see the rest of the team standing on the sidelines waiting for us, the opposing team smirking in anticipation of winning a game without having to play. Sean hurled himself like the conquering hero into the throng. I deposited the oranges and without waiting for me to pull the door completely closed, he drove off again at breakneck speed to get Zara to her ballet class on time.

We were still not speaking to one another as we left her there and crossed the road to a supermarket, where this week we were to break the routine and save some extra time by shopping while Zara was in class. In a silence loud with unspoken hostility, my guilt and his passive aggression, we pushed the trolley through the aisles. I can't recall what broke the impasse. All I remember is me hurling a pack of butter at him and him going one better and retaliating with a can of soup. And then him running up the aisle between the dog foods and washing powders yelling abuse over his shoulder at me and me screaming back and throwing yet more cans and boxes after him.

Perhaps the startled Saturday shoppers thought it was part of a television special (he was currently hosting the nightly current affairs program *This Day Tonight*). He leapt the turnstile. I deserted our laden trolley and pushed through behind him. Outside we faced each other and screamed like two irate red-faced turkey cocks! In the middle of this harangue, a man in a red polo-necked sweater suddenly appeared, and with a grin extended his hand in friendship and said, 'Aren't you the guy who does *This Day Tonight*? I love the show. I watch it every night.' We paused in amazement and stared at him. Then my partner shook his hand and said, 'Yes. Well. Umm. But I'm sorry, you'll have to excuse me I'm just having a row with my wife.' The man stood back, flushed with embarrassment and disappeared into the crowd. I've always wanted to apologise to him.

Anyway, his interruption did the trick. I had a bit of a cry and we laughed and made up. I expect I didn't say I was sorry because I am told I never say I'm sorry. But we had a big hug and went off to pick up Zara and then Sean, leaving the trolley full of groceries to be re-sorted onto the shelves.

If Saturdays were supposed to be active then Sunday evenings were supposed to be quiet, family-only occasions. Where did these self-imposed regulations come from? I don't know. Perhaps from some forgotten memory of my own childhood. But for some reason they were irresistible, ironclad rules for living. They had me in their grip as much as the necessity of celebrating birthdays and Christmas, and I endeavoured in turn to seize the family with them. Learning that they were self-defeating and destructive was a hard lesson for such a chronically organised person, and one which I left almost too late.

Sean had his own way of coping with pointless rules, mine and other people's. He is not a well-balanced Libra like his father, he is an Aquarius, but he has still inherited much of his father's laid-back way of allowing others to let off necessary steam and then getting on with things the way he was going to do in the first place. When I am angry I call it manipulation but most of the time I can see it for what it is — the charm that oils the wheels.

Every Friday, sports day, Sean had to wear a sports uniform of white shorts and a T-shirt the colour of the team to which he belonged. I thought he looked extremely handsome in his purple T-shirt and oh-so-bright white shorts and long white socks. But then I was his doting mother! He loathed the outfit with a depth of hatred only a seven-year-old can muster! Every Friday morning before school we fought. He wanted to wear his tatty, formerly white and now decidedly grey, permanently creased old shorts. I insisted he wear his smart, new, white-white shorts. It was a tussle of wills which of course I won because I was bigger and in control. Or so I thought.

One Friday morning, after the usual confrontation, he left, disgruntled, and in his good shorts, to walk with his sister down the hill to their school. After he was gone I saw a note, one of the seemingly thousands of notes which fell out of their school cases every evening like confetti and which were invariably requests for money for what came to be called in our household 'scursions'. On bad days it seemed if I totalled up the amount of time my children spent on 'scursions' it would more than equal the working time lost to the entire nation through the common cold! This one was a permission slip for an excursion to the Australian Museum. It had to be handed in that day or Sean would miss out and I knew he badly wanted to go. So I ran up the drive, leapt into the car and roared down after them. I saw them before they saw me and I also immediately saw Sean was wearing his old shorts. I cruised alongside him and you should have seen the look on his face when he glanced sideways and realised it was me! He immediately brought his case around and held it in front of him to cover the offending shorts. It was all I could do not to burst out laughing. I tossed him the note and drove off leaving him standing there in disbelief. Later in the day, I laughed some more when I went to check the mailbox and found it stuffed with his good shorts!

What could I say? How could I get cross? He had worked out a way of making both of us happy. He would leave me beaming with motherly pride, wearing what I wanted him to wear, and arrive at school dressed how he felt most comfortable and in shorts which still conformed with the rules. That way I, he and the school were all satisfied. I never mentioned the shorts again. Every Friday we played our little charade. And every Friday the postman squeezed the mail in beside the crumpled shorts.

It wasn't the postman but my girlfriend, who lived next door, who received a big shock when she put her hand in her mailbox and found a full set of dentures! Sean had picked them up on the beach and thought he'd give her a bit of a thrill. He was a great collector of such trophies.

He would accompany his father on trips to take garden trimmings to the tip and bring back trophies such as an embossed leather-covered whisky decanter on a set of wheels made to simulate a nineteenth-century State carriage.

Zara regarded such collectibles with the same degree of distaste as I did. Whereas Sean's room was always a misadventure not to be entered into lightly, Zara's was perfection. Her shelves and hanging space always neat. Ballet posters adorned the walls and her books were arranged according to height. On her windowsill she had plants and a fish-tank. She made her bed every morning and every evening she put her clothes in the laundry and then arranged the clothes she would need for the following day in the order in which she would get into them. Beside this pile she placed her socks and polished shoes.

Every day before school I would brush her long blonde hair and ask her how she wanted it done — separate pigtails, pigtails pinned on top, 'earphones', bunches or a topknot. She hates photographs of herself from that period but my middle-class soul can't help yearning for the time when this true Zara surfaces again. She was then very happy at school too, was elected class captain and was a bit of a teacher's pet. She wasn't very keen on the piano lessons I insisted they both took. But she was generally a delight and so were all her girlfriends. Often when I hugged and kissed her goodnight and tucked her up tight in her bed the way she liked, a sausage in its skin, I would sit on her bed and we'd chat about stuff and I'd think, this is what my mother missed. This is what I missed. Mum was already dead when I was this age. And the emotion I felt was a sorrow beyond sadness. Then I'd hug Zara extra tight and silently hope that she would have a daughter whom she would live to enjoy.

I had finished my first book, the biography of an extraordinary Australian woman, *Andrea*. It had been a hard slog and I needed time to myself and room to breathe. I decided to hitchhike around New South Wales on my own. I wanted to get to Tibooburra, in the far north-western corner of the state, if only because it was such a great name and was always mentioned on the TV weather report as having the highest temperatures in New South Wales. I could have driven there in my own car, or taken trains and buses, but I knew the only way to really meet people was to hitch. So I bought a pack; now I really did look like those girls in London! He dropped a nervous me off on Mona Vale Road. The first lift took me over the Blue Mountains and I was away.

It was the first time I had been away from the children and their father for any length of time. It was exhilarating. I met wonderful people, saw fantastic places and rediscovered myself as a separate person. The only blight on the journey was what I saw happening between black and white people in the outback townships. Even though I had read about this situation and seen it on television, the reality was far worse than I could have imagined and I returned to Sydney only for long enough to pick up Zara and hitchhike together back out to Brewarrina, where I lived for a month researching my second book, *Children of Blindness*.

Zara stayed for two weeks, then Sean flew up, I put Zara on the same plane to fly her back, and Sean stayed for the next two weeks. We lived in the pub because that was a neutral place where all the different Aboriginal factions, as well as the whites, gathered. The children went to the local school. They also hung around with me while I mixed freely with whites and blacks.

We went fishing on the Barwon River with a white farmer who invited us to stay on his property. In the morning he took us out and showed us the unmarked graves of scores of Aborigines who had died in a massacre in the late 1800s. We went up to Goodooga and slept out under the stars with Robyn Campbell, an old Aboriginal fellow in his seventies who told us stories from the Dreamtime. We went over to Dodge City and ate barbecued kangaroo with the Boney family, sitting among the refuse while everyone around us became paralytic with booze. We danced with the Aborigines to the jukebox in the tin shed to which they were condemned at the back of the Royal Hotel and I went to the Whites Only dance at the RSL.

In the evenings we sometimes sat out in the open in deckchairs and watched the movies. In the mornings we sometimes sat on the bench outside the local lockup beside a disconsolate band of sobering Aboriginal drunks who had spent the night inside. We had afternoon tea with the white constable and his wife and dinner with the white school teachers. We attended the monthly Magistrate's Court. The white magistrate stopped proceedings to ask me if I thought it wise for my young daughter to be hearing the sort of language which it would be necessary to have given in evidence. We met the local white Catholic priest, the local white hospital doctor, and a wonderful man called Bert Gordon, a reformed alcoholic, an Aborigine, a born-again Christian who had raised over fifty children without any government assistance. And we listened to everything everyone had to say.

During the time we were there two people died. One fellow was stabbed to death with a knife in a pub brawl. We knew the man who died and the man who killed him. They were both Aborigines. We went to the funeral. The second person to die was also an Aboriginal. She was nine. She was picked up by her feet by a drunk who circled her above him and smashed her head to pieces against the wall. Zara and Sean had been at school with her.

They remember Brewarrina extremely well and I was glad to have shared it with them. That journey was another turning point for me. What I experienced developed in me a commitment to Australia and I took out citizenship.

Travelling like that also made me far less hesitant when their father suggested that he should not renew his employment contract and that we should rent the house and all put on back-packs and head off for Africa to celebrate his turning forty!

It was to be a long, open-ended journey, which meant taking Zara and Sean away from school. At the time I was surprised by how many people asked me if I wasn't worried about the impact this would have on them. It never occurred to me that it would be better for them to stay at school rather than travelling rough with us. Although they were both enjoying it and doing well at school (it had the largest school band in the state in which Zara played flute and Sean played trumpet), I was not madly impressed with what they were learning. The education system was going through a free-for-all stage. Nothing as dull as learning tables by rote or as crushing for their imagination as learning to spell correctly. But there was a curious dichotomy at work here. For while the precious little darlings were not to be constricted by such tedious regimen, there was still this atmosphere of being force-fed through a system, the aim of which was to churn out, at the far end, round pegs for round holes and square pegs for square slots, cyphers to keep our society productive and stable. I felt that somewhere along the line we'd all lost track of the education plot. So — I wasn't at all anxious about taking them away from it.

Guy had also decided to give formal education away despite our trying to persuade him to hang in there and take the HSC, if only because once you have started something you should see it through to the end, and also because he didn't really have any other major plan he wanted to follow. But he was no longer a child, he was a young man and we could only offer advice, not insist that it was taken.

Although he had left school, there was no way he wanted to travel with two young children and Dad and Doris, so he waved us goodbye as we sailed out of the harbour on the *Oriana*. No rainbow this time — instead something even better. It was during the six-week sea voyage to Africa that for the first time we left Zara and Sean alone, without a baby-sitter. Another step forward. Another loosening of the ties that bind. What a relief! We felt they were ultra-safe in their cabin at night and they became so accustomed to being left on their own that by the time we hit dry land we had weaned them and ourselves from that dependence.

The eight months we spent travelling overland from Cape Town to Cairo were a great experience in many, many ways, not the least in living together as a close, self-sufficient and self-sustaining family unit. I think this journey and a subsequent nine months spent doing the same through North, Central and South America, plus a later four-month journey across the South Pacific was the very best thing we could have done together as a family.

Since that time, and because of the three books we wrote about those journeys — *Africa Overland, South America Overland* and *Across the South Pacific* — heaps of people have written and asked for advice about whether or not they should do the same sort of travelling with their children, and I always say, 'Yes! Go for it!' It's no more dangerous now than it was then and the risks are miniscule by comparison with the benefits.

Having the undivided attention of their mother and father for months at a time and going through the good and the tough times together forged a bond which would be hard to achieve amid the pressures of work and school, swimming, piano, trumpet and flute lessons, soccer, ballet, washing, ironing, cleaning, shopping and remembering to feed the dog and cat (who were left with the tenants) and putting out the garbage. They learnt self-sufficiency, independence, confidence, and that they live on a fascinating planet; that it is all there for the understanding and enjoyment and that they should not be overawed by differences or by change. The century in which they will spend most of their adulthood will be full of all that, so the travelling we did together was a brilliant education in not just how to cope but how to make the best of things.

I loved being on the road (I'm still not suited to suburban living), humping my pack and going walkabout. The children carried their own back-packs, learnt what to keep in what pocket and how to have the most essential items nearest the top. We travelled 6000 kilometres through Africa, more than 20,000 through the Americas and 12,000 across the Pacific, using public transport, hitching and living on the cheap. They learnt to sleep on the back of trucks, to eat whatever was available without complaint and to be highly appreciative of unexpected treats. They also learnt to recognise when one of the rest of us was down, either because of being sick (we all at one time or another had severe doses of the trots), or because of being anxious. At one stage we were caught in the no-man's-land of Ethiopia's civil war, unable to travel back to safety while knowing that travelling further on was no less dangerous. Each of them had their own way of coping. Zara became quiet and attentive, leaving plenty of emotional space for the rest of us. Sean told stories and jokes in an attempt to cheer us through.

I have a multitude of memories of them from those years. Zara slipping under the table at the Nairobi Hilton Hotel coffee shop to throw up the rich cake which she had eaten as a present to herself to make up for the short rations she had been on for the past couple of months. Sean pushing off into a crowded Ethiopian village saying that he was going to look for a bottle of Coca-Cola, desperate for a cultural touchstone after several weeks of eating something called foule, which resembled nothing more than a piece of dirty washing-up cloth. Zara red-faced in forty-two degree heat, uncomplaining of the huge blisters burnt onto the palms of her hands by the hot metal side-railings of the truck we stood up in as it barrelled across 100 kilometres of the Sudanese desert. Zara weeping on the side of the road in Tanzania because the young boys she had been playing football with, a football made of rolled paper, were so poor. 'And they don't even know about the rest of the world,' she cried. Both of them hanging onto my hands when I went completely off the air after being told my older sister was dead. Zara sitting demurely among the doilies and making genteel conversation while taking tea with the mother of my ex-spouse. Sean, not yet ten, confidently negotiating, on his own, the tube lines from one side of London to the other in order to visit an exhibition of aeroplanes. Sean imagining that he was a millionaire when his two dollar equivalent in Argentinian pocket money came in a five-centimetre-thick wad of notes. The two of them playing serious card games with Sid Hastie, a wonderful New Zealander in his seventies whom we met while travelling down the Amazon. Sean playing war games with the same-aged son of the Brazilian captain of our little vessel, their only common language an imaginative version of ever-the-enemy German! Zara falling in love with a Ryan O'Neal lookalike on American Samoa and standing in the rain, in the market on Huahine in French Polynesia, to eat a slice of the cake celebrating the coming of her teenage years. The two of them decorating a surprise Christmas tree in our Fijian hotel room with baubles borrowed from the big one in the lobby in an attempt to cheer me out of a bad dose of Christmas blues brought on by the death of my dad.

The wonderful years on the road had been interspersed with less than a year spent back in Australia, where the children slipped with apparent ease back into the old frantically busy routine, and eighteen months spent in splendid isolation in a cottage in my home county of Somerset.

Here Sean went to a primary school which looked like something out of Dickens and we were told by his exasperated teachers that he seemed to have trouble fitting in behind a desk. Zara made the giant leap into senior school and pleased my egalitarian instincts by attending the local comprehensive school. She was still a model student and even went willingly to extra tuition in maths. She joined the Girl Guides, Sean became a Cub and, looking at my homeland through their unbiased eyes, I was shocked to see a rather scruffy, run-down almost third world country! They were completely unaware of the class system, so they moved with total ease from their county horse show friends to those who lived on the local housing estate.

I insisted on taking them to everything that opened and shut and made them keep a project book on England as they had on every other country we'd spent time in. We went to shows, galleries, museums, concerts, stately homes, churches, forts, ruins and historic sites. I went rather overboard in my zealous maternal determination that they should become aware of their bi-cultural heritage. I well remember the occasion which brought it to a halt. We were seated on hard chairs in chilly Bath cathedral listening to a concert of funereal Bach when Sean turned to me and hissed, 'No more, Mother. This is IT!'

After that we went on walks on our own and even left them, eleven and twelve years of age, alone in the cottage for the weekend while we visited publishers and friends in London. It had happened. The Age of Independence had crept up on me and was about to give me an almighty blow to the brain. Looking back over those wonderful years I am staggered that I can have been so ignorant as not to have realised that they would come to an abrupt end. If I had known what was to follow I think I would have relished them all the more. I would also more than likely have left home!

Jan Cristaudo

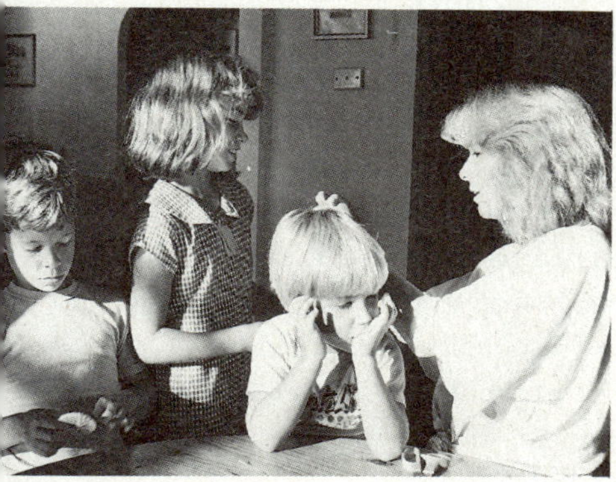

Kids make you more tolerant of other people's needs. But they also bring out a side in you that you would rather not know about.

'If I meet a man socially, at a party or something, and he asks me, "Do you work?" I say, "Too right I do." And when he asks, "What do you do?" I say, "Have you got a couple of hours to spare? Because that's how long it would take to tell you!"'

Jan Cristaudo is one of that often maligned group of women who have chosen to make motherhood a full-time career. Her daughter, Carla, is ten. Her son Kolby is eight, and her son Jay is four and 'the sort of child I used to see other women with and think to myself, thank God he's not mine. He's not hyperactive in a disturbed way. He just doesn't need much sleep, three or four hours and then he's ready to go again. He is into everything and has more energy than all the rest of us put together, including his father, which is saying a lot.'

Jan's day begins at 5.30 am, when her husband, who runs his

own travel consultancy business, gets up to go off to work. 'He's the classic workaholic, though he doesn't like me to say so and doesn't believe he is. He prefers to drive into his office when there is no traffic and to have time on his own there before the staff arrive. That's his thinking time. His creative time. I don't get up with him, I'm not that mad, but I am conscious of his leaving and it doesn't seem long after that the children begin to surface.

'Jay is always the first of them. He is becoming a little more bearable. I used to be able to hear him demolishing his room, talking to himself and the others, though they tried not to hear, drawing on the walls and just generally launching himself into another day. At least now he is beginning to sleep in a little bit later and when he does wake he is a little quieter. But it's all just comparative and I can't even recall what it was like to be able to sleep in until what I consider a reasonable time. Even on those occasions when they sleep over at my mother's place I still wake up early and find it impossible to lie in. All my responses, my entire system, is geared around their hours.

'Carla and Kolby have to leave for school by 8.30 am and before then they have to have breakfast and get into their uniforms. For some reason or other no matter how organised I am the night before there always seems to be one piece of uniform missing, a sock, a shoe, a tie. Then there's the days for special uniforms for sports or the days they can free-dress, those are the worst, all those decisions over what to wear.

'I have to double check they have all their homework in their cases and that I have answered all those notes which seem to come home every other day from the school, mostly asking for money for excursions or special projects. Again I have done all this the previous night, before they go to bed, but there always seems to be something extra to do in the morning, even though I always ask, "Do you have everything ready for the morning?"

'Then there's sandwiches to make for lunch and in between all this I have to keep at least one eye on Jay to make sure he isn't jumping over the balcony, shoving string up his nose or killing the cat. I don't eat breakfast myself. There isn't ever time and even if there was, I couldn't, not with all that going on. By the time I shovel them all into the car I will have shouted at least once at each one of them and they will have had some dispute over some stupid unimportant thing between themselves.

'I have to drive them to school because there's no bus stop near us and once I am in the car I might as well take them all the way. It only takes five minutes but it's just that bit too far for them to walk. It's almost all uphill.

'Jay goes to kindy two days a week. On one of those days I work at the kids' school as ancillary staff in the library. I've been doing that for a year and I love it. It's put me in touch with adults again. One of the worst things about very small children is that they keep you locked away in a world apart from other adults.'

Jan is also president of the School Club. 'I organise outings for the mothers once every couple of months. Last time I hired a bus and we all went into the city and did a tour around various fashion manufacturers, where they all bought things at more or less cost price. I arranged for each woman to be given a little gift as she boarded the bus. We had lunch and held a raffle on the way home. They had a great time, it was on outing for them and a way for them all to meet each other and not feel so isolated. It also raised $350 for the school! That will be spent on specific equipment and books which we cannot get through the Education Department.

'Once a year, at the beginning of the school year, we have a new parents' night so they can all meet each other. It's always the same hard core of people, fathers and mothers, who attend all the functions. They are the ones who are interested in their children's education and want to be involved.

'Last week I organised the Senior Citizens Day for the third year running. It has become increasingly popular. It gives the old folk a place to go where they are treated as someone special. They love it and so do the kids. Even the ones who tend to be a bit rough become surprisingly gentle and protective when they are made responsible for one of the old people. The children take their guests around the school and show them their work and then we give them tea. The parents send food and I get the children to bring flowers so we can decorate the tables to make the place look as attractive as possible. This year over 350 people turned up and they went through 300 teabags, five large tins of coffee, twelve litres of milk and four kilos of sugar. It was amazing to watch! I think even the children were surprised to see the old folk tuck in with such enthusiasm!

'Apart from running the household on my own, I also visit my gran and my mum once a week. My gran lives in close to the city. She's my father's mother and we are very close. She's in her eighties now but looks after herself and is always immaculately turned out. I can talk to her about anything.

'My mum lives on the far side of town, a long way from us. But she visits regularly, often coming the whole way by bus. She is very good with the children and frequently takes them for a few days at a time during the holidays to give me a break.

'It's the after-school performance which I find particularly gruesome. I am usually on top of the morning routine but in the afternoons there is so much to arrange and so many places to get to and they invariably spring something unexpected on me. Like can Leigh come up to play or can Steven stay overnight. All of it when you are least ready for it.

'Carla plays netball and takes piano and musicianship classes. Kolby plays soccer and swims. Jay just runs riot! Sometimes I feel that if I have to get into the car one more time, to pick up or drop off one of them, I'll scream. By the time we all get home and they have done their homework and bathed and eaten I am just about exhausted, especially if Jay has been particularly difficult.

'It's the constant noise and movement and needing to have my wits about me the whole time which is so tiring. It's impossible to relax. Even making a simple telephone call is an impossibility. The moment I pick up the phone either to call or to answer, they start to argue loudly with one another so I can't hear myself speak, or Jay does something particularly awful or frightening. By the time my husband gets home, usually about 8.30 pm, they are asleep and I've tided up the house again so it looks as though it's been that way all day, so when he asks, "What did you do today?" I tell him, "Not much," because there is no possible way he could understand.

'Every now and again when I really go off my brain I open and close the cutlery drawer very fast and loud and then they look at me as if I have gone mad and they know they have gone too far and they go very quiet and well behaved and in this unnatural silence I sort through the cutlery, putting it all back in its right place. It stops me hitting them.

'Anyone who says they can't understand how parents can hit their own children is either unnatural or is lying. I don't mean premeditated cruelty. I mean something done in a sudden rush of anger. I've never done it, but I've come frighteningly close. When I feel like that I say to them, through clenched teeth, "Go away, go right away. Yes, I love you but right at this moment I don't like you, so go away."

'Kids make you more tolerant of other people's needs. They force you not to be selfish. But they also bring out a side in you that you didn't know existed. That you would rather not know about. They are the only ones who can drive you to these lengths. I become cross, very cross, almost violent, and I don't like that. Perhaps this is why I always said I didn't want children. Sometimes I look down on two of me, one Jan with children and one Jan without. All this is in abstract of course, a sort of madness because it can't be. But I would choose to be the Jan without children.'

But then you don't marry an Italian and say you don't want children! Jan and her husband have been married for fourteen years. They have known each other for twenty. 'There was never any possibility of me marrying anyone else. I had lots of other boyfriends of course, but I always knew I would marry him.'

They met on a blind date. Jan was twenty, he was a year older and teaching in primary school. 'He had come to Australia when he was three. His father worked on the railways and his mother in a match factory. They both got up at 4.30 am to go to work and on the weekends they worked in their market garden, which they still have. With that background he didn't really have any chance of becoming anything other than a workaholic! He has a younger brother and sister and takes the role of older brother very seriously. In fact I think he takes everything seriously. He's never been a flippant person.'

At the time they met Jan was doing a designer sewing course and working as a junior in a bridal salon in the city, 'One of those places where they sell those quite awful overdone dresses. I didn't enjoy the work particularly but I liked the girls I worked with and have kept several friends from that time. I didn't have any great career plans. I'd left school at seventeen and all I really wanted to do was travel, but then my dad died and I felt couldn't leave Mum on her own.'

The death of her father, when he was thirty-nine and Jan was eighteen, made a big impact on her life. She still finds it difficult to talk about. 'I was particularly close to him, probably because I was an only child. It all happened so quickly. It seemed like one day he was there and the next he was gone. He had cancer, though I didn't know that at the time.

'I remember going to see him in hospital the day before he died and somehow knowing that I wouldn't see him again. I'd never seen him look so ill, he couldn't be bothered with anything. Only very recently I said to my mother that she should have told me how ill Dad was and that he had cancer, and she said, "I know that now, but at the time I wanted to protect you from it." I can understand that now I have children myself. I have never felt as lonely as I did when Dad died. I wished very much that I had an older brother to talk to. I am now thirty-nine, the same age as Dad was when he died and I often find myself thinking, this is how he felt, this is how things looked to him.

'After he died I stayed on living at home with Mum. When I finally left it was to go to New Zealand with a girlfriend. We hitchhiked around and did all sorts of jobs like picking fruit in orchards. I was away almost five months and when I came back I picked up again with the same guy. He had dropped out of teaching, which was a pity in a way because he was such a good teacher, but he felt too limited by it. He had also always wanted to go overseas, so he wanted to earn good money and he look a job as a salesman for an office equipment company. He was a natural salesman. I took a job repping for a fashion fabric company and we settled into a routine.

'I knew we'd end up getting married; poor chap, he didn't have a chance really. You know how women are when they set their mind on a man! It was his teeth that attracted me. Don't laugh, it's true. He has a great smile. And he's also a good all-rounder. If I said he is decent it makes him sound dull, but he is decent, good, and not dull.

'He was worried that we were just going together from habit. He also wanted to travel. So he decided to go off to London and a few months later I followed him over. He was pleased to see me and we started living together. We couldn't have done that in Australia because neither of our families would have approved. The experience should have been enough to let me know what I was letting myself in for; I saw less of him then than when we were just going out together in Australia! He worked seven days a week for an adventure travel company. The only time I saw him he was almost too tired to speak!

'I worked for an Austrian crystal company, as a sort of girl friday, doing all the jobs the Brits didn't want to do. You know how they are. If the phone rings on Jack's desk while he's in the loo, no one else will answer it. I'd say, "I'll get that," and I'd take the message. They thought I was an oddity because I was willing to lick envelopes if the envelope-licker was away, or do anything else that needed doing, whereas they would only do exactly what they had been employed to do and not one thing extra.'

Jan's partner travelled a great deal in Europe as a courier and she went on a jaunt to Russia with a girlfriend. 'We had a great time. The man who was responsible for showing us around would wait until the rest of the tour group had gone to bed and then he'd take us both out on the town. There's a lot going on in Moscow that you don't read about!'

After eighteen months in London Jan's partner was offered a job back in Australia with a travel company. 'We decided to go back and take it up and also to get married, but for the sake of our families we thought we should wait until we came home to go through the actual ceremony, so we were finally married two weeks after we got back. He was snowed under at work so we took a two-day honeymoon.

'During all these years we never talked seriously about having children. I just knew I didn't want them. I didn't like them. I couldn't relate to them. The idea of having babies was something I put aside. I thought, I'll worry about that when the time comes and I hope the time will never come. Though I do remember one time in London lying in the bath thinking that if I had kids with the man I planned to marry at least they would have dark hair and eyes. I loathed blonde kids.'

Back home again Jan went to work for the Australian branch of the crystal company she had been with in London. Her husband began his meteoric career in the Australian travel business. Within six months they had bought a house overlooking the beach and at weekends they both worked hard at renovating it. After two years of commuting into the city Jan decided to set up a tailoring business from her own home.

By the time they had been married for three years and when they had known each other for nine years, and Jan was twenty-nine, '. . . people began asking, "Are you going to have children?" I would smile sweetly and say, "Oh I can't have children," or, "My husband can't have children." That shut them up. Our families never asked. They knew better. I thought it was no one else's business. They had no right to ask!'

By this time Jan had been on the pill for seven years straight and her doctor suggested that she give it a break. '"Just a couple of months," he said, and he also told me there was very little likelihood of me getting pregant in that time because it would take a while for my system to get back to functioning normally. What a joke. I must have become pregnant within a week of going off the pill. I even know when it was. It was on a wet afternoon in Dubrovnik!'

Jan's husband had been asked by his company to 'shop' Greece and Yugoslavia. 'That means looking at the tourist possibilities in a country. He had been working as hard as usual and they could see he needed a break and this was their idea of a holiday, and to make it rather more acceptable they told him he could take his wife.

'It was the first holiday we'd had since we got married. I sort of knew right away when it happened. You know, the way women do. But I shut my mind to it. We were away for a month and I missed a period and when we got back I had a test straight away and it came out negative, and even though my head was relieved, in my heart I knew it wasn't true. When I missed a second period the result was still negative, but by then it was unmistakable. I had these great boobs and my husband kept telling me how well I looked. He knew and I knew but I refused to face it. After a third test finally showed positive I went straight to my gran and told her, "I'm pregnant and I don't want to be." I burst into tears and she just sat there and held my hand. She knew how I felt.

'Then I told my husband, over the phone, and he came straight home, even though it was only mid-afternoon, bringing champagne and flowers. That made me cry all the more. He was tickled pink and kept saying I'd get used to the idea and I said, "Don't say that, I don't want a baby," and he rocked me in his arms and said, "It'll come, it'll come." I wouldn't tell anyone and I made him promise not to tell anyone either. When I was about five months gone we had some close friends stay over and the husband said, "Your boobs are looking great, Jan, are you pregnant?" I had to say yes and then tell all the rest and everyone was thrilled bar me. I thought, what a stupid reaction, as if having a baby was the be-all and end-all. Who needed kids? Everyone else had them and I wanted to be different.

'It was very late on in the pregnancy that I bought anything for it. I decided I was going to bring it home dressed in denim. Everybody else brought theirs home in pretty pinks and blues but mine would be different from the start. That was the plan anyway, but of course in the end she came home in pink and wearing the little bootees I had worn home from hospital when I was born! I also decided that having a baby was not going to change my life. What a joke!

'I went into motherhood in the same way I go into everything, full pelt. By the time she was born I was a walking encyclopaedia on childbirth. I knew everything, in abstract. I didn't enjoy being pregnant. I felt very self-conscious about my size and I would never get up and dance at parties with my husband. But I think other pregnant women look beautiful and if a man ever puts down the way a pregnant woman looks I'm the first one to leap to her defence.'

Finally Jan's pregnancy ended with an induction. 'I was eighteen hours in labour and I remember lying there and thinking, this is the first and last time I am going to get myself into a situation like this, one where there is no way out. When the baby was born and I was told that it was a girl I was dumbstruck. Only then did I realise that I had been expecting all the way along for it to be a boy.

'My husband was with me all through the labour and when she was born there was this quite indescribable feeling between us. I have never felt as close to him as I did at that moment. We looked at this little thing the two of us had made and we could not have been more surprised if she had sat up and spoken to us! I couldn't believe that she was there when two seconds before she wasn't.'

In that moment Jan went from resistant mother to supermum.

She laughs. Her teeth and smile are every bit as good as her husband's. We are talking late in the evening, 'because it is the only time I have any space for myself. I can't hold a sensible conversation when they are around and even when it's just Jay I can't concentrate fully on anything else.

'It's true that the transformation in me was immediate and complete. It was almost as though what I had been fighting against had suddenly become what it was I had been looking for all my life. Beginning with the birth, being a mother has used me to the very edges of myself. The birth was so difficult that I felt my heart would explode and afterwards I thought that as I didn't have a heart attack then I never would have because my body could never undergo worse stress.

'From the moment she was born she became the centre of my life. I was terrified of being alone with her at first. Frightened that she would die. I delayed going home because I was scared of not being able to cope. She was the first baby I had ever held. It was an incredible responsibility. A whole life entrusted to me. I'd created this life and now I had to learn how to look after it.

'Once we were home I couldn't get enough of her. I fussed over and pampered her. It was incredible. I became a different person. My life changed completely. She was everything. I had no time or interest in anything or anybody else. Of course my husband's life didn't change. After the initial disruption he went on working long hours and the parenting was left to me.

'He told me once that he had never been worried when I said that I didn't want children. He knew I would come around to it and that when I did I would do a great job. In some ways I suppose he knows me better than I know myself. I do feel resentful sometimes that my life has changed so much and his has hardly changed at all. He does all his parenting at weekends and then he takes it as seriously as he takes everything else. But of course it's much easier for him because it's only two days in seven.

'I am very proud of what he has achieved. He's been out on his own now for five years and made a great go if it. But I have never said to him that I want all this.' She gestures around her home. They have moved a couple of times, upwardly mobile is the fashionable description, and now own a large waterfront house. Her great flair and talent for creating atmosphere and beauty is apparent everywhere from the individually designed pieces of furniture to the subtle lighting, unusual wall colouring and well-tended plants. Outside is his domain. At weekends he builds stone patios and walls and does battle with the ever-encroaching bush. It's a lifestyle many would envy. And Jan is conscious that she enjoys a good life.

'Absolutely. I know any complaints I have are so trivial as to be laughable when you compare them with what other women in the world endure. But still there are days when that is hard to put into perspective.

'The funny, or not funny, thing is that here I live in a country where we can make all the choices and yet none of our children were planned. When I became pregnant with what turned out to be Kolby I was taking the mini-pill. I had only just stopped feeding Carla, who was then ten months old. So when he was born she was only nineteen months old. Two children under two is not much fun, as you know, but there was no resistance to having him on my part because I didn't want Carla to be an only child. I had not enjoyed being an only child. I don't believe anyone would enjoy it. As a child you are lonely and as an adult there is too much responsibility.

'When he was born my first thought was, good, a boy for my husband. And of course for his Italian parents. They have been very supportive throughout. Even though I'm a ring-in they treat me just like one of them. I expect that is helped by the fact that neither my husband's brother or sister have children yet. I have produced their only grandchildren so far.

'But once Carla and Kolby were both through that poopy, yucky, chucky stage I thought, that's it, no more. I booked in to have my tubes tied but the day before I was due to have it done I phoned up and cancelled out. I was very apologetic but the woman at the surgery told me, "Don't worry, it happens all the time." I just couldn't go through with something so final. I didn't want to stay on the pill and I'd tried an IUD and had a lousy experience, so I decided to go with the Billings method. This is natural and doesn't interfere with your body. I decided to give it a go because I was fed up with having things happen to my body. I wanted it to have a rest and a chance to be normal.

'We were going through a bit of a bad patch between us, which looking back now I can see was the result of the pressures of motherhood, being constantly tired and feeling hemmed in and suffocated. So I also felt I wanted to control at least that part of my life myself.

'With the Billings method you keep a check on your temperature and your vaginal secretions so that you learn to recognise when you are susceptible to becoming pregnant. The trouble is that it depends on living a fairly regular, routine life and that's pretty well impossible with two small babies. Then we had friends visit from New Zealand. We rushed about doing a lot of things with them so I became a bit overtired and the next thing I knew I was pregnant again.

'We seriously discussed whether we should have another child but finally decided to go ahead. I even thought that I might follow up quickly with another one, to round the family out, two lots of two. But once Jay arrived that idea went out of the window! He's more than two lots of two all by himself. He has totally drained me; pushed me to my limits. At one stage I seemed to almost live at the baby clinic. The sister there was wonderful. She would phone me up in the morning just to cheer me up. She had seen Jay have his tantrums and tempers. She knew how determined he is and understood more than anyone what I was going through.

'Kolby had an allergy to wheat products which took us a while to pin down. Then came Jay and a whole year of sleepless nights. I'd spend most of the time in a daze because of having hardly any sleep. Then my husband tore his Achilles tendon and had his foot in a plaster cast so I had to get up at 5.00 in the morning, shovel the kids in the car, drive him to work, come home and do the daily run-around and then pick him up again in the evening. That went on for three months. Even though friends were very supportive and helped out a lot, it was a period of madness and when I came out of it I decided, no more babies!

'I have a wonderful gynaecologist, whom I trust with my life. It's funny isn't it, the way that through motherhood you develop these close relationships? He knows more about me than many of my friends! Anyway between us, over a few months, we decided the time had come for me to have my womb removed. My periods had become increasingly unpleasant. Half the month I felt as though my insides were dropping out. It was a great relief to have the operation and I bounced back again very quickly.

'In fact I am feeling better now than I have felt for years. Getting back into the workforce through working at the school has been a terrific lift. At first I was frightened I wouldn't be able to cope at all. Even the photocopier terrified me at first! But of course I soon worked it out and now I feel ready to take on a whole lot more. Working in the school library has made me aware of children's literature and what is missing and I am seriously thinking of taking a writing course and setting about writing books for children.

'I am also taking a special sewing course which everyone thinks is very funny, as I have been sewing for so many years. I've started to read some rather more serious books. I have little patches of time for that now, when Jay is at kindy or at my mother's. I feel as though I am coming out of the end of a tunnel. I am becoming more introspective, learning more about myself. It's all tied in, I suppose, with turning forty this year.

'I'm a little bit anxious that next year, when Jay goes off to school and I really do have some time, how I shall feel about that. You never get time as a mother to adjust from one stage to the next, suddenly they happen. One minute you have no kids, then you are a mother, then they are walking, then you have two, three, and then they are gone.

'I don't have specific plans for them but I think I can see the direction they will go. Carla is the academic one, she pushes herself along and gets very cross with herself if she doesn't get full marks in everything. Kolby is the dreamer, the more creative one, and Jay, he'll have to do something physical, active.

'Now that I am getting a little more time to think about myself I realise that I want to go back to work. Not full time, because I don't want to stretch myself that thin. Perhaps in public relations or perhaps something to do with computers. I think it should be something to do with people because that's what I am best at, getting along with and organising other people. Outsiders, non-parents, especially men, don't realise what is involved in mothering; I really do think that if you can juggle your life to cope with three children, their needs and interests, a husband, his job, the school, part-time work, and a social life as well as run a home, well, you could run a country!

'I have learnt an enormous amount through having my children, mostly about myself and my potential. They are now at the particular stage which I have always disliked most. When I didn't want children it was because I would look at ones between the ages of five and ten and think, yuk! But I am looking forward to them being teenagers, because I have always related well to people of that age, and that's not too far away.

'Carla had her tenth birthday recently. She had a dress-up dinner party for a group of her friends. Her dad got done up as a waiter and served them and she really liked that! It was amazing to hear them talk, discussing world issues, like adults. It's then that you realise how quickly it's all happening and what an important job being a mother is. But it's also *so* important to do something for yourself, as soon as they are born. Even if it means moving the earth to do it. An hour, here or there, to do something just for you. I didn't realise this until I was down the track. But it should be done from the word go.

'And you know, when I've had a really awful day I think I would rather not be a mother. I have to remind myself that there are the other times, the good times, too. They take such pleasure in simple things. Walking along the beach they pick up a particular pebble or they stop on the walk up to the house and I'm yelling at them to hurry up and I go back, feeling cross, to get them, and find them looking at a flower, feeling its leaves and touching its petals and enjoying it so much that it stops me in my tracks and I feel glad to have them.'

Dianne Willcocks

Motherhood is the ability to bear, rear and love a child. It's also about building on a foundation.

Gina, Kim, Honi, Arran, Elise, Mec, Shan, Yolana, Leo, Bret, Jodi. No, they're not members of a soccer team, though there is just the right number. Eleven. They are members of a family. The Willcocks family. Not a blended family, where children from two marriages come together as the joint offspring of a new relationship. They are all the children of one mother, Dianne Willcocks, who has been married for eighteen years to the same partner, and who views marriage and children as a commitment not just for this life but for eternity. They range in age from sixteen to one. In an age of zero population growth, the nuclear family and the me-generation, Dianne is something else.

On my way to meet her for the first time I couldn't suppress a growing trepidation, a sense of inadequacy, a feeling of awe. For a mother of two to meet a mother of eleven is comparable to a cadet journalist interviewing the winner of a Nobel Prize for Literature!

In my imagination I had conjured up a house bursting at the seams and that Dianne would be somewhat like The Old Woman Who Lived in the Shoe. The reality couldn't have been more different. Only three of the children are not at school. Only! And they were playing quietly, in a house which was clean and tidy, under the gentle supervision of a tiny, neat, and dark-haired woman who positively glows with peace, calm and happiness. A colour photograph of Dianne's aura would very probably show it to radiate bright blue for a distance of a least a metre! She has a very quiet voice, which I doubt she ever raises, though she assured me she does. But what is most noticeable, and what remains compelling, are her eyes. If you believe that the eyes are the windows on the soul, then it's without doubt that Dianne's spirit is very much alive and well.

In the face of such scale we started with something simple. Though how can anything be simple? For instance, how to come up with enough names you really like. A smile. No doubt she's answered that one before. 'In the beginning my husband wrote a list of the names we both liked and we tick it off as we go. My husband does the final choosing.' A comfortable blend of democracy and leadership. Though in the beginning it seemed as though such a list would not be needed. Dianne was told that it was unlikely that she would be able to have children! (It's not always easy to respond positively to the predominantly male gynaecological profession!)

'When I was a teenager I hardly ever menstruated. I'd go for up to a year without a period. Naturally I was worried. I knew it was abnormal and you know at that age it's more important than perhaps at any other age to feel you are normal, just like other girls. I was taken to lots of doctors and had lots of tests. They thought it might be a problem with the thyroid. Eventually they decided it was something to do with the pituitary gland and that there was nothing which could be done. I remember my mother saying to me, "It will all right itself when you get married." How right she was!'

Dianne was married at twenty-one. 'I hadn't intended to marry that young. I thought I would do so eventually but there were plenty of other things I wanted to do first. I particularly wanted to travel. And specifically I wanted to go down the Amazon. That's still a goal, but it will have to wait.'

She was twenty when she met her husband on a blind date. 'My one and only blind date! I had to explain it to my mother because otherwise she would have blown up, it's not the sort of thing she would have approved of. I hadn't been allowed to date until I was seventeen. Mum thought I should wait until I was eighteen but my brother, who was six years older than me and already married and with children, put in a good word for me. I think he did that because I had told him that I was going to put off getting married for so long that he'd be able to bring his future grandson to my wedding! He was a bit shocked at that and told me I was selfish and in danger of growing up weird. Mum's rules were that I was not allowed to date the same fellow twice running, not without dating someone else in between or going out in a group. This was so I would keep things light, pace myself and also so I would have a look around.'

Dianne left school at fifteen, studied art for three years and then went back to school to matriculate so that she could find work as an art teacher. 'Then I found I was partially deaf and so wasn't able to teach. I decided to take my mum's advice and look for a job with security, so when I was nineteen I went to work for Telecom, in the sales department.

'I'd been there about a year when one of the young men I worked with set me up on a blind date with a new fellow who had started on the technical side. He told this new fellow that I was going to a party on Friday night, which was true, and that I wanted him to take me. He had already made the arrangement and given him my address before he told me what he had done. I didn't really think he'd turn up but I told my mum about it just in case.

'At 7.30 pm on the Friday evening Mum came to my room where I was getting dressed for the party and told me, "Your date's in the lounge room." I thought she was joking. But she wasn't. It wasn't until years later that my husband told me that when he came by that first time Mum had taken him into the lounge and given him a real verbal going over, asked him what his intentions towards me were and that sort of thing!'

'It wasn't exactly love at first sight and the evening was a bit of a disaster because I couldn't find the house where the party was being held and it looked as though I had him along on false pretences. Eventually we gave up looking and went to a movie. He walked me home and asked if he could take me out again the following Saturday, but I told him it was more than likely I would be babysitting my brother's children, which was true. When Mum asked me what I thought of him I told her that he seemed all right but that I didn't think I would date him again. She said something which, considering her usual attitude, really surprised me. She said, "You're becoming a real little social butterfly. I think you should date him again."'

The following Saturday Dianne was not required for babysitting so she accepted her blind date's invitation to the cinema, and as he walked her home he proposed to her. 'I was really surprised. Well, I was and I wasn't. I told him I'd give him an answer in a week. I made him wait the week but I really knew from the time he asked that I would say yes. I think the reason why I had felt nervous about dating him for a second time was that I felt so comfortable with him. I'd never felt like that with anyone else. I sensed that he felt this way too. It frightened me a bit because I suppose I knew it would come to this.'

By 'this', Dianne means a marriage whose bonds of commitment are far more encompassing than most of us are prepared to forge. When she married it was not 'till I get sick of you, till someone even more interesting turns up, till the going gets rough', or even 'till death do us part'. It was for eternity. Because that is a basic tenet of her religion. Dianne is a member of the Church of Jesus Christ of the Latter Day Saints, a Mormon. It is an American-based religion, little known and therefore much misunderstood.

There are 70,000 Mormons in Australia. It's an austere religion; it exacts tithes from its members of 10 per cent of their earnings. Drinking alcohol, coffee and tea, and smoking are forbidden and while birth control is not exactly prohibited neither is it encouraged, except when the mother's health is in danger. But it's also a very supportive religion, partly because its exclusivity gives members a feeling of being special, a chosen people. And partly because those same rules, which the majority of people would find restrictive if not claustrophobic, also give very firm and therefore comforting guidance.

It would be impossible to separate Dianne's religion from her mothering. It would be impossible to separate her religion from any part of her life. 'My religion is my life. We live our religion. It's the basis of everything we do.' She became a Mormon when she was fifteen. Her father, who died of a heart attack when he was forty-three and Dianne was thirteen, had encouraged her to look at a variety of religions. 'Neither he nor my mum or my brother belonged to a particular religion. But they accepted my decision. The very first time I met a Mormon who told me about what they believed it was as if a door had opened. Though it still took me three years to finally make up my mind.'

Dianne's mother insisted that her daughter wait until she was twenty-one before getting married. 'We met in the January and married in the November. By then my husband had become a Mormon. It was a decision he had to make alone and only after understanding all it involved. I was very happy for him. We were married in the temple in Hamilton, New Zealand, because at that time there were no temples in Australia. Before that we also had a civil ceremony in the chapel. The

Australian government insisted on that because the temple ceremony is a closed event.

'When we married it was a sacred covenant we made to stay together through this life, through death and on into life everlasting. So you can see it was a very big step. As a result our children are sealed to us.'

Dianne's husband must also be a very special person, because not only was he willing to take on a pledge of this magnitude but he also knew that it was thought very unlikely that they would ever be able to have children of their own. 'We planned, even before we were married, that we would adopt a family. Adoption is a lovely thing. Children are children no matter how they come to you. But we knew that this could take some time to accomplish, so we decided that in the meantime we would foster children. That was the only reason why we moved out west. Before you can foster or adopt you need your own home so we moved to where we could afford to begin to buy a place.'

The Willcocks moved to Geurie, a little township of 500 people, in central New South Wales, more or less equidistant from the far bigger towns of Wellington and Dubbo. 'My husband transferred to Telecom out there and we found a home for $2500, which had three bedrooms and an acre of land on which we had five goats which we milked and on which we also ran chickens. We paid the place off in two years. It was a good start and a great place to have a foster family.

'In the two years we were there we had ten or eleven children come to us for periods of time ranging from a few days to three to four months. We never had more than three at any one time and we were only supposed to have ones up to the age of seven, but it turned out that we had ones as old as twelve. They came from all over the state, we even had a couple from Queensland and from various towns as well as from the bush. They came from all sorts of backgrounds. A sizeable number were Aboriginal children. We loved them all.'

And then Dianne became pregnant. 'I didn't even know! I

missed several periods but that was so usual I hardly gave it a second thought. I felt a little bit as though I was coming down with something but my husband had had the flu and I just thought I'd caught the same bug. Then a couple we knew well came to visit us and the wife said to me, "You don't have flu, there's nothing wrong with you, you're just pregnant." Of course I didn't dare believe her, even though my husband said that he had sensed this was what it was. The next day I went to the doctor and he confirmed that I was about three and a half months along. I was delighted. We both were.

'Funny thing is that every time I've been pregnant my husband has sensed it before me, and even the children seem to know before me! They tell friends and neighbours, who then say to me, "Oh, the children tell me you are pregnant again," and I say, "Am I?" And they are right! My husband and the children say that I get a certain look about me!

'Gina was born within a couple of days of our second wedding anniversary. We continued fostering children for more than a year until she became so distressed by having so many children coming and going that she started to become insecure. I think she feared that she might be the next to go. So we gave it away and by then I was pregnant with my first son, Kim.'

The Willcocks family now moved into Dubbo. 'My husband was still with Telecom but he really couldn't earn enough money with them, so he started working at other jobs as well. He was not supposed to, of course, but it was a matter of necessity and he has always been a good worker.

'Over the next two years I had another daughter and son, Honi and Arran. I have fed all the children for between one and three months and I have never fallen pregnant when I have been feeding. But once I lose my milk I seem to have one period and by the second one I am pregnant. I have never had any problems or complications with any of my pregnancies. And my labours have all been straightforward too. The first one was the longest, that took eight hours. The shortest was two hours. The last couple have started to take longer again. They have all been natural deliveries and they have all been born healthy big babies. The smallest was eight pounds four ounces (3.7 kilograms), the largest eleven pounds (4.9 kilograms). The only one who was any worry was Bret, the one sitting on your lap, he had a severe milk allergy and that has left him with tooth problems, but that will be simple to get fixed.'

Bret had been sitting on my lap more or less from the moment I had arrived, an unusually affectionate as well as inquisitive and confident boy of three. Occasionally he wandered off to join his four-year-old brother Leo, who was watching *The Never-ending Story* on a video machine. Then he returned for more cuddles and to examine my pen, notebook, earrings and anything else which attracted him. Meanwhile his sister, the youngest in the family, one-year-old Jodi, toddled about the place finding enjoyment and entertainment in every little thing.

The furniture was sparse but eminently practical. This meant that when the video finished and Leo came to do headstands between us, balancing his head on the couch and his feet on the wall, there was no need be nervous of the furnishings or decor. The only rule imposed was no eating in the sitting room. Peanut butter sandwiches were banished to the kitchen. At one point, without being asked, Leo appeared with a plastic bag full of nappies and taking Jodi and Bret by the hand told them they needed changing. When, later on, the two boys became a bit boisterous with one another, Dianne didn't even raise her voice while saying, 'No. You mustn't do that. It's not nice.' They stopped, and I remembered with shame my own exasperated yelling at toddlers.

To a query about whether or not any of them ever fought or ganged up on one another Dianne shook her head. 'Not really. They all of them get along pretty well together. It's a constantly changing situation. As they get older and develop different interests each of them finds they have more things in common with one or another of the others and as those interests change so do the relationships. It's very interesting. At the moment Kim

The most important thing for them is not to waste their potential. They each have the responsibility to make the best use of their abilities and not to take the lesser path just because it's easier.

and Arran, who are fourteen and twelve, have plans to set up a building business together when they finish their schooling. Arran wants be the boss and Kim is quite happy with that. He wants to be the carpenter. They discuss it quite often. And at the moment Leo is particularly close to Yolana, who is six and the next oldest. He missed her a lot when she started school this year. Every morning he asked if he could go with her. That was until she started coming home saying that she didn't like school! I'm just hoping that by the time he can go she will have started to enjoy it. Otherwise I can see a bit of a problem!

'I want all the children to finish their schooling. They all seem to be going well at the moment. Not that schooling is the be-all and end-all and naturally some of them are more academically inclined than others. The most important thing is for them not to waste their potential. They each have the responsibility to make the best use of all their abilities and not to take the lesser path just because it's easier.'

If they follow the example of their father they most certainly won't. After working at three extra jobs at the same time as his main one, he found that there was no further professional or financial promotion to be had in Dubbo, so the couple, then with four children, came back to Sydney. 'My husband had been brought up to believe that you got a secure job and hung on to it until you took your pension. But it became obvious that it wasn't possible to earn enough money that way. There just weren't the promotion opportunities. So he took what was for him a very big step, he went out on his own. I never had any doubts that he would succeed. He is a good man and he works very hard.

'We found a place to live, started paying it off and he set up as a brick-cleaner, using big equipment on commercial and industrial properties. It was extremely heavy and tiring work. He stuck at it for a couple of years and only gave it away because he ended up giving himself a hernia.

'During that time I had another daughter, another son and another daughter; Elise, Mec and Shan. It's not that we ever planned to have a large family. Because of my very irregular menstrual cycle it's not possible to plan. The only thing which would stop me becoming pregnant is the word no, if you know what I mean. Thinking back to the beginning, when I had my first baby and was so surprised and delighted I think I thought then that it would be nice to have four. But we have been more blessed than that. I think of them as mine to care for but that really I only hold them in trust for the Lord.

'I think I have managed to stay healthy because I have been taught a good solid knowledge of nutrition. I have always visited both a doctor and a naturopath and always taken extra vitamins and minerals, in particular calcium. After each birth naturally it takes a little while for me to pick up again and then we sit down and discuss my health and whether it would be wise for me to have another baby. I can see that at some time in the future I shall have more but right now we are going through a bit of a bad patch financially and it wouldn't be the right thing to do.'

The bad patch has hit the Willcocks family hard. After the hernia forced her husband to give up the heavy cleaning work he began selling insurance and was so successful that he made enough to set up a partnership with another man as computer consultants. During these years the family moved house four more times, each time increasing their collateral and buying, or sometimes building, a larger home to cope with four more children. Two years ago the computer business, like many other small businesses in Australia, started to falter from a combination of high interest rates, a lack of support from the bank and a bit of a down turn in the computer business generally.

'It was very sad because my husband and his partner had worked very, very hard. We have had to sell this house to pay off the company debts and now we have to start all over again. He would never declare himself bankrupt, even though he could legally, because he doesn't think that is morally right. It may take some time to pay off all the debts. But we will. We have just started to turn the corner now and see the light at the end of the tunnel. Just so long as it isn't another train we'll be right!

'Anyone can hit financial troubles whether they have one child or eleven. That had no bearing on it happening and I feel very positive that we shall come through. My husband has gone back to selling insurance and we'll have to move back out west probably, somewhere where it's cheaper, so as to be able to start to buy another house. We'll sardine in until we can afford something bigger. This move has hit the children hard, probably because they are older and have more established friendships. I can tell they are distressed because they have occasionally lashed out at one another. But once the move is made and we are resettled they'll be right.

'My husband is naturally upset this has happened. But he sees it all as a challenge and he is not at all cast down. Having so many of us to be responsible for has meant that he has had to be armed six jumps ahead, it has kept him mentally alert and made him very special.

'During this time it would have been possible for us to get some government assistance. But other than the family allowance we have never taken anything. My husband worked out once, just to see, how much we could get in benefits. It was close to $500 a week. That was more than he was earning. He said, "Isn't that wicked? It legally encourages people not to be responsible for themselves." We think the dole is very wrong. It pulls a person down. If people are out of work and need government help they should have to work for it. There's plenty of work to do for the community. It's too easy to get into the rut of not working and not be able to get out of it.

'All our older children work. Gina works in a Kentucky Fried Chicken shop. She buys all her own clothes. Kim earns money babysitting. He has bought a bike and a hockey stick. Honi also babysits and Arran and Elise have a morning paper run. They mostly save their money. They all know we are going through a tough patch. We have family councils and discuss what we are doing. They have even loaned us money when there hasn't been enough to put food on the table. I keep a book with it all listed and when we get back on our feet I'll pay them back. I told them that and they said, "No, Mum, it's all right." But I shall.

'We've always been a close family and this adversity has only brought us closer. They are very special people, my children. All people are special but they are even more so to me. Probably it's true that because our standards are not the more usual standards of today this makes us an even tighter unit. They have had to withstand a great deal of peer group pressure. But that's not been bad for them. For instance if the children at the school are having a party at the weekend they say, "There's no use you coming Gina, there will be drinking and carrying on." And Gina has said to me, "Mum, I don't mind not going to those sorts of parties. I've seen how they are when they've been drinking and it changes their personalities."

'Gina is very mature for her age. She pleaded to take on responsibility for the younger ones long before I would allow her to. She used to get upset and say, "Mum, you don't trust me." But I told her, "No, it's not that. It's because I want you to have a real childhood, to enjoy being carefree." But it's just as if she was born responsible. As if she was born to be the oldest. She is planning to be a nurse and several of them also want to be missionaries for the church.

'It's not as if they don't have fun. Of course they do. Our church runs parties, drama and speech groups, and social events like dinner dances and talent nights. They also go off to fellowships run by the various other churches, places where they can have good clean fun. I don't want to shut them away. I want them to go out and see the world as it is for themselves so that later on when they are adults they can evaluate their own lifestyle against that of others. All the children belong to the church and I believe our religion teaches great self-discipline and also to be conscious of each action and what the consequences of it will be.

'Once a week I try to go to the temple, which is way over on the other side of town, with my husband. We also go as a family to church, which is different from temple, every Sunday. We also say morning and evening prayers together and read the scriptures, quite often during the evening meal. Their faith has definitely helped them during this difficult time. Not being able to afford all the lovely things there are to buy is not such a disadvantage. It can be quite strengthening. It's a matter of attitude, of concentrating on finding the silver lining. We say to them, would you work as hard to accomplish things if either you had everything, or if things came easy? And the more of a load you can take the more you will be able to give and help other people. You can't help others up the ladder if you can't get up it yourself.

Of more use will we be. I think that all this has helped to develop their intellect and their character.

'We were just talking about all of this only last night as we were getting ready to go to bed. My husband was in a funny mood and when I said that what we have been through together had been strengthening and how proud I was of him he said, "Oh, to be a weakling!" He was only fooling of course. Then he said, "I had a bit of a splurge today. I know we can't afford it, but I bought you this book of poems and I want to read one to you which says so much better than I could how I feel about you." It was by Elizabeth Barrett Browning. Do you know it? It begins: "How do I love thee? Let me count the ways. I love thee to the depth and breadth and height my soul can reach, when feeling out of sight for the ends of Being and ideal Grace." It's very beautiful. Then he read one by Christina Rosetti about remembering the first time she had met her love. Then he asked, "Do you remember how on our second date I put out my hand to help you up?" Of course I remembered and he said, "Well, I knew you didn't need help, it was just an excuse to be able to hold your hand because I wanted to so badly." And I said, "Oh you cunning devil you!" But I was very glad that he was!

'I love being a mother. Naturally it's made a few things difficult. I used to paint, but the children started to get into my stuff so I gave it away. Instead now I write poetry and songs in my head, where they can't get at them! Often I write things for special occasions and those I put down on a tape-recorder.

'Having the children has also made it difficult to exercise as much as I would like. I can't leave them alone while I go off jogging. But I have a regular regime of 5BX exercises which I do. It's also been necessary to be a little bit organised. The home is run on a split-shift basis and I have learnt how to catnap for ten or twenty minutes a couple of times a day, just to replenish my energy. I can doze like that and part of me is still fully conscious and aware of what is going on.

'Motherhood is the ability to bear, rear and love a child. It's also about building on a foundation. My parents, my husband's parents, they had their little faults. Hopefully we have learnt and are a little bit better than them. But we have our faults too and I hope that our children are learning what they are and will be better people than us. Their children will go on from them and so on and on and on. All of us children of God and coming closer to Him.'

Marelle Thornton

The whole of life is about communication. If you have speech the fact that you can't walk is not as great an issue.

Ask any pregnant woman, 'What do you want, a boy or girl?' and invariably she will answer, 'Oh I don't mind, just as long as it's all right.' She might already have three girls and be longing to have a boy, but still her major concern is that her baby is physically and mentally 100 per cent.

The fear of giving birth to a baby which is in any way abnormal lurks in the depths of every woman's subconscious. Occasionally such horrors leap forth in the unguarded time of dreams, or when, just as unexpectedly, we catch a glimpse of what could be us or ours on television or in a wheelchair in a public place. But mostly we manage very successfully to push aside such possibilities, to quash such horrors. Safe inside our barricade of self-preservation we tell ourselves, 'That only happens to other people.'

In this Marelle Thornton was no different from any other woman. 'If I thought at all about these things, there was an assumption that it was another sort of person who had handicapped children. Poorly educated people, with low incomes and large families and that in some way or another it was their fault.' Those prejudices were given a severe jolt when Marelle gave birth to her first baby, a daughter, Katie, who is now ten years old. 'In those ten years I have learnt more than I ever imagined possible about myself and other people.' Katie was born with cerebral palsy. In brutal layperson's language she's a spastic.

'I was twenty-eight when I became pregnant and had been married four years. My husband was a Vietnam veteran and when he returned to Australia he started working for an industrial plastics company and went on into design and sales of heavy lifting materials and load restraint systems. He loves his work and is very good at it.'

Marelle is a primary school teacher. 'Ever since I was in primary school myself all I wanted to do was teach. Though I do recall having a little flight of fancy when I was fourteen or so about being a missionary. I was deeply impressed by our scripture teacher, a Presbyterian deaconess, and for a little while there I saw myself as a saviour of the world. It's very common for girls that age to have a love affair with self-sacrifice. It's either that or horses!

'But in the end I went to teachers college. I guess I saw teaching as offering a career and status. It's a caring profession with a high degree of responsibility. It's not something I take lightly. I saw it as a career, not just a job. My mother, who didn't work outside the home, said that I was always the ambitious one in the family.' Marelle's father was a crane driver. Her older sister is a mother of two and a secretary. Her younger brother, who is also married and has two children, trained as a boilermaker. Marelle was the only one in the family to attend a selective high school. 'I have always seen advantage in bettering oneself.

'I was very seriously considering going to the UK as an exchange teacher to broaden my experience when I met my future husband and after a whirlwind romance of a few months we were married. It was a bit of a shock to my parents that it happened so quickly. I had always assumed, ever since I was a young girl, that one day I would have children, probably two. It was all planned. We waited until we had bought our own house and then we thought the time was right to start a family. I was looking forward to being a full-time mum, to being at home caring for my child and husband.'

At no time during her pregnancy did Marelle have any really unusual problems or difficulties. 'Everything went very well. I gained a little too much weight during the last couple of months, a lot of it from fluid retention, and that caused a bit of high blood pressure but nothing too out of the ordinary. My husband came with me to the birth classes. Together we both learnt how to relax and breathe properly so that he could help me at the birth. He wanted to be there, to be a part of it all so that it was as much his child as mine. It was all very ordinary and normal, until the labour.'

Marelle had what is medically termed an incoordinate labour. 'I had no contractions, just one big, continuous pain. The baby was supposedly due on the eighth of April but she wasn't born until the third of May. The doctor assured me this was all right and that I must have just had my dates wrong. In the end I had to be induced and even then it took thirteen and a half hours. It was a very difficult delivery. They did what's called a Kielland's rotation and a forceps delivery. This means putting a clamp on the baby's head, turning it and literally yanking it out.'

Marelle refused an epidural and remained fully conscious and aware throughout this procedure. 'I had wanted a natural delivery and although I was in pain I didn't want to give in and not know what was happening. I thought it was better for my baby if I didn't have an epidural. I was told that they were considering doing a caesarian. I knew I was having a hard time but because it was my first baby I didn't know whether or not it was normal. I just had total faith in my obstetrician. My husband, who stayed right through and was a tower of strength, told me later that he watched with amazement as the obstetrician put his foot up on the delivery bed to give himself extra leverage to pull the baby out and how her neck stretched as he did so.

'When she was finally out she was in total shock. Her head was torn from the forceps and she didn't breathe for several minutes. They rushed her off to an humidicrib in the intensive care ward where she was given oxygen. It was several hours before I was able to see Katie. She was such a beautiful baby. Beautiful. But she had cuts and grazes on both sides of her head and my first thought, after oh isn't she beautiful, was, she's brain-damaged. My own doctor told me there was nothing to worry about but I insisted that a pediatrician examine her and she also assured me, "I can't find anything wrong with her." Right from the beginning there was this unstated but nevertheless quite clear message, "You are just another over-anxious mother."

'We came home and tried to settle into the new routine. To the casual observer Katie at this stage looked perfectly normal but I knew she wasn't. You can call it a gut response. Looking back now at photographs we took then I can see this gorgeous baby girl, but with little gestures, like a turned neck and extended legs, which I know now are symptomatic of cerebral palsy. That's not what I thought was wrong then. No. The words handicapped or disabled never entered my thoughts. The very worst I could allow myself to imagine was that Katie had some slight muscle problem which could definitely be rectified.

'She had difficulty suckling, so much so that I could only breastfeed her for two days. She was markedly right-handed, seemed to have a constantly stiff neck and didn't seem to make the same physical milestones as other babies did, like rolling over and sitting up. When she was six weeks I took her back to the pediatrician who again assured me that there was nothing wrong. But I didn't believe her.

'I'd had some experience with babies. Because I was twenty-eight before I had Katie quite a number of my girlfriends already had children and I had spent time with them. There was also the baby of the woman who lived in the house across the road. She was a nursing sister with an older child and a small baby. She worked evenings and weekends and I frequently looked after her little one. So I was able to make some comparisons. There was also my mother. Katie was her first grandchild and both she and Dad doted over her. Mum never said anything when I voiced my fears to her but looking back I can see she subtly encouraged me to press on with my search for a doctor who would see what it was I could see was abnormal in her. My husband thought I was worrying too much and that Katie was just a slow starter.

'After seven months of being given the run around, one doctor even said to me, "You're just a neurotic schoolteacher looking for a problem." I gave up on conventional medicine and took Katie to a chiropractor. He also told me, "There's nothing wrong." '

It wasn't until Katie was nine months, and suffering from a bronchial infection, for which Marelle took her to a pediatrician, that she learnt the truth. 'I remember saying to the doctor who was examining her chest, "While you're at it would you mind having a look at her neck. She seems to have trouble with her muscles there." He had a look, did some reflex tests and without pause said, "Yes, you're right. There seems to be some spasticity here."

'I remember sitting there. Stunned. It was the first time anyone had used that word. Spasticity. Spastic. I had this sudden image of ugly, gross, deformed bodies, jerking and twitching and drooling. No. That couldn't be my Katie. I instantly projected to my own vision of a spastic adult. I was frightened. Overwhelmed. But my very first thought was not for Katie. It was, how can we tell my family? Next came, how can we hide the fact? I became totally self-absorbed. Worried only what other people would think of me, of my failure and inadequacy at producing a faulty product. I was more afraid for myself than for my baby. I was fearful of other people's reactions.

'These are hardly emotions of which to be proud. But I am being honest. It has taken me many years to come to terms with

Katie's dysfunctions and with the first emotions which I experienced. Perhaps in some ways I am still coming to terms with both. I certainly discover new things all the time. And in a way I live from day to day, unsure what physical or emotional need will present itself next.

'Perhaps the most difficult aspect of it all has been my inability to be in total control. I have always been a very black and white person and need to be in charge of my life and my environment, so it's ironic that I should be the one to have a child who has very reduced control over many of her body parts.'

One of the manifestations of this need to control is the obsessive tidiness which is immediately apparent as soon as you enter Marelle's home. She smiles ruefully when I comment on it. 'I'm much better than I was. Even before Katie was born friends would comment in front of me about how clean and tidy my place always was and I would glow with pride! You could have run your finger along any shelf in the house and not found one speck of dust. It's not like that now, look how dusty these photographs of Katie are.' Framed enlargements showing a beautiful smiling young girl with startlingly clear, intelligent eyes, sitting in a wheelchair holding various awards.

On the fridge door is a certificate stating that Katie Thornton has passed her electric wheelchair driving test. 'That's her black licence. She's very proud of it. When she first got an electric chair she was on a red licence, a bit like P plates. She had to take a series of tests to prove her driving and handling skills before she was given this full licence. It means as much to her as a full licence does to a new young car driver. It represents freedom.'

Beside the licence hangs a tray of plastic compartments. One compartment for each day of the week. Each compartment is in three sections, marked morning, afternoon, evening, and each contains varying sizes and numbers of pills. 'Just this year Katie has begun to have myoclonic jerks, little fits, and this is medication to control them.'

Despite having done a full day's work and then come home to

a couple of hours of caring for her handicapped daughter, Marelle had already set the table for the dinner, to which she had hospitably invited me. Her husband was interstate on business. But Katie was there to greet me, showered, hair brushed, spruced up for bed and showing signs of inheriting her mother's organisational skills. She immediately requested that my car keys be put on the kitchen table. 'So you know where they are and they won't get lost.'

It only took a very little time to adjust to Katie's slightly impaired speech patterns and it was instantly apparent that she comprehends everything that is said or that goes on around her. She is not as shy as many ten-year-olds are of total strangers and contributed frequently to the conversation. But she never interrupted. Her mother is a stickler for manners and a couple of times reprimanded her for showing off. When Katie asked for a glass of juice she held it to her lips and wiped her mouth with an ever-ready tissue. I know that Marelle would resent it but I couldn't help admiring her. Also I couldn't help imagining how I would have handled having a handicapped child.

'Would you like to see my new bathroom?' Katie invited. From behind Marelle supported her daughter's full weight on her arms and together they frogmarched down the hall to Katie's end of the big family home, which has been completely renovated to give ease of access to Katie. Low along the wall there are faint tyre marks made by Katie's wheelchair. Houseproud Mum pointed them out and I winced at what she would think of my housekeeping! The large tiled bathroom has a big shower recess with a chair. The taps thermostatically control the water temperature to an even warmth. 'Katie can now learn to shower herself. It's another important step towards independence. Towards her having some degree of privacy.'

Opposite the bathroom is Katie's playroom, dominated by her wheelchairs, one electric and one manual. And between is her bedroom, perfectly tidy, naturally! On the wall is an array of miniature dolls and other collectibles which Marelle, her husband and friends have sent or brought home for Katie from their various overseas working trips or holidays. At the bottom of her bed are Katie's numerous dolls.

Marelle freed her daughter's hair from its neat topknot and in one deft but spine-jarring motion heaved her onto her bed. Katie suggested sleeping on her tummy but Marelle talked her out of it and arranged her body in a comfortable position. She would stay like that all night, because she is totally unable to turn herself over. A goodnight kiss and a discussion about which companionable light to leave on, and as we walked back down the hall Marelle's relief is palpable.

'This is my time of the day. The couple of hours I get to myself. To do what I want to do. It's a long day. I get up just after 5.00 am to have my shower and fix my hair and face.' Marelle is perfectly groomed and manicured. 'I get Katie's breakfast ready and wake her at 6.30. The bus calls for her at 7.30. That gives us an hour to toilet and dress and feed her. I tidy the house after she's gone and leave for work just before 8.00. My husband leaves at about the same time. The bus drops Katie off every afternoon at 5.30. She attends the Spastic Centre School five days a week. Because of where we live she's the first one to be picked up and the last one to be dropped off, so she spends four hours a day on the bus. It's a long day for her too.

'The weekends are even more exhausting. Though it's been easier since Katie has had her electric wheelchair. She goes off on her own in it. We have to allow her the dignity of taking risks. For seven years she was not able to move from place to place without the assistance of another person. The first time she went out of the house alone I ran from window to window to keep an eye on her, but making sure that she couldn't see me. If I am working outside or in the garden I can hear the chair by the little engine whine it makes as it moves around. She goes off for an hour or an hour and a half by herself. She visits people in the neighbourhood.

'A little while ago she had a crush on the boy who lives opposite and would wheel up his driveway and yell to him, "Scott, come on out, I know you're in there!" The poor boy would cower inside. What eleven-year-old boy wants a girl chasing after him, especially a little girl in a wheelchair? So we had to explain that to her. One of the rules is that she is not allowed to annoy other people or demand their attention. 'She's not allowed to chase other children in the wheelchair or to drive it into them. Fortunately we live in a cul-de-sac and she knows that she must stop whenever she hears a car and look very carefully before she crosses the road.

'Through the freedom and mobility the wheelchair gives her she has met people in the neighbourhood whom even we don't know. One afternoon she came back dragging a puppy on a lead followed at some distance by a young couple who had been out walking their pet when she had accosted them and asked if she could have a go. She also introduced herself to a new neighbour, a young man who had lost his arm in a car accident. We only knew she had met him when she announced at dinner one evening, "Bob doesn't know where his arm is." We paused, and then asked, "Have you been talking to Bob?" And she said, "Yes, and I asked him why he only had one arm and he said he'd lost the other one and then I asked him where it was now and he told me that he didn't know." So you see she's not shy of people. Not yet?'

Over dinner we talked some more about Marelle's first reaction to being told that her daughter was suffering from cerebral palsy. 'After the initial shock we spent a lot of time trying to find out how, why, when, where. Asking questions, poring through medical dictionaries, having tests done; CAT scans and lumbar punctures. I was looking for an answer as to why me, looking for someone to blame. I didn't smoke when I was pregnant. I didn't have any viral infections while I was pregnant. I did have a difficult labour and a violent delivery. And at no time during that labour was the foetal heart monitored, which I realise now was a mistake. But no one person is to blame. It's still a mystery why cerebral palsy occurs. There are some common elements. It happens more with premature babies and at one stage it was found that the RH factor had a bearing on it. But I've given up worrying about it. It took a few years to reach that point but now I live with the problems of today rather than agonising about the past.

'Though I do still feel angry that the medical profession took so long to diagnose Katie's problem. As with any illness or disability, the sooner it is diagnosed the better the chances are of achieving more successful treatment. With cerebral palsy it is very important to inhibit inappropriate movements and muscle spasms, otherwise the body sets up patterns of response which are difficult to control.'

I comment on how attractive Katie is. 'When she was very tiny I was so fanatical about the way she looked, constantly changing her clothes and wiping her clean, that my mother told me, "You'll wash that baby away." The occupational therapists at the Spastic Centre told me years later that they used to call Katie the spit and polish baby, because she was always so perfectly turned out, and that they used to delight in playing games with her in front of me in which she got really grubby and messy. I knew even then that it was my way of compensating. She had to be beautiful, clean and appealing.

'I imagine that even if I had had a non-handicapped child I would still have been over-fussy and protective. That's my nature and I have worked very hard at facing that with honesty. I'll also be honest enough with you to say that when Katie was a baby, although I loved her dearly, I used to lie in bed at night and wish her dead. I would plead, with no one in particular, "Please take this giant trauma away." I imagined putting a pillow over her face or taking her out in the car without strapping her into the seat and driving into a wall. What stopped me was not the thought of Katie gone, but whether I would be able to live with myself if I had actually proceeded with any of my plans.

'I am sure this shocks people. But a public confession helps to expiate the guilt over those thoughts and all I can say is that having Katie has drawn me through an incredible range of emotions that I had never even considered before.'

Marelle's husband also had to handle unexpected emotions in his own way. But by the time Katie was three they both felt they had weathered the worst possible storms and come through together, stronger. They decided to have another baby. A major decision taken with plenty of anxiety. For twelve months Marelle tried, unsuccessfully, to become pregnant. 'I thought that perhaps it was fear that was the problem but finally I went for some tests to see if there wasn't some other more tangible reason why it wasn't happening. The pap smear showed gross cell abnormalities and after an immediate biopsy I had a complete hysterectomy some four weeks later.'

For Marelle this was the final turn of the screw. 'I did the whole "I'm useless, I've failed, I've made your life a misery, find yourself another woman" number. I fell right back into the pit and it seemed deeper and darker than even before.'

It was her husband who dragged her back up again. 'He was fantastic. Husband of the year and father of the year rolled into one. He has always been a very special father to Katie. Every second weekend he takes her to riding lessons. He showers her and now when we are facing the imminent onset of her menstruation I have no doubt that he will not pause at having to change her sanitary pads or attend to any of her very personal needs. Whenever I have felt like giving up he would say, "She's ours and we have two choices, either we keep her with us or we give her up." The idea of putting her into care is so abhorrent to us as to be beyond considering.'

It was after this final blow that Marelle went back to work. 'I knew that part of me was wallowing in self-pity and I decided that I needed to give myself a kick in the pants and get back out into the wider community. I had become very self-involved and somewhat inward looking. As my family doctor put it, "It's time for you to get back into the world of the normal." My husband was extremely supportive, he could see that what was good for me was good for Katie and for him. My mother was supportive too. She looked after Katie for two years before she went to the Spastic Centre School. She's done that for all the grandchildren.

'My father has had more trouble than Mum adjusting to Katie being a little girl with a handicap. He sees her as a handicapped little girl. There's a big difference. He thinks we are too tough with her. On one occasion when she was behaving badly at the table and I gave her a smack he got up and left. But she does manipulate him, which I find quite distasteful. I don't think she should be allowed to take advantage of her disabilities.

'Just like any other little girl she delights in being able to gain attention and sometimes to embarrass her mother. One evening when we had visitors she asked, in front of them, "Mummy, am I going to have clean pants tonight?" She knew just the right button to press! She knew that she would become the centre of attention and I would be embarrassed if those people thought that she didn't have clean pants every night. And I was.

'Another time, also in front of guests, and when feeling somewhat unnoticed, she suddenly pulled her pyjama jacket out and announced, "Mummy, my belly button is dirty." And she got just the response she wanted. I became very flustered and said, "Don't be silly, Katie, it's just that your belly button is a dark hole, like everyone else's, and that just makes it appears as though it might be dirty."

'So you see she knows what she's about. We say that she gets slippery eyes when she has done something or is about to do something wrong. She hangs her head and looks sideways out of them.'

Rejoining the other world was not all easy. 'The first day back at school I remember standing in the playground surrounded by about 400 able-bodied young children, and one of the girls called out, "Watch me Mrs Thornton, watch me," as she skipped, and I felt the tears start in my eyes. Tears of sadness knowing that I will never see Katie skip. That's what is bloody hard, knowing that I will never have the luxury of mothering a normal child. I

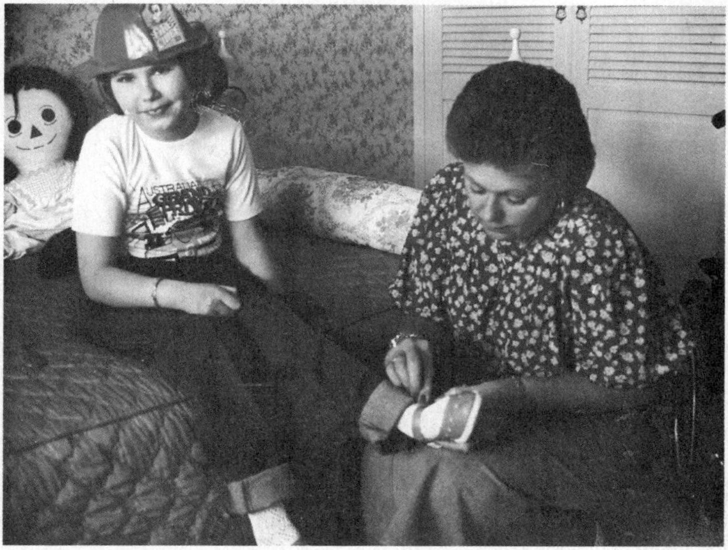

One of the girls called out, 'Watch me, Mrs Thornton,' as she skipped, and I felt tears starting in my eyes. That's what is bloody hard, knowing that I will never have the luxury of mothering a normal child.

hear other mothers talking about what their children can do. The ones with toddlers complaining that they pull the saucepans out of the kitchen cupboards; the ones with children Katie's age complaining that they have to run them here and there to ballet or soccer games and I think to myself, you'll never know how lucky you are.'

For two years, in addition to teaching and caring in the evenings and on weekends for her daughter, Marelle studied at night to bring her teaching skills up to date. 'When I did my original training it was a two-year course. Now it's three years and if you want to keep in line with modern thinking you need to do the conversion course.

'Because of Katie I still suffer some tremendous frustrations and resentments. I am very achievement and goal orientated but because I find that I can only work four days a week and still manage Katie this has meant that I work as a supply casual teacher. To pursue a career path within the Education Department it's necessary to be on the permanent staff and that means working five days a week.

'I need the satisfaction of status within my profession, to have a sense of my teaching worth, some accountability and commitment. I couldn't hack being a relief casual teacher and I have sought out special areas in which to stretch myself, teaching remedial reading and maths and as a language coordinator. For the past three years I have furthered my experience as a teacher librarian.'

As if all this is not enough Marelle has also become deeply involved with the Spastic Centre of New South Wales. She is vice-president and a member of the Board of Directors. 'I guess you could say that's where all the real decisions and policies are made. The centre is a multi-million-dollar organisation which caters for the needs of people with cerebral palsy right through from babyhood to the aged. It is a wonderful organisation and does a superb job. I guess you could say that we are fortunate to live in a country where it is possible to get such first-class care for Katie. Initially I became involved with the centre because of her, but you can't be in there just pushing your own barrow forever, so it has grown to be a far wider interest than that of my own individual need.

It is quite apparent that Marelle's work with the centre, all of it voluntary, is extremely important to her. 'I get a great deal of satisfaction from it and perhaps yes, in a way, it helps to compensate me for not being able to pursue my profession with the degree of intensity which I would have liked. There's only a small group of parents of children at the centre who become involved. The regular hard core. I am in some ways more fortunate than many of the parents because a lot of them have more children than just their handicapped child so their emotional and time resources have to be spread further. Because I have just Katie I can put more in.'

In her neat, tidy and expertly organised office upstairs Marelle gave me brochures about the centre. She spends at least two and usually three nights a week on paperwork and meetings. 'Through the centre I have travelled overseas on several occasions and have studied how other countries, particularly Britain, provide for their cerebral palsied people. I have learnt a great deal about aspects of how society is organised, about politics and about human nature.'

Not all of it has been heart-warming. 'People can be incredibly insensitive. You'd be amazed at how many see me pushing Katie in her wheelchair and say, in front of her, "What a pity, what a shame." I feel like saying, "You unfeeling sod, she may be in a wheelchair but she can still hear." But usually I just give an automatic smile and walk on. Some people just stare. The ones I really can't stomach are the ones who come back for a second look. I feel like saying, "Go on, why don't you, take a really good look," or, "Don't worry, it's not catching." Again usually I manage a smile and say, "Excuse me," and wheel past them.

'Then there are the ones who patronise Katie. Either they say to me, "How old is she?" instead of asking her directly. Or they speak to her in the tone of voice they would use to a two-year-old. As if just because she is in a wheelchair and physically handicapped that means she is automatically stupid too. It really bugs me. And it bugs Katie too. Occasionally she shrugs and turns away from them. Sometimes she just stares back at them as if it's they who are the idiots.

'She knows that children use the word spaso to mean stupid or dumb. And she has said to me, "Mum, tell them I have cerebral palsy and not that I'm a spastic." She really dislikes that word. I have encouraged her not to hide herself away or be embarrassed about herself. But of course she knows she is very different. One morning I went in to her room and found her moving her arms around in studied poses and when I asked,

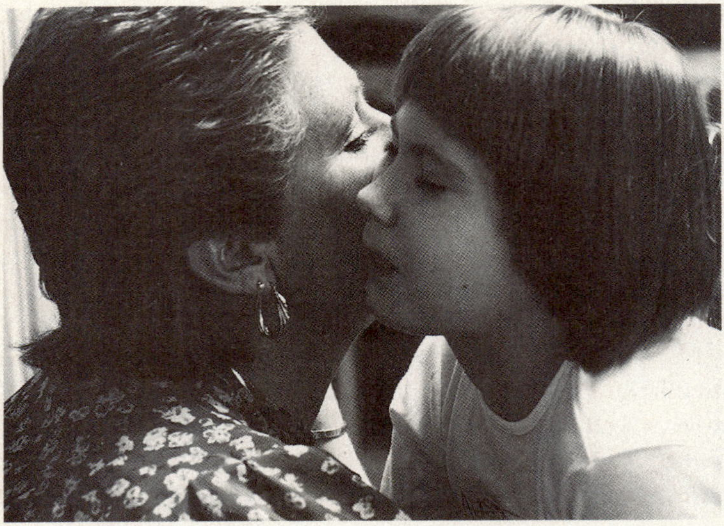

Having Katie has drawn me through an incredible range of emotions that I had never even considered before. I discover new things all the time.

"What are you doing, Katie?" she told me, "I am practising to be a ballerina. That's what I am going to be when I grow up." Then she watched for my reaction. I just said, "Well, that's a long way off yet."

'When she was four she went through a stage of telling me how much she hated her legs. Once she got her wheelchair and became mobile she stopped worrying about her legs. And one day she said, "I don't think I will be a ballerina, instead I think I'll teach ballet." She had worked out that she could perhaps do that from her chair. Now it's her left hand that worries her because she can't control it. Her right hand has about 80 per cent function and she is learning at the centre to be a one-finger typist.

'Just recently, on a weekend, she said to me, "Mum, I'm bored." I said, "Katie, there are plenty of things for you to do.

Shall we read or would you like to have a game of snakes and ladders?" It was as if she hadn't heard me. She just kept talking and said, "Why don't I have any ordinary friends? It's because they get cross that I can't keep up with them and run and jump, isn't it?" What could I say, except the truth. I said, "Katie, you've just got to accept that there are some things you can't do."

'My greatest fear is that she will not develop any sustained friendships. The fact is that she does not have a lot of friends of the same age as herself. It would be better for her if she had brothers and sisters. As it is she is an only child and an isolated child. Her only friends either live some distance away or are other adults and my husband and myself.

'It's very important through all this that he and I don't let Katie become our entire lives. Naturally she is the main focus. But there have to be other facets. They say that a handicapped child means a handicapped family and that's true. For instance, I haven't taken a holiday with just my husband for seven years, and that's not good. It's something we have to be conscious of and try to make separate time just for ourselves. The Spastic Centre has residential space which we can make use of. It's silly I know, but I still feel guilty to put Katie in there for a weekend so that we could have that time off together, just the two of us. I have booked a three-day break for us for later in the year and at this stage I am determined to go through with it. But we'll see what happens.

'As far as all our futures are concerned that is something we are constantly coming to terms with. We have to make realistic goals. Academically she is not on a par with others of her age group, as she suffers learning difficulty, which is something frequently associated with cerebral palsy. But with Katie there are no deadlines she has to meet. There's nothing to say that at twenty she must be able to do this or that. Her greatest goal is to be able to successfully communicate with others. The whole of life is about communication. If you have speech the fact that you can't walk is not as great an issue.

'My hope for her is that she will develop her skills to their fullest and gain her maximum level of independence. I like to think that she will be able to live in a share situation with other young, probably handicapped people. Perhaps it may need to be a fully supported household. At the centre we have married couples in which both partners have cerebral palsy. And I hope that she will be able to have some sort of meaningful employment, to achieve her fullest potential, self-reliance, to feel good about herself, to feel worthwhile, to have the dignity of some private life, to be happy and to love and be loved.'

As I left Marelle gave me a poem. 'I wrote it when I was feeling low and it helped to pull me up.' The last verse read:

For it's love that she'll need more than all else
To live a life that is whole.
From love she will learn to understand
Not her body that counts, but her soul.

THE HORROR YEARS

Trish

Ann Adams

Liz McLean

Paula

Trish

Recently, while doing the dreaded Franklins rush, I met a woman I have known for a very long time but hadn't seen for a couple for years, during which time her children had become teenagers. We stopped amid the piles of boxes and trolleys and I asked her how things were. She gushed on about how much she was enjoying her children. Either she was lying or she need read no further.

I had the distinct impression that she was lying. I recognised a few of the telltale signs. Whereas mothers of young children may look harassed and tired, mothers of teenagers look bewildered, frightened even, wounded to their very core. Who can blame them if they take to the booze, the fattening foods, the Coca-Cola, the Serepax, the pokies, lovers, or the road. Not me. I understand completely.

What I still don't understand is why it's not possible to negotiate these years without such heartbreak and distress. Why as reasonable human beings we can't find a manner of handling all this without ending up on the verge of being committed to an asylum for the insane. (At times such as escape had an extremely positive appeal!) Even having survived it, I still don't have any answers or solutions. What got me through was having a partner with whom to share it all, having work which was demanding and interesting, having a couple of very close friends who realised I was out of my tree but encouraged me to hang in there, and by having, in the end, a sense of self and survival strong enough to surprise not just them but me too. Being able to see the funny or at least bizarre aspect of even the most grievous situations is also an absolute necessity. Laughing most when it hurts most.

It all happened with such blinding speed it caught me totally unprepared. Though nothing could really have prepared me. It seemed as though overnight these two warm, affectionate, intelligent, interesting children turned into absolutely totally repulsive monsters! The only difference between them was that whereas Zara's behaviour became a more-or-less direct attack on me, Sean's had a broader market appeal.

Within three months of our return to Sydney he had broken into the art room of his former primary school with a couple of his mates. They sloshed paint around and made a general mess. And on their way out they were apprehended by the local constabulary. The first we knew of the escapade was when we received a telephone call summoning us to the police station, where Sean had already been fingerprinted.

To say I felt angry would be an understatement. I also felt hurt and terribly ashamed. On the drive home no one spoke. He went straight to his room. I hardly slept and the following morning I frog marched him down to the school principal, to whom he apologised for what he had done and offered to help clean up. Sean was not happy with my humiliating him in this way and I admit that I did it as much for my own conscience as for his.

Two days later he had to appear in front of a magistrate at the children's court. I made his sister come, in her school uniform, in order to witness her brother's shame, in the hope it would make her think twice about doing something equally antisocial. It was an awful experience.

I didn't feel in the least like protecting him. I wanted him to suffer the full blast of possible wrath. Some smarmy lawyer suggested that we should have the case postponed because he would then be able to make sure by legal trickery that Sean did not have to appear in court and run the risk of getting a criminal record. I was speechless with anger that he could make such a suggestion. Sean had broken the law and he was going to pay the price. How would it be if I let him learn that he could wiggle out of copping what he deserved?

It was all over very quickly. The magistrate gave Sean a good public dressing down and then she put him on a good behaviour bond. In the car on the way home I went off my brain and told my son, with a great deal of venom in my voice, that I had stood by him on this first occasion but that it was the last. Any more such behaviour and there would be no backup from me. None. I became so heavy that his father suggested I lay off.

Years later Sean told me nothing I had done or said during the whole unhappy affair had impressed him as much as the look of utter distress on his father's face. That's it, isn't it? Mothers run themselves ragged and all the while the person whose admiration the son needs most is the father! With daughters it's their mother. If you see that as sexism I say it's normal human instinct.

For all of Zara's teenage years it seemed less as though it was her trying to win my approval than me trying to win hers! An impossibility. Zara wanted a mother who was like the ones in TV sitcoms and advertisements. Always turning out enough perfect quiche lorraines to feed the unannounced horde of visiting friends or willing to iron the unmanageable frills on some delicate number one of them wanted to wear to a party. But, and it's a big, important but, doing all that without impinging, without being a person in her own right.

I tried. God knows I tried. I became such a faded version of what I really am that in photographs of me taken during those years I barely recognise myself. I tried so hard to be what she wanted me to be that looking back I cringe with embarrassment. 'If you wore clothes any tighter you'd do better to just spray them on,' she judged me. It would have been easier for her if I had been overweight and not interested in clothes as an expression of personality. At one point I even found myself not caring that I had put on an extra kilo and thinking that perhaps a woman in her thirties should not be so flash; that I should rethink my image, be more circumspect; that I was at risk of becoming something of a joke if I continued to swim topless.

I found myself doing up a couple of buttons on my blouse when I heard her come in from school. If I was going to get particularly dressed up for a dinner or a party I even, and this is really unbelievable, started taking the clothes I was going to wear up to the garage beforehand and dressing in the car on the way there.

Despite voicing her disapproval of the way I dressed Zara and her friends were very willing to 'borrow' my clothes and junk jewellery. Many were the Saturday evenings when she would open my wardrobe to a whole tribe of beautiful pubescent flesh. I would stand back while they rummaged through and while they filled the bathroom with their make-up and hair-colour sprays and the entire house with their music and their depressingly inane chatter. When they left, hardly deigning to notice me, or if they did, only for long enough to fling me a desultory condescending 'thank you' as one might give a small bone to a frantic-to-please dog, I would begin the task of trying to restore some semblance of order to a scene which looked like something from backstage at Les Girls. At least they left the kitchen unscathed. They were not into food — slim and taut though they were, they were all on diets.

Not so Sean and his friends. They would open the fridge and the cupboards and suck out food like human vacuum cleaners! For them an after-school-pre-surf light snack consisted of jaffles and milkshakes. A jaffle was concocted from anything which could be shaken or slopped from a jar or box. For example, a hamburger pattie, half a bottle of tomato sauce and a thick wedge of cheese squeezed between two slices of bread and forced into the groaning jaffle-maker. Two of these savoury items were followed by two sweet ones filled with lashings of peanut butter and bananas. These were washed down with a shake, made again with anything which was easily accessible, and consisted of a half litre of milk, three huge scoops of ice-cream, two eggs, another banana and some highly coloured strawberry or caramel topping. Nothing subtle.

Sean would complain if there were only oranges left from the previous day's gargantuan shopping, the dozen apples having already been ingested, because oranges were too difficult to peel. Bananas were easy. He would half peel three of these, stuff them all in his mouth at once and walk out the door like that, banana skins dripping from his chomping jaws, his surfboard under one arm, a towel and a bag of more fruit in the other hand, and accompanied by a bunch of his mates, all of whom had scoffed similar amounts of food. From the top of the garden, now that the bananas had been swallowed, he would yell, 'I'll be back for dinner,' and I would reel into the devastated kitchen and search for what could be whipped up into something edible to put in front of him in two hours' time.

By contrast with all of this, Guy was light relief. He came and went with an extraordinary succession of the most amazingly beautiful women, all of whom looked like *Playboy* centrefolds. These females never spoke. Well, hardly ever. They just sat there and held Guy's hand and looked at him with adoration while he talked. Mostly he talked about cameras and photography. He had become a very talented surfing photographer and had an idyllic lifestyle following the comps around the coastline. I remember the time he came back from a big comp at Bells Beach in Victoria and slept for a straight eighteen hours. When he eventually staggered to, I asked him how it had gone and if he'd had a good time. 'Sure. It was wall-to-wall women. Trouble is after a while they all start to look the same.' So much for radical feminism!

And so much for all of Sean's eating because he never put on any flesh, probably because he was growing upwards at an alarming rate. In the January he turned fourteen, he measured five feet five inches (165 centimetres). Five months later he was five feet eleven inches. Those articles of clothing he didn't manage to grow out of in three months, he kicked to death instead. A pair of sneakers lasted six weeks, maximum. And he simply wouldn't wear the reasonably-priced brands. They had to be the same as all the other guys were wearing. Life seemed to be a never-ending revolving door of meals and unsuccessful hunts for inexpensive sneakers.

He lived so fast and grew at such a pace, he fell asleep mid-sentence and his knees came undone. That's not the precise medical explanation but that is what happened. He surfed all day Saturdays, partied Saturday nights and surfed all day Sundays, finishing up with a good workout on his skateboard. Just before dinner time on Sundays he'd crawl, whimpering, down the drive and complain about the terrible pain in his knees. They creaked loudly and were frighteningly loose. For six months he constantly had enormous fluid-filled bulges behind each knee, for which he received ultrasonic treatment and an admonition from the specialist not to use his knees so much.

Sean gave the doctor the same look he gave me when I caught him skateboarding down the very steep hill on which we lived and warned him of the extremely dire consequences of falling in front of a vehicle, unprotected, off a board which was travelling at thirty kilometres an hour and had no braking system. I confiscated his board but he just borrowed ones from other fellows.

His knees were not the only part of his anatomy which suffered due to the sudden surge of growth hormone. He casually let drop one day the fact that he frequently had little blackouts. 'I sort of doze off and come back a few seconds later.' My God! My mind leapt at all the worst possibilities, fuelled by the fact that my older sister's son suffered from petit mal, having as many as 200 little turns a day. Within twenty-four hours he'd had a brain scan which showed, of course, totally normal brain size and patterns. The specialist pointed out on the computer print-out how completely his brain filled his skull and told me that as people age the brain shrinks and of course if the person suffers from, for instance, Alzheimer's disease, it shrinks abnormally. 'Why don't you have a scan, Mum,' Sean suggested, 'to see if that's why you have your funny turns?' I protested indignantly and didn't tell him that in fact I did have a scan the following week.

It transpired that I was totally normal too (or at least as totally normal as any mother of teenagers can be) and it wasn't until a couple of years later that it was discovered, by accident, as these things always are, that I have a slightly dicky heart. The specialist immediately started talking pacemakers and daily pills for life and was most put out when I told him that, as over the years it had been variously suggested that I was a manic depressive, that I needed a hysterectomy, that I should take Valium and that it was all Woman's Troubles, I was quite relieved to find that what I had was something even a mere man could have and that I was sure it would all get much better when my children left home. It has!

The other portion of Sean's teenage anatomy which seemed to have worked itself loose was his lower colon. He and all his friends became such proficient farters they had competitions to see whose fart, when lit with a cigarette lighter, burned the bluest and for the longest time! Unfortunately for Sean, and for us, he always created his most magnificent expulsions of wind when he was asleep, so these could never be entered for the title. To force my way into his room in the morning to rouse him from his deep sleep of exhaustion was to battle against a fug, the pressure of which made his bedroom door difficult to open, and to risk immediate asphixiation.

What a way to go! And if the foul air didn't get me it seemed likely that there were at least another dozen terminal diseases lurking under the bed and in the dark corners of his disgusting room. I had stopped cleaning their rooms years previously and I also no longer ironed their clothes. I had even managed to stop caring that they didn't iron their clothes either. For a while I insisted that if they were coming out with me they iron whatever clothes they were going to wear. But after a few ugly tussles of will I gave even that wan hope away. I was learning, slowly, that it was better to save my depleted energies for what really mattered.

Still I did feel that out of consideration for the health of other members of the family, not to mention unsuspecting visitors, I should insist on Sean fumigating his personal space every six months. It was a risky business and I did it in dread of what might leap out at me, but twice a year I waited until he left for school and then made a swift attack. After flinging open the windows I first bundled up the bedclothes for a double run through the washing machine, then I dragged the mattress out into the sunshine, next I pulled the bed into the middle of the room and then I emptied onto it everything, and I mean *everything*, from his drawers, shelves, cupboards and wardrobes.

Along the wall beside which the bed had stood there were little fungoid heaps of mouldering, barely recognisable banana skins. In the bottom of the wardrobe were pairs of totally destroyed sneakers, which he had grown out of months before, still stuffed with socks so ripe with sweat they had coagulated and were actually stuck to the sneakers. There were cigarette papers and packets, well-thumbed copies of *Hustler* and *Penthouse* and other detritus too personal to mention. Sometimes I found shirts of his father's or jackets of mine which had gone missing ages ago and which Sean had solemnly sworn he had never seen.

It was impossible for Sean to sleep amongst all this, so he was forced to bring it to order, cleaning up as he went. The odd thing was that he didn't seem to mind. On the contrary he quite enjoyed going through it all, no doubt discovering all manner of lost treasures which had become buried over the months.

The other room in the house which Sean more or less monopolised and where he seemed to excel himself at farting was the rumpus room, where he was to be found slumped in front of the television. This occurred when the waves were breaking too far out, were dumping, or were too flat (I learnt a whole new vocabulary during this period and could even comprehend the literary delights of *Surfing World*). He would loll back on the couch surrounded by the debris of jaffles and shakes, and channel change during each commercial break with his toes. This habit drove his father to distraction, which prompted Sean to suggest that what his father was really mad at was that his own legs were not long enough for him to be able to perform the same delicate task.

Throughout our withering bad-mouthing of him Sean remained good-natured and complacent about his accomplishment. I well remember the journey home from town, after the four of us had been to a concert (I could still very occasionally bamboozle them into attending a cultural event), during which Zara and Sean laid the back seat down and dozed off. Fatal. Sean's rectum immediately began to whistle. His father's yell woke him and he mumbled an apology. Seconds later he dozed off again with the same vile result. Another yell. And a less respectful response from Sean to the effect that he couldn't help what happened when he was asleep. 'Then bloody well stay awake,' his father ordered. 'And if you can't control your bodily functions then I think you should see a doctor.' Throughout this exchange I had been trying to remain rapt in the beauty of the music we had just heard, but this really was all too much. We halted at a red light and I jumped out of the car slamming the door on a few choice words about what I thought of them all and suggestions about where they could all go. The car was driven off at high speed and I was left in a dark forest to walk home. A few minutes later there was a screeching u-turn, the car door was thrown open, I got in and we all drove home, wide awake and silent.

The following morning Sean left a note on my desk. 'Dear Mother, please make appointment with doctor about possibility of operation to stop farting. Your loving fart of a son.' I replied in a note left on his desk saying that an operation was available but that the doctor was out of stock of the necessary rectal clips, which were made in Japan and would not be available for a further two weeks. We maintained this ludicrous but amusing communication for a few more days and I kept his notes so in good time he can show them to his own farting son.

Such low humour was light relief from Zara's dramas, which were now daily occurrences. From the moment she awoke until the second she dropped asleep Zara created scenes in which she was invariably centre stage. Exhausting!

It was during these years that I developed the routine of a daily morning run. Raising children forced me into patterns of living which were in constant flux, changing with the ever-changing situation. We now got up at 6.00 am and while their father put their breakfast on the table I did the ironing. Then at 6.30 we woke them and left them to it while we took off for an hour's run and swim, coming home just a few minutes after they had left to catch their bus to school. That way I at least started the day in a calm state.

Occasionally Zara would stagger, bleary-eyed, into the laundry where I was ironing before I managed to make my escape and always with some preposterous demand. Then she would either burst into tears or scream foul language at me if I was foolish enough to react in either a negative or a positive manner. It was a total no-win situation, so for three whole years I tried very hard to avoid ever being in the same room alone with her. In the company of others her attacks were somewhat modified, though not always. She managed to stage quite a number of award winners in restaurants and other public places.

I did feel compassion for her because it was obvious that she was not happy within herself. But I'm not a saint, nor, thankfully, a martyr, so my sympathy was worn pretty ragged and I frequently lashed back. We must have been hell to live with. Both of us.

Everything she did was a rejection of us, and of me in particular. For starters she began to slob around in an unbelievably grotty manner. Post-nuclear-urban-aggro okay, but unwashed underwear, greasy hair, scuffed shoes and torn hems not okay! Both she and Sean started going off to school in personalised uniforms. They also started wagging school and because of the laisser faire attitude of the staff and in particular the headmaster they were able to get away with this behaviour. Other, more self-disciplined, students did just fine. Rhodes scholarship material is not lured from the straight and narrow by a good set of waves or by the promises inherent in being a surfie's moll. Lesser mortals are more easily persuaded to a life of hedonism. It's not easy to raise non-academic children in a beach suburb!

We tried to arouse their enthusiasm by becoming deeply involved in school activities. We joined the P and C, helped to raise money for equipment, worked on the gardening committee, which spent weekends planting trees in the school grounds, and joined the roster of parents who helped in the school canteen. But the more we put in, the less they seemed inclined to do so themselves. Eventually, and with deep personal regret at choosing a divisive over an egalitarian system of education, I agreed to send them to a private school. I realised I had been reluctant to make the decision not out of concern for their best interests, but from my own prejudices.

We told them of our decision at breakfast one morning. If you think we should have discussed the matter with them first, my reply is that you obviously don't have children and that I was trying to run a family, not a democracy! Zara stacked on an enormous turn, slamming glass doors and yelling red-faced abuse, but she and her brother joined the scores of other young people on the long daily bus journey to and from the city. Truth to tell, she enjoyed the social intercourse of those trips and also the far stricter discipline at the new school. Sean sat in the back seat of the bus with the headset of his Walkman glued to his ears while the focus for his apparel attack moved from bottom to top. He took such inordinate pride in wearing the school's most battered straw boater that he was incensed when his father made the umpteenth new one totally destruction-proof by lining it with fibreglass mat and resin. Sean waited a respectable time — two days — and then 'lost' it.

He was told, 'You'll have to buy the new one from your own pocket money.' What a ridiculous threat! They both were given five dollars a week. A new boater cost three times that and if his pocket money was spent on a boater, who would pay for the surfing magazine, the visit to the local cinema or support Sean's addiction to video games? He played video games with the same fervour press magnates and television stars play the horses! He concentrated so hard that sweat would pour from his brow as his leaned across the flashing screen jiggling his forefinger too fast to be caught by the human eye.

So as to have more money to waste in this manner, Sean took on a weekend job. I encouraged this move because I thought it would give him a better sense of values if he had to work for what he threw away and that it would also instil in him some regard for the value of the work ethic. Silly, silly me! Sean's job cost us far more than he ever made from it.

All he had to do was sweep up and hose down the paths and patios around a large house in our neighbourhood every Saturday morning. The first few Saturdays Sean managed to cycle up there on time and get the work done. But on about the fourth Saturday I had a phone call mid-morning from the man who had employed Sean asking where he was. Sean had left home two hours before supposedly to go to work, but I made some puny, protective-mother excuse for him and said he would be up there very shortly.

His father was hopping mad. I scrambled after him into our van as he shouted, 'I know where the bastard is.' He drove at breakneck speed down to the next beach along from us, came to a squealing halt in the car park and, leaving the engine still running, leapt out and ran down to the edge of the surf, where he began shouting and gesticulating wildly. He looked very funny but I didn't dare laugh. Sean came out of the water, wearing his wetsuit and with his board under one arm, and his father gave him a verbal lashing right there in front of his mates, who lounged about enjoying the ludicrous spectacle.

When they reached the back of the van his father grabbed Sean's board and hurled it in, threw his bicycle in on top and went to grab Sean by the neck of his wetsuit and push him in too. As he did this he tore the third finger on his left hand, but he was so angry he hardly registered the little spasm of pain. He then drove us at the same crazy speed, shouting all the while at Sean, who was struggling out of his wetsuit and into his clothes, up to the paths and patios which awaited the cleanup. Here he pulled to a sudden stop, Sean scrambled out, his father threw his bike out after him, along with a few more choice adjectives and we roared off back to our home, emotionally drained. But there was more to come.

Two hours later the phone rang again. This time it was a woman who said in quiet, well-modulated tones designed to calm me, 'There is nothing to worry about, but your son has had an accident. Please don't panic,' because I already was! 'he will be fine. He's been hit by a car.' At which point I freaked and his father had to come to the phone.

For the second time that morning we leapt into the van. Guy was with us. We had been strapping the windsurfer on top of the vehicle to take it for a sail. We zoomed back up towards the house where we had recently dumped Sean so unceremoniously. The narrow road zigzags back and forth up the hill and on one of the most treacherous tight corners the stuff of nightmares, a potential death, occurred. The clip holding the back of the windsurfer on to the car-rack came undone and the board swung out like a scythe over the footpath just avoiding the decapitation of a startled pedestrian. Trembling with relief and fear we reattached the board and proceeded at a slightly slower pace a little further up to where Sean was lying on his back in the grass beside the road.

He was conscious, with no visible injuries, but white-faced and obviously very shaken. Also shaken was the driver of the vehicle who had met Sean coming down the hill on his bicycle on the wrong side of the road. Sean had careened over the front of the car, into his windshield and rolled up across the top and down into the grass. The man was overweight and a smoker and it was a miracle such an awful experience wasn't the final cause of a heart attack.

Guy and his father followed, at a sedate pace, the ambulance which came and took us to the hospital. Inside I sat beside Sean grasping his hand and babbling on while the wonderful paramedics monitored and checked him. The hospital staff were also fantastic. They kept an eye on Sean, who lay there looking incredibly vulnerable, all long-limbed and gangly, for a couple of hours, anxious about the possibility of internal injuries, and then said he could go home if he was kept quiet. But not before he had been visited by the police, who very rightly gave him a talking to about his irresponsible behaviour.

Only after the sister said he could go did I burst into tears and then I couldn't stop. His father said, 'What's the matter with you, they said he's all right!' But the sister gave me a cup of tea and a cuddle.

Sean's bike was a write-off and we paid $250 for the damage Sean had done to the man's vehicle. But that wasn't the end of it. Over the next few months his father's finger seized up and became permanently locked in a bent position. For a while he wore a small brace on it during the day and at night a full arm one, which meant he could only sleep on his back, in which position he always snores and keeps me awake, or on his left side. Being on the road working five months of the year has made it more or less impossible for him to keep up regular physiotherapy, so the finger is now arthritic and probably inoperable. I see it as a legacy — a reminder of those years.

By mutual consent with the owner of the patios, Sean didn't go back to the job. No doubt the man was as relieved as Sean! Sean is not cut out for such work. He now has a tiny mid-city garden and patio of his own, but he pays someone else to maintain it. By contrast Zara always had a job. She worked as a checkout chick at Franklins, she watered the gardens of homes which were used only as weekenders, she served behind the counter of a deli and she took around the canapes at privately catered functions. What she earned she spent but at least when she dyed her beautiful blonde hair a ghastly jet black, or when she bought a one-off designer cloak which drowned her petite shape and made her resemble a moving Jackson Pollock, she did it with her own money.

By comparison with what she earned the pocket money which we continued to give both of them was a paltry sum indeed. In exchange for this five dollars they were supposed to take it in turns to carry up the garbage, and alternately either clean the car or sweep and hose the patio. One piece of advice for future parents of teenagers. If you are considering a fee-for-service arrangement with your children over pocket money, don't! Take the car to the drive-in car wash, sweep the patio and put out the garbage yourself. It's not worth the hassle. Just give them their pocket money with your blessings and save yourself the headache and the increased heart rate which come with all the shouting which is necessary to get them to do those jobs. Take the easy way out of this one and save your energy for the ones that really matter — like dope and booze and sex!

When you are a non-drinker and non-smoker like me it would be easy to come across as a wowser to your teenage children, and that would not be at all helpful in the constant battle for their hearts and minds. In fact I think it would encourage them to go to the other extreme. I have strong opinions about these socially acceptable drugs but like all other personal values these come under heavy attack from teenage children. It's very good to have your beliefs challenged, it helps to prevent ossification of the mental faculties! But how to hang in there without losing touch with either them or what matters to yourself? The only way is to listen, to talk, to be always available. (Never mind the pressure of work, the time of night, your own emotional state or the fact that you have your period coming and feel like stabbing anyone who comes within reach of you.)

We were fortunate in that none of our children got into heroin, even though it is so readily available. But they did try cocaine and street stuff like Ecstacy. Still they managed to resist peer pressure enough to stay on course. They all smoked dope. Guy went through a macho drinking phase. Sean and Zara went to places where alcohol was being served long before they were eighteen and I accepted that because the social climate makes it difficult for that not to happen. Where is there for them to get together with their friends other than places where hard liquor is sold? They are as much a victim of our hard drinking history as are the heavy social drinkers and alcoholics of my age. Zara drank very little, she's a natural non-drinker. Sean knocked back a few and eventually it was the incidental cause of a major change in his life (of which more later), but the most important thing was that I kept talking and listening about it all.

Perhaps that was the most important thing. Look, I don't know. Even having been there, done that, I still don't know. I don't know why some young people handle it and others don't. I just know that the risk, the very high risk, of them becoming involved in a scene which was too hard for them to cope with and finishing up destroyed or even dead was a very real and ever-present fear all through those years. I lay awake for hours waiting for them to come home from parties which they had been given special permission to stay at until past the normal weekend cut-off time of midnight on the grounds that they were being given a lift home with someone we knew; some of the longest hours of my life.

Sex, by comparison, was a dead cinch. Perhaps it frightened me less because I'd had more personal experience of it than the drug scene! I just kept feeding them information about contraceptives and saying that anything goes just as long as you behave responsibly and with caring towards the other person. Zara reacted to my attempts to bring such matters up for casual conversation with the same buckets of withering scorn she poured over me continuously. She sneered audibly when Sean asked, 'Mum, do you know what a homosexual is?' Except that is not the word he used. It was far cruder, more anatomical and to the point. But unfortunately unpublishable, which is ridiculous. I had thrown the evening meal on the table and was rushing to get off to a P and C meeting, wearing the one middle-class, suburban-mother-of-two-and-a-bit outfit which I reserved for such occasions. Sean knew the answer to his question. He wasn't asking a question. He was testing me. Seeing how I would react to such blunt language. What could I do except sit back down at the table and talk about sexual preferences, prejudice, caring, love, and contraceptives and listen to his thoughts. I was half an hour late for the meeting and didn't feel I should be too precise in telling the chairman what had delayed me!

And for those mothers who want to and think they can protect their daughter's and son's virginity by keeping a scrupulous eye on them, I have yet another cautionary tale. Our last family holiday with Sean, but minus Zara (who was suffering from too bad a dose of puberty blues to want to join us), was spent on a journey of tribute through Ned Kelly country and finished up with a beach camping expedition. Here we were joined by close friends of long standing who had with them their two teenage daughters and their slightly older girlfriend. Years later Sean told me that it was this friend, a girl so presentable as to warm the cockles of any middle-class mother's heart, who right there on the beach, within earshot and more-or-less under the beady eyes of over-protective adults, who were at the time lying on their backs around the campfire oohing and aahing over the beauty of the night sky, knocked off my son! So there you go, but so what?

At least the holiday was a brief respite from Zara and her dramas. We always encouraged them to bring their friends home. But even this was fraught with problems. I well remember one of the times when Zara had a girlfriend stay over. We all took to our beds at about 11.30 pm, but for some unknown reason I woke an hour or so later and found my partner already awake beside me. Without speaking to each other we lay there — listening. There was a somehow unnatural quietness. Without discussing anything we both got out of bed and went downstairs into Zara's room, where we found the beds stuffed with pillows and extra blankets and no signs of Zara or her girlfriend.

We clambered into tracksuits and into the car and with an uncanny sixth sense, well-honed by parental experience, we drove through our little village and down to the beach, where we very quickly found Zara wandering along alone. After the initial angry words we asked where her girlfriend was. They'd had a row and she'd gone off on her own in the direction of the changing sheds and toilets. Anger turned to anxiety. We searched these buildings and the scrub behind them, terrified that we would find her battered body. (Such improbabilities become very definite possibilities in the middle of the night.)

Mixed with the fear was the feeling of guilt that I had not been responsible enough towards some other mother's daughter. After half an hour of fruitless searching and calling we decided we had to face telling the girl's mother that her daughter was missing. Zara, who had started out by being sulky and aggressive, was now as anxious as us. We drove, slowly, to her friend's house. The knot in my stomach twisted tighter and tighter. What the hell was I going to say? What was this woman, whom I had known for ten years, going to think about me letting her daughter wander off into the night? We let ourselves in a side door and crept into the front room, where to our astonishment we found Zara's girlfriend asleep on the couch, the television silently flickering away. I felt like throttling the two of them. Instead we crept out as silently as we had entered and I never told the girl's mother how close she had come to losing her daughter.

But Zara didn't need the assistance of her girlfriends to create scenes. She was quite capable of doing that all on her own. For her penultimate ballet exam she insisted that she had her entire costume in her bag and refused to let me double check. When she began to dress at the examination hall she announced that she had not brought the correct tights. Classical ballet does not make allowances for idiosyncracies of dress. Even Baryshnikov would fail an exam if he was incorrectly attired. Without saying a word I rushed out to the car and drove, with my hand on the horn, a story of distress for any police officer who tried to stop me formulated in my mind, home and back again, with the necessary tights, in just on eleven minutes. A journey which should normally take at least twenty.

Zara snatched the tights with a hostile glare and I retreated with a thumping headache, to the car, where I sat and hated her. But I also hated me. Despised me. Why did I do it? Why didn't I just let her fail? Was it that her failure would be my failure?

The following year, two weeks before what would have been her final exam, after twelve years of being toted to and from ballet lessons on three continents, sometimes through (with no exaggeration) hail and snow, she announced that she was giving up ballet. Yes. That's right. Fear of failure. Even I, her mere mother, knew that. But I didn't care any more. I had turned the corner. The process began on the day I found myself having fantasies about killing her!

I remember it very clearly. We were driving up the hill out of the suburb adjoining ours and I had to slow down because of heavy traffic. She was sitting in the seat beside, having a go at me. I can't put it any better than that. Yap. Yap. Yap. Yip. Yip. Yip. On and on and on. Niggle. Niggle. Niggle. I stared ahead trying to obliterate her voice. I pulled out to overtake a slow-moving truck and in that instant the thought came unbidden into my mind. If I swerved suddenly now and at the same time leant across and opened the door on her side she would fall out and under the wheels of that truck and *then* she would stop talking! At the time I was not shocked by the thought, I was too anxious to reach wherever I was ferrying her to and get rid of her. It was only later that I was staggered by the enormity of what I had daydreamed. It was another weight to add to the distress which caused me to wake up in the night crying. Not wake up and then cry, but cry in my anguished sleep and wake already in tears.

It was obvious, even to me in my frayed state, where all this was leading me. One mother of a teenage daughter girlfriend of mine had already been committed to care for R and R. I considered going for outside help but baulked at this because I thought it would only fuel the fires of Zara's already spectacular theatricals.

And then one day her father came across me sobbing into the ironing about the fact that she had once again turned her cheek aside when I had gone to kiss her and he said, 'So what? Why the hell do you go on attempting to kiss her? Are you so desperate for her to love you that you are going to lie down and let her shit all over you for the rest of your life? Because if you do you're a fool.' And something clicked in my emotion-drenched brain. I thought, uh-huh. I thought, he is losing respect for me. And my God I didn't want that to happen. What on earth would be the point of going through all this with him only to find when they left home that we were two strangers staring at each other over the debris of the years? And I put all the emotional garbage about Zara at the very back of my head and pulled down a shutter on it.

What a relief. From that time on, with some notable lapses, I remained detached from her scenes. It was as though there were two of me. The one she continued to hound and the other one who stood aside, aloof, and kept saying, 'Remember now, don't get sucked into all this.'

One of the lapses occurred when she gave her father a verbal lashing. That she could attack the man who had loved and supported her in truth in a far more generous-hearted manner than I, despite all the stuff she had thrown, was so insupportable that I flew down the stairs to her bedroom like one of those cartoon characters, going so fast my feet didn't touch the floor, and hurled myself at her, throwing her back against a huge plate glass window. If her father hadn't separated us I think we would have done each other a great damage. But in general I did manage to maintain an emotional distance.

Now you are thinking, I know you are, that none of this will happen to you. But you are wrong! You may be presented with a slight variety of this terror and you may handle it differently, but you'll get the boot in the guts too, and that is said not with smug pleasure but with a sense of shared sorrow. At least you will be better off than me because having read this you will be ever-so-slightly prepared. I know the whole scene was a little less trying for my spouse because he had been such a teenage hoon that he anticipated their tricks, though perhaps not quite the degree of Zara's fine-tuned tortures.

He knew they would have huge parties the moment we left them in the house alone and they would get so boozed they'd jump off the balcony to fall three metres into the rocky garden. He knew they would 'borrow' any money we left around. He knew they would drink the gin we kept for special occasions, fill the bottle with water and then deny having done it. He knew they would stay out until the wee small hours and spin ludicrous yarns about how they had missed buses, the car had run out of fuel, or they had given a lift to an old lady who lived on the other side of town. He knew they would 'borrow' the car and sneak it back with a bump or two and that even if we hid the keys they would try to jump-start it. (It became stuck on one occasion in the difficult drive.) He knew they would 'borrow' our clothes and sell them to their friends. (Sean was most indignant when I found one of his mates in my denim bomber jacket. 'Well you never wear it!' he said.) He knew they would stuff their beds with pillows and sneak off on midnight assignations. He knew they would shoplift and run foul of the law. He knew they would blow the guts out of our stereo system and similarly destroy the accoustics of the car radio and tape deck. And he knew they would be slack at school and more interested in the waves, the opposite sex and having a good time.

He knew all this was more than likely to happen because he had done most of those things, plus a few others, himself. But I couldn't anticipate such behaviour because I had been such a revolting little goody-goody. At least that's what I thought, until a couple of years ago when my younger sister asked, 'Do you remember Boko?' I should have been forewarned by the studiously casual way in which the name was dropped into the conversation. Silly me. I walked right into it. 'Boko?' I pondered. 'No. No I don't. Who is he?' 'It's not a he it's a she,' her voice hardened. 'Boko was my black doll whose head you ripped off.' (Uh-huh, here we go.) I had to admit that I couldn't remember committing this heinous crime and tried to steer the conversation onto lighter topics. (Family! You travel more than halfway around the world to see them only to have them rake over cold, bitter coals!) But my sister was not to be deflected. 'Well, I kept Boko, her body and her head, until last year. She came everywhere with me.' (My sister had lived in England, the Canary Islands, South Africa and now Canada. Could she really have packed the two-part Boko along with her lingerie through all these places? It seemed so.) 'Last year, for my fortieth birthday, my husband gave me a new black doll and we buried Boko in the garden.'

My God! I mean this was not a David Williamson play I was performing in. This was real life! But of course I knew immediately that Boko was not really what my kid sister was on about. She was telling me that I had been such a nasty, rotten, mean, miserable bitch when I was a child that I had made her life a misery and she had coped by keeping Boko as the symbol of all her very real hatred of me. We hugged and kissed and cried and I kept saying how truly sorry I was for how I had been, but the terrible truth is that I don't recall being awful enough to so badly wound her. I remember our childhood with pleasure and her as always being smaller and more vulnerable than me and my memory tells me that I protected her.

Which just goes to show how selective memory is and persuades me that neither Zara nor Sean will truly remember the emotional mincer they put me through when they were teenagers, at least not until they have teenage children of their own. Then will I be able to resist standing on the sidelines and cheering the little bastards on?

Ann Adams

All the struggling through the teenage years does have its compensations; and the best rewards are seemingly the smallest ones.

Ann Adams' first awakening to the trials and tribulations of having teenage children came in the mail in the form of a bill for $150 for ambulance services. 'You know how it is, as a mother you develop a sort of sixth sense about them and immediately I knew it was something to do with my oldest son, something I wasn't supposed to find out about. I was right. It was a bill for transporting him from the Police Boys Club to the local hospital some months previously.

'I confronted him with the evidence when he came home from school. He was visibly shaken and eventually it all came out. He was with a group of older boys, who'd bought a flask of whisky on the way to the disco. He'd drunk it rather rapidly, to gain greater impact I guess. Apparently he had actually *wanted* to get drunk, perhaps to appear more assertive and to lose his inhibitions. Lose his inhibitions he certainly did, and came perilously close to losing his life also.

'The alcohol, combined with the heat in the club and the frenzied activity of the disco caused him to collapse. According to some interested bystanders I was told that he had aspirated his own vomit, turned blue and stopped breathing for some time. If their description is true he probably suffered a respiratory arrest. However, luckily, he was resuscitated and taken by ambulance to the hospital.' Ann is a nursing sister and so understands the seriousness of all this.

'I was cross with him and let him have it. Such a stupid thing to do, though at least he would only have harmed himself. And I was furious with the police and the hospital, both supposedly responsible organisations but neither of whom had let me know. I rang up the club and the response from the officer I spoke to was, "Well madam, what d'you expect, we get hundreds of these kids up here, we see all sorts." I informed him, curtly, that this was not one of his hundreds of kids, this was my son and that he was not a street kid, and that I had encouraged him to attend the club because I thought that being run by the police meant that it was a safe place for him to go. Huh! He didn't apologise or try to explain or anything. He was very casual about it all which made me even more furious by the time I went in to see the people at the hospital.

'The guy there in charge of casualty was initially very offhand. He admitted that my son had been treated as an assumed drug overdose and that they had given him an injection which assists in reversing the effects of a narcotic overdose. He filled me in on the statistics about the kids who pass through casualty daily suffering the effects of drug and alcohol abuse. As my son was still a minor I questioned the legality of treatment and in particular the hospital's failure to make any contact with us, his parents.

'He could have died. I've seen that happen with alcohol and vomit. It's not something to be taken lightly. I took most of my distress out on the hospital and the police who were so slack. I didn't need to say much to my son. He'd had a big enough fright and has never done anything so stupid again.

'That's the thing isn't it? Their stupidity. It drives me crazy. How do they think they can get away with all these things? And that they never think of the consequences. And that you get dragged in to it all. Left to clear up the mess. I suppose we were the same as kids though I didn't have an opportunity to get up to the same tricks.'

Ann had a very different childhood from her own children. She was raised on a 3000 square kilometre cattle property in the Gulf country. 'It sounds like a cliché, but it's true, I had a *wonderful* childhood. I was the second oldest of four. My dad ran the station and my mother is a writer, but of course out there the woman runs the homestead and the family too. There was no school of the air then so we did correspondence school and Mum had to supervise all that.

'By lunchtime we were finished and then we'd go off looking for bees' nests or fishing or picking wild vegetables. Learning the lore of the land. The Aboriginal kids were our friends and we learnt almost everything we knew from them. They were very sexually aware from an early age. There was nothing in it to be ashamed of as far as they were concerned. They gave us the hard, cold facts, not in a hush-hush, dirty way. More, "Well, there it is kids." And the reaction was, "So what?" My closest friends were Rosie and Moana Mudd, Ruby and Rexie, who was quite mad.

'I had this wonderful dog, who died when he took a strychnine bait put out for the dingoes. I was heartbroken and insisted that he had a proper grave dug about a mile away from the property. It developed into a little animal cemetery. A bit morbid, but girls are like that at that age and I think I got the idea from *Girl* magazine. Anyway we buried a turkey that died out there and a pig and then I had this idea that the place should be made attractive and planned a cobbled pathway to it from the homestead with poppies along the edges. Complete madness out there in that country where it's dry for 90 per cent of the year!

'Anyway I roped the Aboriginal kids in on my dream. I was the foreman, you see. I armed them with boxes of matches and told them I wanted the path cleared but that they must make sure to beat out the fire on each side of the track. Well the inevitable happened. We forgot to keep an eye on mad Rexie, and he was so engrossed in setting fire to it all that he forgot to beat out, and the next thing I knew I looked behind me and there was this wall of flame. It burnt half the property and Dad and the men fought for two days and two nights non-stop before they put it out.'

At eleven Ann went off to boarding school in Brisbane, an all girls Church of England school. When she finished at seventeen she spent a year on the property teaching correspondence school to the two children of the property mechanic. 'It was a great year, like a coming-out. I went to bush race meetings to which people from hundreds of miles around would come. We'd go to the races all day and then party all night. Then I went down to Townsville to do my nurses training. As a kid I had ideas about becoming a vet but that idea got lost and anyway I always thought I would get married and be a full-time mother. That didn't come to pass, thank God. I'm very glad I have my career, it's helped so much, especially during their teenage years, when it's always seemed as though one or other of them has been up to something.

'There was the business of my daughter sneaking out at night.' Ann laughs. We both laugh, so loudly that the other patrons in the restaurant to which we have made good our escape, away from husband and children, turn to regard us with disapproval. They would probably disapprove even more if they knew what we were making light of — but we have both been there and know the only way to stay relatively sane is to joke about it.

'We had rented a beach cottage for a week and my daughter had brought a girlfriend along. They were fourteen.' An expression crosses Ann's face which only mothers of fourteen-year-old daughters can fully appreciate! 'I thought they were spending rather a long time making themselves glamorous before going to bed, you know the sort of thing, lots of blow-drying the hair.

'Anyway we all went to bed and in the middle of the night their alarm went off and woke us up. My husband shouted out for them to switch it off and when they didn't he got up and went into their room and found it empty. They had obviously set the alarm on the repeater mode by mistake.' More laughter from us and more frowns of disapproval from the patrons.

'My husband went out into the night to track them down. It was a wild and isolated area and my main concern was that they would be raped and murdered. It sounds silly talking like that here, but in the middle of the night it seems very real. There was also the very real possibility that they could drop over a cliff. Matters were not made any easier by having my in-laws staying with us on holiday and there was this tut-tutting atmosphere.

'Anyway of course he found them, wandering along the beach, I suppose in the hope of meeting some young men. They hadn't arranged to meet up with anyone. It was really just a lark. They were unharmed, and after abusing them both and telling the friend that she would have to go home in the morning we all went back to bed. But he had our daughter up again at 5.00 in the morning. She was a championship swimmer at that time and he had her out there in her swimsuit, goggles and cap swimming 100 metres out into the channel and back again. All I could think about then was the danger of sharks. You know how fathers are about their daughters, the majority of them anyway. They just don't like to see them growing up I think. Perhaps it's because they remember what they got up to with girls when they were that age!

'What did I do at that age? Well — there was this ghastly creature who worked for my dad. He was a bit simple really, overweight, about twenty-four and obviously admired me. He used to throw stones up at my bedroom window and I'd go down and meet him and we'd kiss. That was all. That was my brush with illicit romance!

'So perhaps I was prepared for my kids to explore romance. What I certainly wasn't prepared for was their brush with the law. More than just a brush really: caught shoplifting, fingerprinted, children's court, the works! It still leaves a nasty taste in my mouth.

'The humiliation is the worst part. Sitting in the police station in the presence of dozens of nonchalant police officers, hearing the offence read out in bored, heard-it-all-before tones. An offence of gargantuan proportions to my shocked ears. Maintaining a dignified silence in court while the magistrate ripped my child to shreds, obviously a good deterrent tactic, but still, hard to take. This child of mine who had been brought up on *Blinky Bill* and *Five Go to the Moon.* Who had been fed nutritious meals, taken to concerts and ballet, encouraged to read the newspapers and, above all else, to be honest; what were we doing in this sordid courtroom? We didn't belong there! But we did. My well-brought-up teenager had broken the law. The whole business completely rocked me.

'My emotional response when I first heard what had been done was something to be seen. Wild swings of emotion. The hurt caused me to react like a shrew towards this stupid person who had let the side down so badly and then in the next instant I became the oh-so-loving mother who wanted to comfort and console this innocent victim of circumstance. In the end the mother in me won and I only wanted to protect and exude words of wisdom, brush the whole incident under the carpet and start all over again.

'That's the worst any of them have got up to. At least as far as I know it is. D'you think they do things we don't hear about? Oh heavens!

'I had to take a day off work to go to court over this business and when I told the women I work with where I had been and why, I could sense that a few of them thought, tut, tut, my children won't ever do anything like that. But of course they will! Perhaps not that, but something else equally awful! I didn't think mine would either. I remember some years ago a girlfriend, who had teenagers, telling me some of the things hers had got up to and I thought exactly the same: mine won't do that. So there you are.

'By the time the youngest started getting into trouble, I was more or less expecting it. Mind you, that doesn't make it any easier. He had a friend who was two years older than him and somewhat lacking in the social graces. I worked on the theory of aversion therapy. I took a certain amount of pleasure in trying to engage this lad in conversation at the table. He had absolutely nothing to say and my son would see this and get twitchy.

'I suggested to my son that he should upgrade his friends, but apparently this one's appeal was that he was a "cool dude." You know the sort, into rap dancing and graffiti. One evening my son asked whether this friend could stay over for the night. He made the request in front of the friend. Don't they always do that? So of course in order not to look like a mean mum I had to say yes. It sound ridiculously coincidental but it was a re-run of the alarm clock story. In the middle of the night the alarm went off, only this time it was me who went in to check it out and found they had gone, but not before stuffing the beds with extra blankets!

'The knapsacks were missing and as we knew they were into graffiti we had a good idea of what they were up to. They could have been anywhere, so we just sat up and waited for them. By 3.30 am we were so worried we phoned the police. They asked for a description and my husband asked them if when they came home we could bring them down to the station for a bit of a razzle, just to frighten them. The two of us sat there smoking cigarettes and getting more and more worked up and anxious. We went through three packets of cigarettes between us. No wonder I had a blazing headache. We took it in turns to go down to the all-night service station to buy one packet at a time. The man down there said, "Having a heavy night eh?" And I said, "You're not wrong about that!"

'When they finally came home at 5.00 am they tried to sneak in without walking us up and when they saw my husband standing there, they almost fell over. When they were told the police had been out looking for them our son nearly wet his pants. "We've just been out for a walk," they said, "because there was nothing else to do!" But when we told them that we knew they had been spraying walls with graffiti they both admitted it. They had walked for miles along the railway tracks, dodging trains. I was horrified at the risk they had taken, it would have been so easy for them to have misjudged a train and been killed. They just don't seem to realise most rules are only made for their own protection. My husband insisted that they came with us down to the station and this time the police were great. They gave them a real dressing down.

'That was the last time we saw this particular friend and our son was profusely apologetic about it all. They aren't bad kids at all. In fact they can be wonderful and I have great faith in them all coming out right. By "right" I mean as decent human beings, after all most people do, even us! We even survive all our self-induced traumas. You start out thinking life is straightforward but it becomes increasingly complicated. For instance, I know when I got married I thought it was forever.

'I married within a year of finishing my training. I was twenty-three, he was a year younger. I fell in love. He was good-looking and I wanted his children. Corny, huh?' A year later she had David, who is now seventeen. He was quickly followed by Megan, now sixteen and then Christopher, now thirteen. 'The first one was planned, the second two were not. My husband worked as a technician in the sugar industry and his job kept us on the move. We lived in Innisfail, Babinda, Tully and finally Cairns.

'It was about this time, when my youngest was only three, my first marriage broke up. Of course it was a time of terrible trauma and heartbreak for all concerned. The grief and guilt goes on for a long, long time and I always feared the children would suffer in the long term. The second time around is difficult for everyone, step-parents and children, but we've weathered the storms and I can look at the children now and say, with all honesty, here I have three sound, happy people. If anything, they are more mature and wise for their experiences.

'My second husband's own children came back out to Australia to visit when they were sixteen and fourteen. I could sense that they were determined to hate me but we ended up the best of mates. His son went back and did his apprenticeship and has come back and is now living with us and working with his father. He's twenty-two. His daughter also came back, got married, and now they have a baby girl and are living back in Cairns. Her mother came out when the baby was born and we all got along just fine.

'Between all of us we've raised five incredibly stable, normal children who don't appear to have suffered at all from the stigma of coming from broken homes. I don't think that any of the things they have got up to as teenagers are because of this. They are just behaving like normal teenagers. I know that now, though as I said I wasn't at all prepared for it and I can't say I much enjoyed it!

'Though I am very close to Megan. She and I are good mates. She is very honest with me and when she tells me things about myself I listen because I value her judgement. We are more like sisters than mother and daughter and I prefer it that way. I am not comfortable with the all-powerful parental role. But she can be very aloof and that slices me up. When she wants to she can just switch off and if I am shouting at her about something she has or has not done I can see a look of distaste on her face which says, "Pull yourself together, Mum". It's then that I understand why parents hit their children. Only your children can make you feel like that. Teenage children more than any other age. Teenage daughters more than teenage sons. But on the whole I think I have come off rather lightly.

'Megan is the least tidy of them all, and that's putting it mildly. She is always so immaculately turned out but you wouldn't believe the things you find under her bed. I don't clean up any of their rooms any more, but one time when she went away for a holiday with her friend we thought we would give her a surprise and paint her room. We found ten empty cigarette packs under her bed. They are not allowed to smoke at home, though that's hypocritical because both of us smoke, so I find it very hard to impose that rule on her.

'Another thing that drives me crazy about her is that she borrows anything of mine to which she takes a fancy. I used to have lots and lots of earrings. Now I have none. I also used to have a very nice pink fluffy sweater. One day I was doing some shopping when I saw Megan and her friend walking along towards me. The friend was wearing my pink sweater! And you know what, when they stopped to speak to me I was such a wimp I didn't even mention it!

'I wonder why that was? I would never have done that to my parents, but then it would hardly have been possible. My father was the least materialistic man I've ever known. I loved him dearly. But he rarely gave us presents. It wasn't till he died that I understood why. When he died all he left were some small things of sentimental value: an old radio, a stockwhip and a collection of photos. That was about it. He didn't own anything else. So it had never occurred to him to give us presents.

'With our own kids of course it's different, they expect you to be able to provide everything and we move heaven and earth to do just that. I feel as though I brought them into the world so they are my responsibility and come first. I have stayed at work because I wanted to do as much as possible for them. That work has become a career which I really enjoy.

'Last year I took a cardio-thoracic course and I am now

working in a cardiac catheterisation lab, which is very demanding work. This year I wanted to do a coronary care course but it coincides with David coming home for a holiday from the United States, where he has been for the last year as an exchange student. So of course I put the course off. I'll do it next year. The kids come first, I guess!

'I'm looking forward very much to David coming home. He went away a strutting youth and he'll come back a young man. He's good-looking and gentle. He is very self-conscious still about having been badly burnt when he was a small baby. He fell into the fire and had burns to 25 per cent of his body. Fortunately his face was not marked but his body was so bad that the kids at school called him barbecue features, and on more than one occasion he was beaten up. My maternal instincts urged me to intervene but my dad, bless him, said, "Don't do that, he's got to learn to stand on his own feet and fight his own battles." He was right and now when people ask him about the scars he tells them his mother attacked him with a blowtorch when he was a baby!

'I did the same with Megan when a particular teacher at school had it in for her. She eventually sorted it all out herself and learnt the lesson of self-reliance.

'I was not at all keen for David to go off to the States, I didn't want to lose him, but I knew it would broaden his horizons and he was set on it and kept nagging until I arranged it. I guess I knew when he left it was the end of an era and I would miss him a lot. He wrote me a wonderful letter shortly after he arrived there, saying how much he appreciated all I had done for him and how much he missed and loved me. I expect he was homesick.

'His American "mother" tells me, "David is a wonderful boy and he is always offering to do things around the house for me." I was incredulous when she said this because of course he never did that around here. I guess he's growing up. He has fallen in love with a young girl whose whole family are very religious and he is asking me now why I am not a practising Christian and why I didn't insist that he learnt about it all when he was growing up.

I see life as a road. A wide road. And all I can do is nudge them gently towards the middle of it. I totally believe in them coming out all right and I think it's important that they know you believe in them.

If I had, and he had been forced to go to Sunday school, that would have been wrong too. You can't win. The sooner you realise that with teenage kids, the less grief you will suffer.

'Megan wants to go into journalism. She also is going off as an exchange student; she is going to Denmark. She wants to go and we are doing all we can to make it happen. It will be very expensive, the two of them, the living is free but of course it costs heaps because we have to send a hell of a lot for pocket money. I don't have the same resistance to Megan going as I had to David, probably because that has been such a success and because the break in family life has already been made.

'Of course I shall miss her, I am still the clutching mother hen. It's very different for men. They are never as committed to a child as a mother is. It's a very different, worthwhile but different, relationship they have.

'I may be naive but I do think that children basically turn out the way you want them to. I would like them to be more academic, if only because they might then find it easier to get and hold on to a job. But on the other hand I don't think school is the be-all and end-all, and I think the HSC can be a sham, there's far too much emphasis on it. It's far more important that they get out and experience life. It goes so fast. I am forty-two and I envy them their youth.

'I see life as a road. A wide road. And all I can do is nudge them gently towards the middle of it. I *totally* believe in them coming out all right and I think it's important that they know you believe in them. The trouble is that in the rushing about of everyday living it's too easy for these sentiments to get buried under a lot of debris.

'Just the other day I came home after a ten-hour day of very heavy and stressful work. I was completely pooped. All I wanted was to sit down and put my feet up and relax with a cup of tea. Instead I was met by Megan saying, "Where have you been? You were supposed to take me swimming." And by Christopher who said, "What's for tea? I'm starving." I felt like crying, but I didn't. That's what being a mother demands of you; what it's about. And it's hard then to remember the really good things about them and what you want for them and to have an overhead, long-term view, but that is also what being a mother is about. Holding on to it all.

'However, I have found all the struggling through the teenage years does have its compensations. We dragged ourselves out of bed at 5.00 am every morning for several years to take Megan to swimming training. And went again in the afternoon, no matter how much we would have preferred to sit down and relax after a day's work. But I was amply rewarded on every one of the many occasions I saw her standing on the winning dais.

'David too has excelled at sports. All those cold mornings we stood on the sidelines of soccer ovals, cheering his team on to victory, and all the miles we've driven to training and sporting fixtures has paid off. He has a roomful of trophies that he, not his doting mum, displays with pride. He even came first in New South Wales for weight-lifting in his age and category and I hadn't even known he was doing weight-lifting!

'Christopher, my extrovert graffiti artist, plays baseball and does karate, which involves me in more running around, but I know by now that it's all worth it.

'Quite apart from their sporting achievements, the best rewards are seemingly the smallest ones. Like an older one giving a younger sibling a serve on table manners or correcting their speech. Isn't that an echo of my own tired voice plugging endlessly on? Or watching David run forward to help an elderly person cross the road; or Megan glare at me in indignation because I hadn't seen fit to give any money to the old tramp begging for his next bottle of plonk. Or just for Christopher to say in all earnestness, "You're still very young for your age, Mum," while a haggard face looks back at me from the mirror.

'These are the little things that make you realise you are accomplishing what you set out to do in the very beginning, and that is simply to be a good mother.'

Liz McLean

It's been tough, I wouldn't deny that. I guess the toughest thing has been having no day-to-day backup.

'He was sheer lovely madness. The children loved his wonderful cooking. He was not a plain old sausage-and-mash man. Even when there were lots of other children visiting he'd still go to great lengths. He'd make the sausages into boats or buses and cover the mash with peas to make into a beautiful green field and when he served it all up it was like a work of art. The children and their friends still remember all that. We were very spoilt.'

Liz McLean is recalling her husband, who died almost exactly four years ago. As a widow Liz has had to be more than a mother to her four children: Sara, seventeen, Sallie, fifteen, Samantha, twelve, and Steven, seven. 'It's been tough, I wouldn't deny that. I guess the toughest thing has been having no day-to-day backup. My brother and parents have been great and so have my husband's family. But of course it can't be the same as having another adult to share the daily ups and downs. I do try to keep an eye on areas of their lives where a father's input would have been most beneficial. I am more anxious about Steven than the girls because he's stuck with a whole houseful of women. He's a very butch little fellow but he's happy to sit around with the girls plaiting their hair. Fortunately the fathers of some of his own friends have been very good at taking a special interest in him.

'But you know how it is; you are mostly just so caught up in the day-to-day things there's not much time left to worry about the broader issues. I'm too busy turning off the television set and the heater.' Both had been left on full blast when her daughters left en masse. It was school holidays and they were going to 'check out the shops and then hang around in town'. The doors were all left wide open too, of course! 'As you can see, I don't tidy their rooms any more! And I haven't ironed their clothes for years. If they want to get around like that it's okay. Occasionally, if they are coming out with me, I do insist they iron a blouse!

'I am conscious about not wanting to lay extra responsibilities on them, especially by asking the girls to look after their young brother. I don't think it would be fair. It's me that should bear the major burden of there not being a man about the house, not them. I don't want them to miss out on being children. I still do most of the general housework myself because to be honest it's quicker and also I know then that it's done. I'm not fanatical about it and in the holidays I let things go a lot because otherwise I'd be driven crazy.' We make our way out through the kitchen, an area devastated by the teenage breakfast onslaught. Even while she walks and talks, in a skill finely honed by motherhood, Liz shuts the door to the microwave oven, retrieves a peanut-buttered knife from the floor and rescues the tea-towel from imminent danger of catching fire. She makes coffee and we escape to the winter sunshine at the bottom of the garden, escorted by the McLean's deaf and elderly spaniel, Dotty.

'I never planned to have four children. I know there are women who start glory boxes when they are teenagers and many who think about marriage and children as the ultimate goal. But I can honestly say I never thought about marriage until I met the man I married!'

Liz was born in England, was brought to Australia as a baby, spent eight years here and went back to England when she was eleven. Both her parents were Congregational ministers and her father was posted to Australia as the principal of a theological training college. 'Mum was the first ordained woman minister to practise in Australia. Congregationalists have become amalgamated in the Uniting Church now but I still think of Mum and Dad as Congregationalists. I can't say I'm religious. I do believe in a personal God but I also believe in free will and that we are all responsible for our own actions. When I was growing up I found it a bit restricting, not being allowed to do things on Sunday other than go to church. But I got used to all the jokes — she was only the vicar's daughter, you know the sort of thing. And now I'm very, very grateful for that upbringing, for the morals, the knowledge, the beliefs and for the value system it gave me. It's a great backstop.'

Liz finished her education in England, did a three-year training as a physical education teacher, taught for a year and then decided to take a year's working holiday in Australia. Towards the end of that time she fell in love and three months later her mother flew out from England to officiate at her wedding.

'Mum married us, which was lovely. We were married in a Congregational church, even though he was Jewish. We couldn't be married in the synagogue because he was "marrying out." Marrying me more or less meant his being excommunicated. Not that he minded. He was never a devout or even a practising Jew. He'd been barmitzvahed but that was all. His mother was Jewish, a Jacobs, and his father had converted to marry her but they hadn't been religiously observant. His only sister is now more strictly observant than either of her parents were.

'When we married I was twenty-three and he was twenty-four. It seems young now, but it didn't at the time. It seemed right. We didn't talk before we were married about having children. I think we just assumed that we would. When we met he was working on and off in his parents' shoe shop, but that was only between writing, which was always his first love and all he really wanted to do. He started writing when he was at university, writing for the various student revues and magazines. He attended several universities: ANU, Sydney and I think Macquarie too. He'd enrol in a course but never finish it. He wasn't interested in getting a degree. He was only interested in writing.

'Shortly after we married he saw an advertisement in the paper for a writer. It didn't say what it was for, but he applied anyway and it turned out that it was for an English television production company which had come out to Australia to produce a series and was looking for local people. The senior writer must have been impressed with the raw talent my husband had because he employed him, took him under his wing, and polished his skills. It was just the start he needed. From then on he never did anything else.

'Mind you, it was a very precarious way to make a living. It was either feast or famine. But he loved it so much that he always used to say that it wasn't like working for a living.'

To begin their married life the couple moved to Bowral, a small New South Wales country town, 100 kilometres from Syndey. 'The rents were cheaper out there and it meant we could live on my salary while he established himself as a writer. I took a job teaching phys. ed. at a local school. But his work took off so well that he spent a lot of his time commuting back to Sydney for meetings with producers and directors, so in less than a year we moved back to the city.' Shortly after the move Liz became pregnant for the first time and gave up work.

'Sara was born two years after we were married. Two years later we had Sallie and two years after that along came Samantha. The three girls were all planned. With Sam we were hoping for a boy but when she was born we gave away the idea of trying again for a son. When I became pregnant five years later it was a hell of a shock. I didn't tell my husband straight away because I wasn't sure that I wanted another. I took the girls away for a few days' holiday to think it over. I was considering having an abortion. But then I thought, well, I suppose we can afford to have another. The deciding factor was when I had an amniocentesis which showed that I was having a boy. That was it. We had Steven. If anyone had told me when I was twenty that one day I would be the mother of four, I would have run away! And now I'm the sole parent of four.'

What really established her husband's career as a television writer was the weekly series *Spyforce*, which starred Peter Sumner and Jack Thompson. The couple started paying off a big home in an attractive suburb and settled into the routine of family life. 'Except there was nothing routine about it. There couldn't be. The finances stabilised a bit when he went to work on a very good salary with Grundy's, who employed him to devise new programs. But there were always deadlines and sudden decisions to be made. He was constantly having to fly off at very short notice or having to instantly produce a story concept or script idea. The entire industry is like that. The pressure is enormous. And for someone like him, who already had health problems, it was literally fatal.

'Both his parents had a history of heart attacks but it wasn't until he went into hospital for a lumbar fusion that he was told he had inherited their problems. The doctors told him they were astounded at how high his cholesterol level was and at the obvious signs of stress. They immediately put him onto medication for both. After that he went for regular checkups and we both kept an eye out for any of the usual signs of heart problems — a stiff arm or a pain in the chest. But he didn't do anything about the stress. In fact things became worse because he left Grundy's, he was a bit fed up with the red tape there, and went out on his own to set up a production company in partnership with another man.

'He wasn't satisfied with being just the writer, he wanted to do it all. He had a happy, positive outlook on life but he was a very driven man, highly motivated, a classic workaholic. The company did well, but the pressure was incredible. He had always worked twelve hours a day. Now he was working seventeen hours.

'They were planning on making three movies in cooperation with the Queensland Film Commission. For three months he was constantly flying backwards and forwards to Brisbane. He kept suggesting that the children and I move and we set up a home up there. I told him that I had seen too many of the ups and downs in the business to want to uproot the children on the strength of a few movies and I am very glad we didn't make the move, because what finally happened was they made three movies but were only ever paid the money for two, so the company folded. This really shocked him but he wasn't the sort who gave up easily.

'He had another idea he had been trying to get off the ground for a while. He talked it over with someone he had known for a long time, a man he thought was a friend but who played a very shabby trick on him and took the whole thing over as if it was his idea. Ron was shattered. Completely shattered. He couldn't believe that a man he had known for years could treat him like that. He was very angry and even more hurt. He went to solicitors but they advised him not to press charges because even if he had won the costs would have been crippling.

'All this was what killed him. He died on a Sunday. Sallie and Samantha were staying overnight with friends. So only Sara, who was thirteen, and Steven, who was three, were in the house. About 8.00 he got up and had a shower and he came back into the bedroom saying that he felt faint and could I get him a towel. I got up and fetched a towel and when I brought it back to him he was dead. Just like that. A massive heart attack. No warning. Nothing. I called an ambulance. Then I yelled to Sara to come and help me. I still don't know whether that was the right thing to do. But I wanted to give him mouth-to-mouth resuscitation and put pressure on his chest to try to get his heart going again and I couldn't manage to do it all on my own. I suppose Steven was wandering around wondering what all the fuss was about but I don't really remember. I phoned my brother and he and a friend came over immediately. Then the ambulance came and they took him away. I didn't go to the hospital. I knew he was dead and I didn't want to go there.

'My brother went to the hospital and he told me later that they had continued trying to revive him, but that even if they had, he would have already suffered tremendous brain damage. So I am glad they didn't succeed because he was the sort of man who would not have wanted to live with an impaired intellect. I thank God he didn't suffer. He was just forty when he died. We had been married for sixteen years.'

In the conversational lull the McLean's cat appeared, his tail held high and twitching, from out of the shrubbery where he had been stalking his prey. 'He catches lizards, poor things,' Liz told me as we moved our chairs beyond the reach of the encroaching shadow of a tree.

To a question about how her children handled their father's death Liz responded, 'Only Sara attended the funeral with me. Sallie wanted to come but I wouldn't let her and the other two were definitely too young. I wanted them all to remember their father as he was, not as a box sliding through the curtains into the fire. I thought that was too frightening a concept for them to handle. I'm not sure even now that Sara should have come. My parents gave the service, which was the hardest thing they had ever had to do, but it made it easier for me. Usually it's all very impersonal because the person who gives the service doesn't even know the person who has died. At least his funeral had the comfort of being a family occasion. During the service he was described as being kind, generous, without malice, a great raconteur and cook, and above all a family man. All of that was very true.

'I can't recall much of what happened immediately after the funeral. I know I sent the children back to school within the week because I wanted as little disruption as possible to their lives. We talked about why their dad had died, of course, but I didn't dwell on it and sometimes I wonder if even now I try to shield them from the pain it must cause them. They were immediately uppermost in my thoughts and decisions.

'I knew I would muddle through somehow, even though financially things were in such a mess that I couldn't even afford to make the payments on the mortgage. Because of the company folding we had been forced to re-finance the house. We were in the middle of doing all that so there wasn't even any insurance to cover these payments. Fortunately my husband did have a life insurance, although that took longer to come through than it should. I don't really know how we lived in the very beginning. The relatives took over. The Jews have an incredible set-up for handling such situations. Someone was with me for every hour of every day. There was nothing for them to do except to clean so they took the books off the shelves, cleaned them and put them back over and over again. I sat for hours at a time in the bath.

'I didn't ever think, why me? I didn't rant and rave at God and I didn't feel any anger towards my husband for dying. I know all those are classic symptoms of loss. One odd experience was a dream I had. I never dream, or at least I never remember my dreams. But this one was so vivid it astounded me. I dreamt that he hadn't really died. He had just played a joke on me. I was furious with him. In fact I was so angry I woke up. Then of course I realised it was just a dream.'

Throughout our conversation Liz had smoked cigarettes nearly continuously. 'I smoked about the same amount before my husband died. What would I have done at the time without the Scotch and the ciggies! I had to get back into the swim quickly because of the children. There was no time to go into a slump or feel terribly sorry for myself. You cope because you have to; there's no choice. I tried to get everything back to normal. I thought I was coping reasonably well until I started to get frequent attacks of feeling faint. The doctor said it was delayed shock. But I got over that too. I never panicked or felt like running away. My main concern was to protect the children.

'It took about a year before I started to feel I was functioning like a normal human being again. During that year my brother had helped me sort out the finances and I had sold the house and moved into a much smaller rented place. By the time it came to the move I was ready to go. A group of the relatives wanted to put in together and buy the house outright for us but I said no. I wanted to move. Without my husband it wasn't a home, it was just a house, there was no point in living there any more. And I wanted to keep my independence and not be obligated to anyone. We have moved back into the area so we still see the old house, it's big and sits up on a hill on an acre of its own land, and the children sometimes say, "Wouldn't it be nice to go back to the old house?" But there's no way in the world that I would go back.'

The McLean's first move was not such a success. 'The three children went to three different schools and because none of them were either near enough for them to walk to or on a convenient bus line I did an hour and a half run-around to drop them off in the morning, and then the same, only in reverse, in the evening!'

But it was during this year that Liz began to socialise again. 'Until then I hadn't wanted to go out. I wasn't ready to mix. I knew when I was. It was my brother's secretary who got me going. She was a single woman about my age who knew the singles scene in Sydney. It's a whole other scene that I'd completely lost touch with during sixteen years of married life. We had never been great party-goers, or eaten out a lot. We'd always run an open house and because my husband was such a great cook and really enjoyed entertaining there were always people at our place. Almost all our friends were married and had children and now I was confronted with learning to be a single woman again. It was most odd. I was out of the habit and it was quite difficult to relearn how to relate to people on a one-to-one basis again.

'To be honest I quite often found it boring. It was all very new but not very exciting. We'd go out every Thursday night to either a club or a bar and sit around and chat. Most of the people we mixed with were either single or divorced. I didn't go out of my way to tell people I was a widow. If the question came up I would say so. I remember telling one man who had assumed that I was divorced, "No, I'm a widow." He said, "Well, it's the same thing." And I said, "No, it most definitely is not!" And it's not.

'What I really missed was the adult male companionship. It would have been nice to have someone I could phone up and say, "What about coming out to dinner?" After a while the Thursday night habit got to me. I thought, I'm becoming more set in my ways than a married couple! and I gave it away.'

By then Liz had moved back to the same suburb she had lived in before her husband died, 'because it's on a direct train line into the city', and was having trouble with her oldest daughter. 'It was her first real push against parental authority. She just lay in bed and refused to get up and go to school. No amount of cajoling or shouting from me would shift her. In the end I phoned my brother. He came roaring over and as he set his foot through the door she was out of bed! She's over it now but for a year or so she wouldn't speak to her uncle!

'Fortunately she seemed to do her rebellious growing up overnight. One quick burst and it was over. She left school at the end of Year 10 to try to break into the modelling scene. The previous winter she had been chosen as the Helena Rubenstein Face of Winter. She took off to New Zealand for three months on an exchange modelling contract.

'Naturally I was worried. What mother wouldn't be? But what could I do? Anyway in my heart I knew it was the right thing for her. Both the older girls are more mature than most young teenagers. Perhaps it has something to do with not having a father and perhaps they would have been that way anyway. I know they go to the pubs even though they are under age. But I also know they are not into dope.

'We all talk very openly about everything. Sex and drugs and rock-and-roll, you know. I am sure they have their heads screwed on the right way and I do believe in them and trust them. I do also think that once children become young adults, they should leave home. They should experience living with a group of people their own age. It should be a time when they learn a great deal about themselves. They can't do that if they go on living within the security of the family. But I am more than happy, while they are still students, to provide them with a good home base.'

It was three years after she was widowed before Liz formed her first close relationship with a man. 'It was my first sexual encounter in all that time. I couldn't believe it myself because I am a physically affectionate person. It was partly because my upbringing makes it impossible for me to have casual sex but also because I'd not met anyone in all that time that I fancied!

'Looking back on it now it was doomed from the start. He was separated. He hadn't wanted children and when after nine years his wife decided to get pregnant the marriage began to fall apart. Eventually she returned to England with the child. I was attracted to him because he was brilliant, had a good sense of humour and was great company. I must be one of those people who when they fall, they fall. Because I fell head over heels. He met the children and they liked him and four months later when we decided we might all share a house together they were all for it. I think they thought it would be good for me! The lease on my place was coming to an end so we moved again and he moved with us.

'I am very glad his divorce hadn't come through because I am

I think my husband would be happy to see the direction they are going. It's a great pity that he didn't live long enough to enjoy them as young adults and it's a great pity for them that they didn't ever know him as a man rather than just as their daddy.

sure if we could we would have married and it would have been a disaster. As it was he only stayed in the house for four months. He couldn't take family life. His father had died when he was a child. He had one sister who was eighteen years older than him. So he'd never had a family life. And suddenly he was plunged into a teenage household. Well!

'I have always preferred that the children bring their friends home rather than they hang about the streets or go to places I don't know. The house is always full with not just my four but with their friends. There is never peace and quiet. Life is lived at full volume. There is no way to turn it down. The noise. The coming and going. The constant demands and interruptions. He couldn't cope. And he couldn't see why I wouldn't change my lifestyle to fit in with his rather than theirs. He couldn't understand that it wasn't possible for me just to drop everything and go out. He felt I should put him first. He loves music and it irritated him that there was never space or peace enough for him to enjoy it. And once that first flush of love wore off, as it inevitably does, instead of something more precious developing I began to find his complaints irritating.

'Also I must admit that I wasn't used to having a man, another adult, coming into the house every evening at 5.30 pm and demanding attention. It was like having another child. Only worse. He couldn't understand why I couldn't be all me for all him. He was even silly enough to take it out on Sara and Sallie. That was the final straw. So he moved out.

'It was a relief. We still see each other. But only as friends. When he comes to the house the children are pretty cool towards him. All except Sam, she really took to him and was sorry to see him leave. I get the feeling they want to protect me because they know I was hurt over it all. You can't hide that sort of thing from your children, or you shouldn't anyway. But I certainly don't want them to feel sorry for me or trapped in any way by having a sole parent. That would be a terrible burden to lay on them. I want them to feel free to move off into their own independent lives.

'One thing I did learn from the experience is that I don't think I'll have a live-in relationship again. It's not only because the children are too important to me to shuffle them aside to make way for a man, it's also because I've become accustomed to living on my own with them and I don't think I want to make the sort of adjustments which are necessary if you are going to share your life with another adult. I enjoy my freedom too much! It's been a bit of a battle to get to the point where I feel like that and I don't want to throw away what has taken a lot to achieve. At some point in the future what I would like is a good relationship with someone who understands. But I'm not holding my breath for that. I don't have time. There's too much going on.

'Sara came back from New Zealand, I think she was surprised at how homesick she felt, and has started a graphic arts course at tech, which I am delighted about. She gets a small grant to help her while she is a student and I've agreed to provide a roof over her head and food but all the rest is up to her. She earns some extra money babysitting and she is learning to manage her money very well. She has had the same boyfriend for eighteen months, which I suppose may have something to do with having no father and wanting that stability in her life. But I like him a lot and I am glad that she has this close friendship. He is a little bit older than her and she spends a lot of time with his family too, so I find that is a sharing of the burden.

'Sallie is in Year 10 and intending to leave at the end of the year. She wants to get into the television industry, I think because she can only remember the more glamorous side of it and not the heartbreaks and financial ups and downs. She has a natural writing flair and enjoys her drama classes. I can't say I am too keen on her trying to get into the industry because I have seen its worst aspects. But I can't say no and I can't push. All I can do is offer advice when she asks for it. She is still going through the gang of girlfriends stage.

'Samantha is in her first year at high school and we call her our absent-minded professor. And Steven, he's the one I have to watch medically. The doctor has told me that by the time he reaches his early teens he will need to be checked for cholesterol levels because he may have inherited my husband's medical problems. At the moment he's still only in infants'. So there's a long way to go; sure is, my word yes!

'But I think my husband would be happy to see the direction they are going. It's a great pity that he didn't live long enough to enjoy them as young adults and it's a great pity for them that they didn't ever know him as a man rather than just as their daddy. There are still many, many times when I miss him. It would be good to have someone else apart from me to say no to them. They must get sick of hearing Mum's voice. But apart from sharing the parenting there are other times I miss him, especially in the evenings when the older ones are out and the younger ones are in bed.

'Each year on the anniversary of his death we have gone to the crematorium together. But I hope that this year they won't want to go. I don't want to. It doesn't do any of us any good. I want them and me to remember him as he was, full of fun and life and not as a little plaque on the wall. He had always joked that when he died he wanted to be stuffed and used as a bar ornament!

'Thinking of the past doesn't help much. It's good to have great memories but I have to look forward and make plans. Up to now we have managed to live off the insurance money, a bit of rent for a front room which I let to a boarder, and the pension. The pension is the same as for a divorced person. The forms are full of questions relating to your spouse and maintenance money. It's all too little to be able to live a decent life on and so I am going back to work next term as a full-time casual teacher of physical education. It will be the first time I have taught for seventeen years!

'I can't say I am really looking forward to it. But I need to so as to get some sort of secure future. Thank heavens I have the certificate. Once I am in regular employment I can use the bit of money left over from the sale of the house to put down as a deposit and start to buy my own home again on a mortgage.

'I'm really too busy with getting the day-to-day necessities organised to have time to plan far ahead. But I do know I don't want, further down the track, to be a weight on them. I never want them to feel "Poor Mum", or obligated to stay with me. That's very important. I don't think they do. But of course it's good to know they love you and have some understanding of how you feel. Before you go I'll find a letter Sallie wrote the year after her father died. She was going to send it to a woman's magazine for Mother's Day. I found it when I was cleaning up her room. She never got around to sending it; typical isn't it! But that doesn't matter.'

To Whom It May Concern

My mum is the best in the world and I think she should be awarded 'Mother of the Year'. You see my dad died late last year and Mum hid her depression very well. Though we were all sad Mum just kept her cool. Now we have to move house because we can't pay for our big house because Mum hasn't a job. Mum isn't going to let this incident pull the family apart, she's going to help us stick together. Although Mum may lose her temper sometimes who can blame her with four kids and now no husband. I feel so sorry for Mum that I cry for her sometimes. Mum is taking this as well as she can, which is quite well. I think she's been great and I love her very much. Please put Mum on your list as Mum of the Year (because she definitely is). Thank you, from Mum's second oldest child, Sallie McLean.

Paula

My poor relationship with my mother is being repeated in my relationship with my daughter. But I'm determined to break the cycle.

'Overnight she turned from an open, free little spirit into this sullen, brooding thing who kept her diary sealed and locked the door to her bedroom and the bathroom. I can be feeling cheerful and positive about life but when she walks through the door it's as if she brings with her a cloud of doom and gloom which emanates from her into every nook and cranny.

'She is totally unresponsive and sullen. There's a lot of door slamming and the only conversation we have is when she spits out, "I hate you. I don't want to live with you. You don't understand me." Her aggression is all aimed at me. I understand that and would be surprised if it wasn't. I've read the books and I know that all this is what's described by psychologists as "infuriatingly normal behaviour". She is totally self-absorbed.

All that pent-up anger and frustration could be used as a positive force if she knew how. The trouble is, it has control of her instead of her having control of it. She almost vibrates with unhappiness and I want to say to her, "What you are saying is not what you mean. Let go of all this or it will eat you up. I love you, I know you love me, so let's stop all this and just love each other." But she's not listening and I've stopped talking. I get so worked up about it all that I take it out on myself. Just recently I kicked a hole right through the cupboard door with my bare foot. I know it's not productive but I can't prevent myself from feeling guilty at being a failure both as a mother and a daughter. Rationally I can tell myself it's unacceptable to feel like this but it's the emotional response which is so difficult to control. The fact is she is very like my mother.'

Paula is talking about her thirteen-year-old daughter Vanessa. But she is also talking about herself. And her mother. And the terrible, searing cycle of unresolved mother–daughter, daughter–mother emotions. Paula is extremely self-aware; almost painfully so. She is also bright and verbal, but none of this has helped her solve the puzzle. Perhaps it has even made it more difficult for her. 'A friend once said to me, "Paula, if you spent all the energy you put into going in circles, into going in a straight line, you'd be light years ahead," and I knew he was right. But I have the feeling this is the final circle because I'm getting bored with going round and round. I'm going to see this one through and break the cycle once and for all.'

The cycle began when Paula herself was born. 'My parents were disappointed I was not a boy. When they did have a son, three years later, he was a sickly child and my father also had a run of bad health when I was young. Our house seemed to be constantly full of nurses and nannies. It was hard being the only healthy one and I must have driven them mad. I was always being farmed out, all for seemingly reasonable causes, either to my paternal grandparents or elsewhere, and by the time I was nine I was sent off to boarding school. I guess, to put it bluntly, my parents didn't much want me. I was a bit of a nuisance and got in the way. Yes, I felt rejected.

'They too were both victims of their upbringing and their conditioning. They have what I describe as a "terminal marriage"; it seemed to be always on the point of collapse. It took me years to work out that their fights and arguments were the only way they knew how to communicate. One result of all that is that I can't bear tension. Very early on I developed a sense of humour which I use to defuse situations.' It's true. Throughout our conversation Paula dropped in funnies and made light of incidents which could just as easily have been the cause of tears.

'Not that it made it any better but the schools I was sent to were good private schools. In the material sense my family are very wealthy. I grew up in an exclusive suburb with a swimming pool and tennis courts. Mum didn't work outside the home other than charity work such as Meals on Wheels and the board of the Crown Street Women's Hospital. Dad ran the family metal manufacturing business. He was an engineer. When I was a child I told people he was a train driver because I thought that was what an engineer did. When he retired he became a gentleman farmer with a property west of Sydney. Outside the barn the Rolls is parked between the sit-upon plough and the sit-upon tractor. The landscaped garden is a delight, my mother is the world's best gardener, and she keeps peacocks, geese, pretty chickens and ornamental ducks.

'I left boarding school of my own accord, in the early part of Year 12, fraying the umbilical cord considerably. I finished my schooling at the local co-ed high school, from the sublime to the ridiculous educationally speaking. Immediately after I sat the last exam of the HSC I left home. It was a fiery exit but I was free at last.

'First off I shared a bedroom with three guys and a motorbike. Then I moved into a house with my then current boyfriend. I did a very short stint as a secretary and then started dental nursing.

This was the start of a not too good period. My boyfriend had a violent streak in him and he would often let it out on me. Sometimes he beat me so black and blue I was unable to go to work. It sounds bizarre that I accepted this sort of behaviour but in a way it meant he cared and that was all that mattered to me.

'I left dental nursing after I had been accepted into a kindergarten teacher's training course. I've always loved children. My one ambition since I was a child was to get married, have six children and live in the country. I love *The Waltons*! The extended family is my ideal, probably because I never had one. I'm a romantic to the nth degree! I loved kindergarten teaching but not the archaic establishment way the college had of running things. They still wanted the image of the kindergarten teacher in the twin-set, Fletcher Jones' skirt and sensible shoes. I wanted to wear jeans and take the children on nature walks.

'Then my childhood idol died. He was like a brother to me and more, because on many occasions I had been farmed out to his family and he and I had become very close. He was an epileptic. He had a fit one night, suffocated in his pillow and wasn't found for two days. His death affected me profoundly. I dropped out of college, split up with my boyfriend and went into a suicidal phase.

'On the third major attempt my father turned up to have me hospitalised in a private psychiatric home. I was there for two months and really loved it! Really. The other people in there were so genuine and real. I used to help the staff with other patients. I felt useful and cared for. It was great. But it wasn't solving the underlying problem and I couldn't stay there forever.

'When I came out my mum and godmother took me overseas with them. We went to England, where I stayed with my mother's sister, who lived in the country. While I was there I received a letter from the dentist I had been working for in Sydney asking me if I would like to go and work for his wife's brother, an Austrian who was also a dentist. He wanted a dental nurse who could also teach him English. So off I went to Austria.

'He lived in Bavaria, which is a beautiful, gentle place, and the nine months I spent there were a very beneficial experience. Because I couldn't speak German and no one in the tiny village could speak English I had to start from scratch and learn again, beginning with essentials. We waste so much time and energy filling in the void with mere noise which passes as conversation. When you have no access to this idle chatter you have a chance to look at and consider everything you say. It was as if I was born again through language. The dentist was quite eccentric. In addition to my work in the surgery, for which I fortunately didn't need much language, I was employed to converse with him in English and to have breakfast, lunch and dinner with him every day. We sat on opposite sides of the table in a small room, the walls of which were covered with the stuffed trophy heads and skins of animals he had hunted and shot. For almost every meal we ate vension which he had killed. My vegetarian leanings didn't translate too well.

'He told me that I should be careful and not cross the bridge to the cafe on the other side of the bridge, because the young men there were "bad boys". So of course I did! Naturally they thought I was great because I was Australian and different. Looking back I realise I was very innocent. I started going out with one in particular. I'd been on the pill for a few years and I thought I should give it a rest. The next thing I knew I nearly died from an undiagnosed ectopic pregnancy.

'I didn't even realise I was pregnant. I had a period that went on for six weeks but I didn't tell anyone because I didn't have anyone to tell and I didn't realise it could be dangerous. I didn't even know I was in trouble until I was unable to get off my bed, to move or even to talk for three days. Then suddenly I felt good. I experienced this beautiful, all-encompassing white light and a feeling of bliss and euphoria. It was wonderful, magical. Then I suddenly realised what was happening to me. I was dying. I panicked. I shouted to myself, "No! Not yet!" Somehow I managed to pull back. I focused all my energy into getting off the bed and because my body wasn't functioning properly all I could do was elbow my way along the floor to the feet of the nearest person, and collapse. I don't know what happened after that. When I came to, there was one tube in one arm and another in the other arm and tubes coming out through the bandages that went from my middle to my thighs.

'They told me afterwards that I was very lucky and that I'd had only six hours to live. The egg had adhered to the outside of the Fallopian tube and when it burst it had ruptured the tube. They'd had to whip out half my bits and pieces and they told me, "You'll be lucky if you are still able to have children."

'I was ten days in hospital and when I came out I decided to go home for a couple of weeks. My father had been ill and I wanted to see him and also to recoup myself. I had no intention of settling back in Australia. I really liked Austria. I stayed four weeks and then went back to Bavaria. I started going out with my former boyfriend's best friend, who was the spitting image of the boyfriend I'd had in Australia, the one who beat me up. Except this one didn't. Within less than two months I was pregnant again. Carelessness I suppose. Because I believed them when they told me there was little chance of my getting pregnant again, I wasn't taking any precautions.

'I couldn't have an abortion. Not after what I had been through. If it was true that the operation had put me at grave risk of never being able to have children I felt this might be the only chance I had to have a baby. But the essential basics for a long-term relationship and committed partnership were not there. He was nineteen and I was twenty. There was no future there for me as an unmarried mother; no support system. Because I couldn't write the language I would have been limited in what sort of employment I could find. The father wanted me to stay but I decided to go home again.

'I phoned my father, who was in England on a business trip, and told him I was pregnant. He suggested I join him there, which is what I did. Then he tried to persuade me to have an abortion. He said things like, "Your mother will have a fit and your grandmother will cut us off." He went as far as taking me along to see a Harley Street specialist. Fortunately the man sensed how I felt and said to me, "You want this baby, don't you?" and I told him, "Yes I do", and he said, "Well, you go ahead and have it."

'So I came home with a disappointed father to a mother who told me I would be a social disgrace for them and that they would have to resign from all the committees they served on. Their attitude was, "How can you do this to us?"

'They set me up in a little flat and I was in seventh heaven. I became an unwed, beaming earth-mother! I wore silver and pink and caramel long flowing Indian dresses and put on so much weight I was up to eleven and a half stone at the end. And I didn't even think I was fat!' — Paula is a naturally petite size eight. 'I read everything I could lay my hands on about pregnancy, childbirth and babies. I became absolutely involved in the wonder of it all. I was totally at peace and happy. I positively glowed. I think I looked very beautiful.

'All this made the actual birth a terrible disappointment. I had a very difficult time, which was made even worse by the attitude of the sister in charge of the ward, who made it apparent that she did not approve of unwed mothers, and by the fact that I had to go through it all alone. My mother drove me to the hospital and waited outside. From then on I was on my own. It was before the time when fathers were permitted to attend the birth of their child and anyway the father was on the other side of the world. I didn't even have a girlfriend who could stay with me and rub my back and comfort me. As an unmarried mother I had put myself outside the usual support system. I remember that her birth was accompanied by a gigantic electrical storm. Afterwards I learnt that during that storm a big tree had been uprooted at my parent's house.

'Vanessa was born six weeks premature and I had great trouble feeding her. It was two weeks before I could take her home and we never became bonded during that time. When we did finally get together alone she was difficult and colicky and jaundiced. I went from having no milk to having breasts like Sabrina, which were continually overflowing with enough milk for Cleopatra's bath. Vanessa didn't sleep and she cried constantly. I realise now it was because she was premature and her gut was underdeveloped but then I didn't know anything about babies other than what I had read and I had no one to ask. It's assumed that mothers have an innate knowledge but that's not true. I just stumbled along, learning as I went.

'Looking back on this time all I recall is feeling like a zombie from exhaustion. I've never admitted this to anyone but it was then that I became a *Days of Our Lives* addict! I would flop in front of the box at 1.30 in the afternoon, something I had never done before, to watch it. I grew to love the family in that program as if it were my own, only better, because nothing too traumatic ever happened to them. It was safe, comforting. I still watch it whenever I can. Isn't that awful?'

Paula moved back into her own apartment and settled down, as much as anyone ever does, to adjusting to her new role. 'I took advantage of my celebrity status as an unwed mother and began to enjoy it all. I started mixing with old friends again. One of them was the guy who had also lived in the place where I had shared a room with the three fellows and a motorbike. His name was Nigel and I wasn't in the least surprised when he telephoned one night and said, "I just rang up to find out if you'd like to get married." I said, "Yes", and in less than a month we were married under a tree in a park in Queanbeyan, just outside Canberra, where he was teaching.

'It was a non-marriage marriage. I knew that before I did it. I suppose I married for the security of being with someone I loved but was not "in love" with. There's a big difference and I think it was the same for him. He was five years older than me, a zany, extreme character with a biting wit. He adored Vanessa. He called her Pink Thing and carried her around in a paper bag and told people she had no legs.

'He moved up to a job in Sydney and we bought a house in the Blue Mountains from where he commuted up and down every day. I think my parents were a little relieved. When I was growing up they had hoped that I would marry some ambitious young man with a promising career and settle into serving savouries and smiling and saying the right things at cocktail parties. My marriage to Nigel was a far cry from that but at least it was a marriage.

'It was good for most of the two years it lasted. We only ever had one fight. The worst thing was that he went off on the train at 6.00 in the morning and by the time he came home again at 7.00 in the evening he was so exhausted he didn't want to talk or do anything. He'd grunt, eat the dinner I had spent hours preparing and disappear into his study.

'I loved those first couple of years with Nessie. She'd point out all the little things that you miss once you become an adult. We'd play and do things together. It was fun showing her the world and building our relationship. But while that was growing better and better my relationship with Nigel was getting worse and worse. I became pregnant. He didn't want me to have the baby but I did. It ended with me having a miscarriage at four and a half months. I think it was brought on by the stress of knowing that he didn't want me to have it. After that the marriage became more and more hollow and empty. I started to do with him what I have now got down to a fine art in my relationships with men. I manipulate it into an intolerable condition where the only way for the man to react is to reject me. I can force a relationship straight down the gurgler faster than any other woman on earth!' Paula laughs, but it's the laugh she has taught herself to make so as to diffuse the situation. 'It finally came apart when Nigel fell in love with one of his sixteen-year-old students. How's that for a blow to the ego?'

'After that I moved back down to Sydney and went to live in the maid's quarters at my grandparents' house. While I was there my grandfather became very ill and died and my grandmother decided to move into a much smaller place. She asked me to help her auction off the possessions she didn't want to keep. I adored my grandfather. He was head of his own family business, held the chair of many other successful companies and had lived a fascinating life. Granny didn't allow him to smoke so he and I used to sneak away to a room at the very top of the house where he had a secret cigarette and there we would talk about everything. Every birthday since I had turned ten he would always give me the same thing: a dozen pairs of French stockings and a bottle of French perfume.

'When Granny sold her house I moved out into a house of my own on the North Shore and I decided that I could either jump off the Gap or do something constructive with my life. I decided to go to university and because my teachers had always told me that I would never be able to understand anything scientific I decided to study science. My major was palaeontology. I loved university. Loved it. I studied part-time for three years. But I didn't finish the course, although I can always go back and do that, because my private life fell apart again.

'I had a long drawn-out relationship with an actor who broke my heart into a million pieces. He really screwed me up but it was just as if he had me under a spell. It was terrible. By this time Vanessa was in primary school and a very aware little girl. Poor Nessie watched me disintegrate. She was a party to our fights and she saw what a mess I became. In the two and a half years we were together I went down to six and a half stone. I fell pregnant again and because he was so indecisive about whether or not he wanted me to have our child I had an abortion when I was thirteen weeks gone. Not a pleasant experience. In the end the only way I could escape him was to get married. While he was away doing a play in Melbourne I met this guy and the moment he told me his name was Nigel I knew I would marry him.

'He thought I was wonderful. He laughed at what I said. He liked the way I looked. Within a month we were engaged. I told my boyfriend over the phone. All he said was, "You might at least have waited until I came home." But I knew if I had done that I wouldn't have gone through with it. I stayed married to Nigel Number Two for less than a year. I thoroughly liked him. I still like both my husbands and get along well with them and their new wives and children. The only reason why this second marriage didn't last was because of philosophical differences. He joined the Orange People and I couldn't go along with their beliefs nor his need to join a group. I am first and foremost an individual and believe in individual responsibility. The time we did have together was very productive. We spent a lot of it questioning and looking for some meaning to life. He taught me to begin to be not so hard on myself and it was his impetus which encouraged me to seriously pursue yoga. Yoga has given me a great deal. It has taught me a lot; opened my eyes and my heart and helped me come to terms with what I am and what I feel.

'I studied to become a yoga teacher. It was not easy. I worked my body, mind and soul off and I was so proud of myself when I completed the course that I took the certificate around to my parents to show them, to say, "Look. I am good at something. I can see something through and finish what I start out to achieve. Here is something I didn't give up on but have seen through to the end." Instead of the usual emotional smack in the face I wanted a pat on the back. I felt I deserved it. Mum just glanced at the certificate as if it was meaningless and put it to one side saying she would show it to Dad later. After a couple of weeks when I phoned her and asked her for it back so I could have it framed she asked, "What certificate?" I thought for a moment she had lost it but fortunately she hadn't. When I went to collect it Dad handed it back to me folded up. Imagine that! Folded up with a big crease through it! I was so angry. So hurt.'

The added resonance in her voice expresses the depth of her distress and is strong enough to activate AG, the stuffed bear with the electronic voice which is propped at the far end of her leather sofa. 'That's right AG,' she agrees with his synthesised retort. 'Comes to something, doesn't it, when your closest friends are two teddy bears and a cat!' Paula's extremely handsome all-black feline friend, Vegemite, is stretched out in the sunlight on the patio of her top-floor apartment. It's an attractive home decorated with warmth and style. Everywhere there is evidence of two women living together; from the piles of freshly laundered underwear to the photographs and the shopping lists. 'Nessie doesn't like it here. She is accustomed to a big house and she finds this too small. In a way it is, at least with her as she is now. If we were on good terms it wouldn't be like that but when she comes home and fills the place with her anguish and then shuts herself in her bedroom it feels very claustrophobic. That's why I spend so much time on my patio garden. I *love* my garden. Gardening is great therapy.' Judging by the fine condition of her plants and colourful flowers it seems that among the things Paula has inherited from her mother are her green fingers. But I think it wiser not to mention this genetic link.

After her second marriage broke up Paula formed what she describes as a 'lean-to' relationship with a man she had known for some time whose wife had died of a heroin overdose. 'He had two children and I had Nessie and we knitted together a family unit. But he was taking amphetamines and I hated his addiction and didn't like the sleaze that surrounded it. I wanted to save him and us. I loved him and the family we made together. I was totally devastated when he phoned one day to say he wouldn't be coming back. He'd found another woman who liked sticking needles in her arm and he wanted to alleviate his guilt and save himself by saving her. I sold the house and we moved into this place. We've been here nearly three years and I've become a bit of a social ostrich. It's easier and anyway there aren't any decent men out there. I've given up on romantic love. I'd just like someone with whom I could be comfortable, relaxed and happy. Are you married?'

We talk for a while about love and marriage and, inevitably, children. 'When people ask me what I do I say, "I'm a single parent." And then they say, "Yes, but what do you do?" And I tell them, "I look after my daughter." She is my job. But she is also my love, my responsibility. There's nothing I wouldn't do for her. I'm sure we'll get through this patch. But it's tough I can tell you. Vanessa is a pubescent Gemini and I am a Virgo-Libran. We are both headstrong, so it's inevitable that we should clash. She has just woken up to the resentment she feels about the failures I've had in terms of relationships. She hasn't had enough experience to understand the whys and wherefores of all that. I am only just beginning to understand my own parents and I'm thirty-five and have been through a bit. But at least, unlike me, she knows her mother has always loved and wanted her.

'At present she is pretty unlovable most of the time. She looks awful. She's a stunner, gorgeous, but the way she dresses denies that. All her clothes are black, as if she's saying, "Look at me, I'm suffering." But I never comment on it. I also don't make any remarks about her smoking. I know she does it in defiance of me and that she knows I don't approve, but I feel that is one of those decisions she has to make for herself. I don't even say anything about her foul language, or, worst of all, her habit of expectorating everywhere. You may laugh but it's not funny. Not to live with. I don't worry about her getting into drugs. She has seen first hand the result of such escape routes. Losing half a "family" was a bad enough experience to put her off drugs forever.

'Nor am I anxious about sex. She's very pretty and doesn't have to do much to attract a positive response. She's probably learning how to kiss and what is acceptable and not acceptable to her. There's lots of strutting and posing and that sort of thing. Apart from the outrageous antisocial behaviour she shows me she's pretty straight and terribly modest and shy. My greatest worry is that she will get herself into a situation which because of her innocence she is unable to handle.

All that pent-up anger and frustration could be used as a positive force if she knew how.

'The very worst thing about our present situation is having to cope with it all on my own. If I had a man around who occasionally said to me, "I love you", or told Nessie when she was behaving abominably, "Don't speak to your mother like that", it would be such a comfort. Parenting is not designed to be a single job. You have to have another person to share it with. It's an impossible load for one person to carry on their own.

'I am trying to share some of the burden at the moment by going to a counsellor with Nessie. It was a decision I made almost from desperation after she left home. She roared into the flat one day and screamed at me that she hated me and didn't want to live with me any more and that she was going to live at her girlfriend's place. I sought to diffuse the situation by sending it up slightly and I said, "Okay, you want to go, I'll help you pack." But she was for real. She took some of her stuff and left. I went over there the next day to bring her home but she just screamed at me, "Leave me alone. Give me some space." So I told her, "I love you, Nessie. I want you to come home. I can't force you but I want you to know I'll be there whenever you want me."

'She stayed away two months. I was devastated. But I kept the lines of communication open at my end and I made sure she was still attending school and I didn't force or even push her, because I thought it might make things worse. Eventually she came home of her own accord and when I then suggested going to a counsellor she was quite agreeable. It's done us both some good. We've been able to talk to each other through this third person and she's been able to bring out a lot of stuff which until now she has kept pent up inside. She's a very frightened, very concerned and very angry person. She has taken on the responsibility of worrying about me and my up-to-now pretty hopeless relationships with men. She has said, "I could see this man was going to leave Mum, to hurt her, and I wanted to protect her from all that." She has interfered a lot in all my relationships. It's a question of which comes first, the chicken or the egg. She's worried and so she interferes and the relationship falls apart. Which comes first; her interference or the relationship foundering?

'At the moment she is dark about me having a Fijian boyfriend. I've just come back from spending a week with him in his village in Fiji. He's a fisherman and farmer. A big, gentle, innocent man. He lives totally off what his land and the sea provide. It's a fantastically simple and appealing lifestyle and when I look at photographs of myself taken there I can see the total peace in my face. I am content. But it's a pretty impossible relationship. I can't live there permanently because of schooling for Nessie and he can't live here permanently because of visa requirements, and in any case what sort of work is there here that he would like to do? I think Nessie is worried that I will do a moonlight flit and disappear over there to join him. But I wouldn't ever let her down like that. She says that he sees me as a rich white woman and is taking advantage of me. And she complains that I spent the money going there to stay with him instead of spending it on her. But I took the cheapest possible flight and stayed with him for nothing, and besides I worked my bum off, twelve-hour days, seven days a week to save the money while she was off staying with her girlfriend. I am very glad that I have my job. It's a very positive input into my life.'

Paula is the manageress of a place called the Balloon Shop, which sells balloons for every occasion from huge commercial displays to individual parties. 'You can't help but be cheered by a balloon. You can't be miserable and have a balloon. They are joyful things. They tie in very closely to my philosophy about life. There are more ways of teaching yoga than by giving classes. I've just had a new business card printed, combining the two professions, which says, "Breath is Life. Life is a Celebration". There are a lot of things about life that I can't hack; for instance people hurting one another. But a balloon is the complete antithesis of anything like that. It is light and peace. Being around balloons has helped me a great deal during this time of stress.

'I'm an intrinsically happy, bubbly person. When I'm down I hibernate, have a bit of a wallow and keep myself to myself until I get over it. I am often badly affected by premenstrual tension, especially if I don't do my yoga. Vanessa is even more badly affected. I certainly think this adds to the emotional trauma which we are going through at the moment. But even though I get pretty jack of it all I tell myself it's just a matter of battening down the hatches. I think our love for each other will get us through. I am conscious of the pattern in my life. Of my poor relationship with my own parents, particularly with my mother, being repeated in my relationship with my daughter. They talk about the sins of one generation being heaped upon the next and this is what has been happening. But I am really determined to break the cycle.

'At the moment Vanessa is miserable. I want her to be happy. It is possible to work at being happy in the same way as you can work on other areas. That is just one of the things I have learnt from yoga. You *can* do it. I want her to resolve these emotions. I want her to unpack that mental suitcase, take out the junk and put in something nice for a change, instead of carrying all that harmful stuff with her on through her whole life. It's non-productive. It's destructive. I should know. I've been there, done that. What I want for her more than anything else is peace of mind and happiness of spirit with just a fraction left unresolved to give zest to her creativity. She is a very talented writer and cartoonist. She has heaps going for her if only she can just let go enough to let it all happen.'

LETTING GO

Trish

Chris Sumner

Cynthia Stanley-Jones

Anne Wood

Trish

So, they are gone and what a relief it is! But more than that, it's terrific fun. We have become friends again. We actually enjoy each other's company and look forward to seeing each other and doing things together. Yes — there is life after teenage children!

Mind you, it didn't happen all at once. It took me quite a time to re-centre myself. In fact it's only now, more than two years since they moved out, that I have ceased to continuously marvel over being able to have a shower in peace (without having first to mop the floor and pick up mountains of wet towels) and being able to use the telephone whenever and for as long as I like. It's just great to be able to listen to my own music, to eat when and what I want, to be able to either sleep in or get up in the middle of the night and read or just wander around. Best of all is the freedom to come and go and do as I like (taking into consideration only one other person), including being able to sit and stare at a blank wall, or better still the ocean, for as long as I want.

Unexpectedly, it was a very long time before I could deeply enjoy these freedoms. Eighteen years of being a full-time mother had left me so revved up I found it impossible to change gear automatically. My head wanted, so very badly, to stop racing, but my system couldn't let up. I felt compelled to keep to a strict regimen and order. To fill those 'sixty seconds'worth of distance run'. I remained mad for months.

Slowly, slowly, I've come back to sanity. It really is like no longer bashing my head against a brick wall.

Frequently women ask me, with an edge of desperation in their voices, 'How did you get your children to leave home?' And I know they are deeply shocked when I say, 'I just told them, "When you reach eighteen you have to go." ' But having survived teenage children plus almost two decades of peer group pressure from other parents about my children's education, their sexuality, dress, behaviour, attitudes to drugs, life, death and the whole damn thing, I am now totally impervious to what those mothers think.

I have stood beside Zara in a crowded theatre foyer on an opening night while she hissed and catcalled at women wearing dead animals — her description for fur coats! I have been shopping in up-market boutiques with Sean looking like an extra from *Clockwork Orange* and all the time that I was trying to elicit information from sales people, they were too busy keeping a wary eye on this outrageous person, who they were certain was shoplifting, to be able to give me any assistance.

I have cringed beside Zara as she informed the snooty waiter in the dining room of the gentlemen's club where her grandfather had taken the entire motley family crew to dinner that she did not eat 'dead flesh'. And I have flushed with embarrassment as Sean told a specialist physician who had cared for his father for more than thirty years that his own sharp chest pains became acute 'only when I smoke a lot of dope'.

How well I remember the expression of distaste on the face of the specialist who, having told Sean, suffering frequent attacks of tonsillitis, that he didn't think he needed to have them removed, watched Sean turn to me and ask, 'Are we paying for this operation?' and when I replied in the affirmative, turn back to the doctor to tell him, 'Then I shall have my tonsils removed'. After the operation the doctor came by Sean's room and apologised for suggesting he keep his tonsils because, 'They were some of the most enlarged and diseased I have ever seen'. His conciliatory visit helped me cope with the stares of outrage from the nursing staff, who viewed Sean's black beret, heavily gelled hair, dagger earring and ferociously torn, sleeveless T-shirt emblazoned with atomic explosions and obscene messages as less than appropriate hospital attire.

And how grateful I was to Zara's father when he introduced the camera operator, the sound recordist, me by my own name as the production assistant and only himself as the parent of Zara to the head of the Harvard Medical School. She was accompanying us on an interview he was conducting into state-of-the-art research into AIDS and was half wearing a pair of crutchless, kneeless, grubby jeans, with her unwashed hair tumbling from a scruffy beret and the unstitched hem of her full-length, shabby, ancient, originally black overcoat dragging on the floor.

After all that I should care what other mothers thought of me giving my children the royal order of the boot at eighteen!

In fact Sean didn't hang about long enough to get the flick. He flicked himself. I had thought that for their last two years of schooling they, and just as importantly we, would be better off if they boarded. The decision was made partly as a sanity-saving device and partly because we had a joint work project on which we were about to embark which would have meant us being away from Australia for large hits of time. As it happened this particular project didn't eventuate, but by then the decision for them to go away to boarding school had been made and so off they went.

We chose schools which were far enough away from our home that it wouldn't be possible for them to take evening pass-outs, but close enough that they could come home for weekends. Zara, who, though she would vehemently deny it, has strong leanings towards the autocratic, settled into her new surrounds very quickly. While just as quickly Sean ran foul of the sensible rules and regulations.

One evening, together with three other students, he babysat the children of one of the housemasters and while they were at it they drank a flagon of wine. Their indiscretion was discovered because they left unwashed wine glasses lying around. The others were suspended and sent home a week before the end of term but we insisted that this would be no punishment for Sean, who would simply spend his time surfing. So much to his aggravation, Sean was kept at school and made an example of by having to paint the school fence, 'Like Huckleberry Finn,' he complained.

He was also warned very strongly by the headmaster that if he broke school rules again he would be expelled and warned by us that if this happened, we would not go looking for another school for him. Less than six weeks later that is what happened. He came home for weekend leave by train and as soon as the train left the station he and his mates changed out of uniform into civvies, went to the bar and started drinking. Some kind-hearted, caring woman passenger, who no doubt had no teenage sons of her own, saw what they'd got up to and when the train reached Sydney she phoned the headmaster. When Sean returned from his weekend break the headmaster was waiting with his expulsion order and Sean was on the next train back down.

I was away, in the United States researching another book, so it was his father who received the headmaster's phone call, and pleaded with him, unsuccessfully, to give his son another chance. Later the same evening when Sean arrived by train at Central Railway Station, he phoned home, with a borrowed coin because he had no money at all, asking to be picked up along with all his bags. His father, still furious over the incident, told him, 'You're not welcome here, Sean. I don't want to see you until you have a job.'

Now I admit that I wouldn't have been able to do that. I'm too much of a wimp, or too much of a mother, or both! I am really glad I wasn't around for this particular drama because I am sure it would have been the cause of much conflict between his father and me. I am also very glad that his father had the courage to stick to his guns. Because as Sean himself will tell you, 'It was the best thing that ever happened to me.'

He also says he put down the phone and wasn't sure which he would do first, faint or throw up! His father says he was so angry that for twenty-four hours he didn't care what happened to Sean. During the next twenty-four hours the anger wore off and at the beginning of the third day he started to worry that what he had done might have pushed Sean into doing something even more stupid than getting expelled from school. So he began to ring around his friends and when he reached the young woman Sean had been dating for several months and asked if she knew where his son was, she told him, 'Sean's at work.'

So there you go! At the weekend Sean came up to the house and the two men (for he was a man now even though he was only sixteen), father and son, embraced and made up. Sean said he was sorry for upsetting his dad and his dad said he was sorry for getting angry and that was it. Sean has never been out of work since. In fact he is often a good deal more solvent than us!

I have always made it very clear to the children that if they take the dole they will not be welcome in my house. The same applies to their friends. I think social security benefits should be available for those who really need them. But I don't think my children, with everything they have going for them, their education, experience and background, will ever need them, so they should never take them. They are there for people who are far less fortunate than my children, or the majority of their friends. I know this rule has caused a few heartaches for them because taking benefits has become so socially acceptable that when, for instance, Sean gave up his hairdressing apprenticeship and started out on his own as a freelance self-employed entrepreneur there were a lot of his friends who told him he was a fool for not taking the dole. I told him what I think: that it's a soft option and like all such options is destructive of self-respect. I know it takes a lot of guts to stand up to peer group pressure at that age and so I was very pleased that he did and told him so. He told me that this year, his nineteenth, has been the best of his life and that he feels just great about making his own money, renting his own house and running his own life.

Recently he was employed as a model in an advertisement for a well-known soft drink. Half of the sizeable fee he was paid disappeared in tax. He was horrified. I rubbed salt in the wound by telling him, 'That goes to help pay the dole to people you know who shouldn't be taking it.' 'Mother,' he groaned, 'will you ever give up?'

When it came to Zara it was my turn to be tough. She hung in there and took her HSC and then she came home and from the kindness of my heart I told her that although she had just turned eighteen she was very welcome to stay on with us until the end of the school holidays but that by the end of January she should be on her way. They had been left a little bit of money by my dad and much against my wishes this came due to them when they reached eighteen. I thought they were far too young and even tried to get it deferred until they were twenty-one, but this wasn't legally possible. It wasn't a fortune, but it was enough to buy an airline ticket to the other side of the world and have enough left over to knock about for a year, which is how Zara spent hers, or to buy a second-hand car, which is what Sean did with his.

So I wasn't quite throwing Zara to the wolves when it came to the last weekend in January and I said to her, 'Time to go, Zas.' She asked, 'Can I stay until I take my driving test on the seventh of February?' I know you, as a caring mother, would have said yes, but I had learnt my lessons and knew that once I started giving an inch a mile would be taken, so I steeled myself for the anticipated reaction and said, 'No, Zas. But I tell you what, you can come back the night before, in order for you to get a good night's sleep and a decent breakfast, so you are in good shape to take the test. How's that sound?' Her reply is unfortunately unprintable!

So she packed the treasures of her childhood into three carefully labelled tea-chests, supervised her father nailing them shut, extracted a promise that they would not be opened except in her presence, then organised us into lugging them up to the far, dark recesses of the already overburdened garage. We were being punished.

Her brother and his girlfriend picked her up from home on the last Saturday in January and whisked her away to her new life in an orange BMW convertible. She perched in the back with her suitcases and ghetto blaster and waved goodbye with a nonchalance I knew she didn't feel. And of course I had a little weep. And of course I worried about all the things I hadn't told her. In fact that's how this book started. I thought I should write her a long letter; to join up the dots and colour in the picture. Had we talked enough about drugs, AIDS, birth control? Did she know how much I loved her? Or did she feel rejected? I lay in bed that night, picking away at my anxieties, unable to phone her because I had purposely not asked where she would be staying. I knew that in an emergency her brother could tell me but this was not an emergency for anyone except me. And as usual a mother's emergencies don't count.

During the next few months I began the adjustment to being a non-day-to-day mother. Fortunately I was preposterously busy with work, so the strange void, the lack of noise, the sudden space in the house, the freedom to leave things — the car, food, jewellery, clothes, records, books — and know they would be in the same place when I returned, was not as gut-wrenching as it might have been if I'd had the time to keep mulling over it.

Zara's departure coincided with the enormous step of launching out into our own business with a couple of colleagues. Suddenly, rather than being independent freelance operators, we were employing people, which meant being responsible for them, and instead of having no children at home we took on an extended family. It seems to be the nature of the industry in which we work that the large majority of the people who are involved in it are in their twenties and thirties and few of them have children. So suddenly I was surrounded by people, twenty years younger than me, whose judgements of me were based totally on my professional ability. And I was made to realise how much I had grown to depend on being a mother as part of my persona. Not, 'I think, therefore I am', but 'I am a Mother, therefore I am something worth while!'

I was using being a mother as a form of protection, a shield or a banner behind which I hid, only coming out to be judged once that information had been digested. Being a mother gave me status, though of course only in my own eyes! I felt that what I had come through, what I had achieved, should somehow be apparent to everyone. I became conscious that I needed to let people know, early on, that I was a mother. Stupid, because people who are not mothers don't have a clue what is involved and so are not at all impressed.

I recall being politely quizzed by a twenty-nine-year-old production manager about what experience I'd had which would enable me to run an overseas crew on the road. He looked at me blankly, as well he might, when I told him, a little waspishly, that having survived eighteen years of children I didn't think two months of organising three men to travel around the world would prove too difficult!

So I made a conscious effort not to talk about my children, especially to other women, because I knew I was doing so to make myself more acceptable to them. (I might look a bit flash but really I'm okay because I am a mother!) I still recall the first occasion on which I let a woman, pregnant with her first baby, tell me how it felt and talk to me as if I wouldn't understand what she was experiencing. I let her rave on for twenty minutes before subtly letting her know that I had been there, done that. Gradually I've been able to let go of motherhood as a badge of honour and only occasionally do I flash my membership to gain admittance.

The other unexpected reaction to my loss and to my freedom from daily irritations was that I entered into a relationship in which I could indulge all my need to care and nurture. My partner has always been self-sufficient. He has never needed or wanted me to organise the detail of his life, 'to run around after me', is how he would put it. So when I began to do it for someone else he looked on with surprise and sometimes slight annoyance. Perhaps it was just that when the children first left I needed to be needed at that very basic level. To dismiss this friendship as only that would be to denigrate it. There is a warmth and sharing and learning which is much more than just something to fill the void. And fortunately my central relationship is of such honesty and quality that it has never demanded a closure to the rest of the world. To be caged by other people's perceptions of wifedom would be as intolerable as to endeavour to live up to other's expectations of motherhood.

Now I've reached the exceptionally pleasant stage of being able to enjoy everything about my life, including being a mother; because of course I haven't stopped being a mother just because they no longer live with me.

Zara went overseas a few months after she left home. She has studied and worked in the United States and Britain (she is in the highly enviable position of being a triple national and so able to live and work in both those places with no legal worries) as well as travelling in Europe. Because our work takes us overseas frequently we have seen her at least every six months and each time I have enjoyed it more. We've done some fun things together and she likes to introduce me to her friends who are an eighties version of the Flower People; very caring and supportive of one another, they hug and kiss each other a lot. A born vegetarian, she knows all the best cheap restaurants and has introduced me to new delights like shots of eye-popping wheat-grass juice and delicious spirolina soup. She'd run a great restaurant.

Now that she has gone through her money she's learnt to cope with having very little. The apartment she shares is in an okay part of downtown Seattle but has no furniture other than a double mattress. One evening, after a long international flight, I collapsed there while she and her dad went grocery shopping and then rustled up an enormous spaghetti cooked in borrowed pans and eaten off borrowed plates by about a dozen of her friends.

Zara is like a delicate indoor plant in need of careful nurturing. She's an emotionally complicated person and there are many convolutions, much tough stuff to get through, before we touch base. She isn't relaxed enough with herself to lie back and wallow, confident in my love. She needs constant reassurance and gentle care. But we're getting there.

She's a brilliant organiser, as I am sure her longtime boyfriend has learnt! He's a West Coast Jew with long, curly black hair and startling blue eyes, a drummer with a group called Skin Yard. Zara has toured with the group, taking photographs of life on the road, and she organised him into working straight jobs to earn enough money to bum around Europe for a summer. Then she organised their travelling. The feminist in me would like to see her use the energy she pours into him put to use for herself. But I understand what she does for love. For her up-coming twenty-first birthday present I am giving her a ticket home for a visit and I am looking forward to that.

Her greatest skills are still verbal and written, though she hasn't recognised that yet. I have tried to persuade her to keep a diary of her experiences and to write to me. But in an era of instant everything it's difficult to impress the worth of the written word. She's more into lengthy reverse-charge, long-distance phone calls!

It's a matter of each generation's change in values. A very close pal who is seventy-one (and a great-grandmother) still turns collars! When her husband's shirt-collar becomes rubbed thin on the inside she unpicks and restitches it so the raw patch is turned under. The collar never sits as well. Her two sons, neither of whom is short of a bob or two, try to dissuade her from her frugality. 'The war is over, Mother,' they josh her.

But she finds it as hard to adjust to the decadence of throwing out frayed shirts as I do to long-distance phone calls or taking the helicopter into Manhattan from the airport. That's what Sean and his lady did on their visit to the Big Apple. I was aghast! 'It's so expensive!' I said. 'It costs $50,' he told me, 'and it costs at least $30 in a cab, more if you get stuck in traffic, and think of the savings in time and aggravation. It's the way to go, Mother. It's class. That's what is missing in your life, class!' (Where does he get these ideas from? How come he is so at ease with ordering cocktails which resemble miniature Pacific islands, complete with greenery? How come he knows the maitre d' at the newest restaurants in town?)

Sean has got on with his life at an enormous pace. He did two years as an apprentice hairdresser. (I knew people were saying, 'Well what else could you expect with a mother like that!') And now he says, 'You can tell them I am an entrepreneur.' He and a mate have formed a company organising large-scale parties which people pay to attend. He has a most impressive knack of knowing what people want in the way of entertainment and being able to target a very specific market: people under thirty with style and money who want to be seen in the 'right' place.

The laziest, most grotty bum has become an extremely hardworking spit and polish person! A few months ago when I dropped in at his place in Darlinghurst and found him polishing the black laminated fronts of his kitchen cupboards, I asked him what he was using. 'Spray and Wipe,' he held up the can. 'I've tried other brands and this is the best. It's more expensive but it doesn't leave smears'. Was this the same person whose teenage bedroom was a breeding ground for germ warfare?

He also has had a long-term relationship and despite a multitude of offers is happiest committed one to one. There would be those who see in the fact that both he and his sister have this type of friendship an indication that they are searching for the comfort of the regular home base they have been denied, but I view it more as an affirmation that they liked what they saw up close of our shared life and would like to replicate it in their own.

Sean and I lunch together more or less once a week and then often we go window shopping, which is great fun because he has such a terrific sense of style and fashion. Quite frequently we sort of fall into a shop by mistake and he talks me into buying something by telling me how well it suits me! We also eat at his place where he and his girlfriend go to great trouble to make us special vegetarian delights. He makes the soup and salad while she makes the main dish. They both make the dessert and he lays the table, decorating it to a colour scheme down to the napkins and flowers. Pretty amazing stuff for the Slob of the Century!

It's so easy with him, he loves me and I love him and we confide in and trust and cherish one another. We can and do talk honestly about the most personal stuff. He's got my number, so even if I try a little bluff I can't get away with it. He is like a sturdy tropical plant lapping up the sun and the rain, and whatever else chances by. His life is full of extraordinary people and experiences and he revels in it all.

He is most anxious that any woman with whom he is involved should be independent with her own career and life plan. He told me, 'It's important for a woman to have her own dreams and go about making them come true, rather than relying on a man to make it happen.' It makes me happy not to have lumbered the world with yet another man who only wants a woman to be half a person.

And now that they have left home my friendship with Guy has finally blossomed too. I think he was pretty amazed when I did what I had always told him I was going to do and pushed them out of the nest at eighteen. Now they are all equal it is easier for him to handle. I will always feel sorry that he suffered for our happiness, but as he goes into his thirties he seems to have been able to put all that behind him. A few pretty dramatic love affairs of his own have no doubt helped him to better comprehend the choices we made.

He has developed into a fine photographer, winning international awards and being widely published. He has just returned from a working visit to the West Coast of the USA and Fiji, where he shot surfing contests for a series of professional video tapes which he is going to produce and distribute. I see him frequently too. He drops by the house, he's done some work for the company and this year we went skiing together. He is particularly close to Sean and sometimes when we are all together I think we should all go into business together. We'd be an unbeatable team!

Being with the two sons and their father has taught me a great deal about men and particularly about how they regard women. Very enlightening! But then everything about motherhood is enlightening. I've plumbed depths in myself which I would never have discovered if I had not been pushed to it. Some of it I could most certainly have done without. I have put up with stuff from all three of them that I would not have tolerated from anyone else, not even their father. But I think I am a better person for that: more tolerant, accepting, open-minded, and less self-centred. Perhaps the very best to come from mothering is the impact not on personal values, but on the wider scale of issues; through creating life I feel connected to it at the most basic level, to the flow, the ultimate energy, the ongoingness of it all. If I was to die now, at this very moment as I type these words, because of those other human beings I would not feel the time spent as this particular collection of atoms which forms me had been useless, misspent, wasted. They have given purpose and direction to my life and no doubt will go on doing so. They are my reason, though it's pretty hard to see it that way when the telephone bill comes in!

Several months ago Sean and I were strolling through the lunch time crowds when he asked, 'Tell me the good things about having children. It can't all be bad.' I stopped in my tracks, astonished and aghast that he could think that was how I viewed being a mother. As so often happens, another vital conversation took place in a bizarre setting with him towering above me, irritated office workers having to break their stride to stream past us and me fumbling to explain what I've tried to say in this book. He could sense that I was agitated so he gave me a hug. 'It's okay, Mother. I'm not complaining. I couldn't have had a happier childhood. It's just that I would like to have children and I want to know what to expect.'

It hasn't happened yet, but as we are extending the house anyway, we're building extra bedrooms so as to be ready — for visits only! I am most certainly not willing to raise my grandchildren. I have friends who have taken on the next generation in this manner and I don't think it is good news either for the child, its parents, or its grandparents. That way nobody grows up and moves on. I shall be there only as backup. I am better prepared for grandmothering than I was for mothering. I am looking forward to it. I feel confident I shall be a terrific grandmother! And so the river flows on.

When I told them I was planning to write this book Sean said, 'Can I sue?' and then grinned; Zara said, 'You must be bloody joking!' and then laughed; and Guy said, 'Huh!' I wonder what that meant?

Chris Sumner

The way I feel about a forty-four-year-old woman is not the way I feel about myself.

'Oh it was too soon, I wasn't ready for her to leave.' The answer came without hesitation to my query as to how Chris Sumner felt about her seventeen-year-old daughter, Katie, leaving home and going off to the United States. 'I felt I wasn't ready to let her go, to say goodbye. I'd seen her in my mind as going on to university and having her close for another three years. But part of me knew it was the right thing for her to do and that part of me is proud of what she is doing. It was important for her to establish herself separately from me. We are very alike temperamentally. We also look alike, but who wants to be constantly told, "Wow, you're so like your mother"?

'I got into a terrible panic, thinking perhaps I had not taught her enough to keep herself safe. Over the last three months I told her everything I could think of, even to the point of what to do when she arrived in San Francisco if her luggage was not on the carousel! The one thing I forgot to tell her was what to do if the people who were to meet her at the airport weren't there. And of course that was what happened! And of course she did exactly the right thing, without any advice from me, she hung around until they turned up. So much for needing me!

'For her it is very much a break for independence. She understood that what she was undertaking was much more than a physical journey, it was a journey into herself. I could see how vital it was for her but, oh, it's been so difficult for me — to lose control, to let go of my responsibility for her. I've always been able to do something, to physically take care of her, to keep her safe, but now I can't do that. I have to rely on her.'

Katie had left home a week before her mother and I had dinner together and the rawness of the wound left by her daughter's leap for adulthood was very apparent, even though Chris's own upbringing has given her a strict sense of propriety which allows little room for displays of emotion. But the conversation, far from being all doom and gloom, was brightened with a great deal of levity about women's foibles and terrifying emotional vulnerability, especially with regard to their offspring.

Chris has two daughters, Joanna at sixteen is sixteen months younger than Kate. It is immediately apparent, even on first meeting, that the sisters are unusually harmonious and what's more that the three of them, mother and daughters, are also exceptionally close.

'I suppose that's true, though it's hard for me to know how close others are by comparison because I am part of it. The girls themselves have told me that they can talk to me about everything and far more easily than many of their friends can talk to their parents. I suppose it's true that some of that has come about because for almost seven years I was a single parent and this unavoidably changes perspectives and emotions.

'One thing I have been very, very conscious of is trying not to make up to the girls for not having a full-time father around all the time. I have tried not to make them feel smothered or responsible for me. I expect I have failed in that, all mothers do to some extent or other. You have to accept that. But I can honestly say I have done my best. And Kate's going away like this is in many ways an expression of my own success in not making her feel she is tied to me by feelings of guilt. That would be too awful. So I am glad she has gone.' Long pause. 'I think.' Longer pause. 'The joke is that I left home myself at seventeen!' And we laugh.

Chris, who is forty-four, was born in Edinburgh, so she is quick to point out that she is not only British, but Scottish. She has three brothers, all of them younger than herself. 'It was inevitable that I should take on some of the role as an assistant mother even though it was not specifically required of me. They are all now married and all of them have children. My mother, who has a BA from Oxford University, did not marry until she was twenty-eight, partly because she had been acting as hostess for her father, who was the Archbishop of New Zealand. My father, an Associate of the Royal College of Science, was works manager at an aluminium rolling mill during much of my childhood. But they have always been keen on animals and farming so we lived in a village twenty miles from Edinburgh and grew hay and kept hens and pigs and sheep.

'All of us went to good private schools. It must have been a tremendous financial strain on them. I wasn't unduly aware of it at the time but I guess Mum never had many new clothes. She devoted her life to being a full-time wife and mother. But she is a great deal more independent than she might at first appear. She has always been a socialist. So she and Dad go along to the polling booth together and just cancel out each other's vote! She doesn't say much but when she does it's apt and worth hearing.

'I don't really recall anything in detail about my childhood other than being generally happy, that we had a lot of space around us and I liked that, and that Mum and Dad never argued in front of us. Of course even as kids we could sense tensions but we grew up in an atmosphere of politeness. Even now it's difficult for me to express anger, instead I tend to cry.'

Chris finished school with the Scottish Leaving Certificate and because she was still too young to begin her training as an occupational therapist, she went to France to work as an au pair for a year. 'I don't know why but my going to university then was never within the range of possibilities and I'm not even sure where the idea for doing OT came from except that I had always been interested in medicine and in doing things with my hands.

'Recently, because of Katie leaving, I asked my mother how she had felt about me leaving home at seventeen and you know what she said? "I had faith your innocence would protect you!" She was right. The closest I came to getting into trouble was when a complete stranger came up to me in the street and gave me a rose!'

When Chris was in the middle of her occupational therapy training her parents immigrated to Australia. 'I stayed on to finish my training and came out to join them two years later when I was twenty-one. I found a job with the Crippled Children's Society and became engaged to a man who'd had polio.

'Looking back I realise what a disastrous relationship it would have been if we had gone on and become married. I have this very strong caring instinct. I think it's strong in many women. It's one form of love of course, but it's not a good basis for a marriage. I very much wanted to be married and to have children. I'd never seen my life in any other terms.'

Two years later she did marry. 'I was quite prepared to do what my mother had done, that is put my own life second, both to him and the children. I worked until I was seven months pregnant and then I stopped, I thought to take up full-time motherhood. Giving birth was a fantastic experience. It gave me an incredible sense of my own mortality. Kate was continuity. It was important to present her to my own mother as proof of my own fitness to stand beside her. I was aware at the time that I could date becoming an adult myself from the time of having my first baby. It was only then that I began to see I had other options.

'Kate was only seven months old when I became pregnant, by mistake, with Joanna. I had wanted a large family. Oh yes. I would probably be happiest having six kids and living in the bush. The one slight hitch is that it would have to be with the right person, someone with the same values and who wanted the same things.'

Chris's husband was an actor. 'He was very good but it's always a chancy business, so to put some stability into our lives we opened a bookshop, with some help from Mum and Dad. It was a good move at the time but in the end it didn't help. We loved each other very much but we were unable to reconcile our very different attitudes.

'The break when it came was very hard for both of us. Oh yes. My primary focus was my marriage. I saw myself as his wife and as Katie and Joanna's mother. I was happy fitting my life in around them all. I had gone back to weaving, something I had first learnt as an OT, and I was running workshops and teaching as well as selling my work. I had found a path. I had a life of my own which I could combine with the children and with my husband's irregular lifestyle.

'We could never make definite plans because something was always more than likely to come up: a play, a film, a voice-over, a series, or a casting. I am by nature an organised person so this unpredictable lifestyle made great demands on me to adjust. I've also always been good at managing money and partly what went wrong was that he wouldn't let me do this and of course I couldn't insist because he was the provider. Anyone who does not have economic independence does not have the rights over their own life. If someone is paying then you are beholden to them.

'My first husband is talented, creative and never dull. So it was a difficult break. The turning point for me came when I realised that the difficulties could not all be my fault. We are both complex characters and did not have the maturity to deal with that. I did not see myself as someone who was difficult to live with but for someone like him I was. We decided to try living apart. We'd been out of Australia for a few months and rented our own home so I went up to the farm my parents had moved to and he stayed at his brother's. When our place became vacant I moved back in with the girls and he eventually bought another house.'

Chris gave up weaving. 'It was too solitary an occupation for a time of such trauma. So I brought out the handy old diploma and polished it off and went back to occupational therapy. But I was pretty demoralised and when you are caring for the sick you need to have plenty of your own resources to carry you through. So I sat down and thought about what I wanted to do with my life. It hadn't turned out to be the way I had always anticipated — happy wife and mother. Now I had to face the fact that I was going to be a single parent and to be realistic about that, could look forward to twenty-five years of earning an independent living and should not hang about waiting for another man to gear my life around.

'I find it really hard to make decisions but when I do I tend to see them through, and I decided to be an anthropologist and get a job in a museum. Yes, I suppose you're right, it was a fairly unusual decision to make. It wasn't quite out of the blue. I had always been interested in anthropology. We had taken the children on a long journey through Indonesia and that had confirmed my interest, so it just seemed this was the right direction to follow.

'I enrolled as a mature-age student and for the next four years I lived off the Supporting Parents Benefit, Tertiary Education Assistance, a series of part-time jobs and child maintenance from my husband. He has always been very good in providing for his children. I made very sure it never went towards anything for me, only for the girls. He was resentful and felt that he was helping me through university, but he wasn't. My parents were very supportive of what I was doing and also helped me financially. Putting it all together I was able to stay in my house and provide a secure and unchanging base for Katie and Joanna.

'I actually had very little money but I managed to juggle it. I think that has made quite an impression on the girls, who were six and seven years old at the time of the split. Katie in particular. She is a natural born consumer. She is sick of being broke, of having to manage on very little, and that is another reason why she wanted to have a break between school and university. She wanted to work, to have her own money and to be able to buy, buy, buy for a while.

'My being at university fitted in very well with being a mother and a single parent. I think women are fantastic, and that's not blowing my own trumpet, the way we juggle our lives around our various roles. Being a student meant that I could always be there when the girls went to school and when they came home and also during their holidays. It was also good for them to see their mother was doing something which was important to her and separate from them. I was also aware that it was vital they saw that I could cope with being a single parent. A woman on her own, with children. Because ultimately it's not what happens in life but how you cope with it that counts and I wanted them to understand that so they can put it into the context of their own lives.'

Chris did very well at university. After one year she changed to major in ancient history and archaeology. 'I *loved* it! Mature-age students are very motivated and bring more to bear on their studies. I was getting good marks for my assignments, working very hard and enjoying it all.'

In 1979 Chris joined a university archaeological dig near Tel Aviv in Israel. 'It was everything I had anticipated and more. The next two summers I went back to Israel as a member of staff, learning more each time. I got my BA and decided to do Honours. Life was going so well for me, I felt so together in my professional life that it even seemed possible to get my private life together again. In the years we had lived apart our relationship had got better and better. He had always kept close to the girls, who love him dearly. So we decided to try being together again. But it was doomed, I see that now, by us being very different from one another. All we did was reopen old wounds, I suppose, but we both found it difficult to let go finally.

'I was forty that year. On my fortieth birthday I filed for divorce. It seemed the right thing to do. Cut my losses and look forward. Just after my birthday I went back to Israel for my fourth season, taking the girls with me for the first time and on the second day there I met my present husband. He asked me to come for a walk in the moonlight with him and I said no. I didn't want to get involved. I tried to run away from it. But that's the trouble with life. Things happen at inconvenient moments. I fell in love with him. Simple as that.

'We share lots of interests, particularly archaeology, but we are really very different. There is so little likelihood of me being able to change him in any way, even for what I might see as his own good, and out of love for him, that I have never tried. I respect that in him.

'I sometimes wonder if there is some deep-seated reason why I go for difficult men! He was a single child, a year older than me, who had never married and never had children. He had lived with a woman, but only very briefly. He is an academic, totally committed to his work. And what's more he's an American, from Berkeley, California, so we couldn't let the relationship develop slowly back home. Right from the beginning it involved making decisions; the very thing I most dread!'

A surprising remark from a woman who has made many major decisions, the majority of them on her own. 'Yes I know. But each one has been agonising!' The next one was how to fit their lives together. 'He went back to the USA and I came home. We wrote very frequently. I still treasure those letters. He says more in his letters than he does face to face. He came to Australia six months later to see if what we had was worth pursuing and we decided that I would join him in the States. I had finished half of my honours degree and the girls were at a stage where it wouldn't be too disruptive to their schooling.

'We spent six months in Berkeley and I loved it. The girls did too. They made friends and enjoyed the life. It's such a fantastic place. So much happens there. He was marvellous with the girls. Small children love him but he has no desire to have children of his own, so he was entirely happy to have them provided for him. I think part of my appeal for him was that he could see the quality of the relationship I have with them and he wanted to be part of it. The only problem was that because we were not married I was unable to work in the United States and that was vital to me. I was not going to give up what I had worked so hard for.

'Our visa was for six months and after that the three of us came home, but by then we had decided to get married. In many ways it was a far bigger step for him than for me. After all I knew what was involved but I think he had reached the stage in his life where he didn't want to be alone any more. He applied for a National Research Fellowship in archaeology in Australia.

'He is extremely highly qualified, one of the top people in his field in the world, so he got the job. We were married to avoid the problems of residency and all that, otherwise I would have been just as happy to live with him. I went back to California by myself to get married because I had done it once with my family and friends here and he had never done it so it seemed more appropriate to have the party there. Then we came back here and settled into life together.'

That was three years ago. 'I am not going to pretend that it's all been easy. It's astounding to think about what he took on: new wife, new country, new job and new teenage family, all at the one time. So I have had to make allowances for all of that. But he is *very* tidy, *very* precise and *very* organised. He lives a regulated life and we have no choice but to do the same.

'Right from the start we split our expenses down the middle.

He also suggested that we run a communal house. Each person cooks dinner one night a week and on Fridays we eat out, just the two of us or with friends. Left to myself I would probably still be cooking all the meals. As it is now the girls have become good cooks. They are able to make a meal from whatever is in the cupboard. He still thinks they get away with too much around the house and makes few allowances for them being teenagers.

'All this can only have been good for them. They have learnt to deal with an adult male at close quarters and I have generally managed to restrict my meddling to interpreting between them, which comes from my natural desire to keep the peace. I think this is a traditional role for women. A role we play the best — juggling emotions, trying to keep everyone happy. We do it better than men because, well, I often think a woman's mind is as multifaceted as a fly's eyes. Men tend to be far more single-minded.'

Apart from her daughters and her new marriage the other major facet of Chris's life is her new career. She is an assistant curator at a major museum and her skills and personality are so highly regarded that she is presently in the enviable position of having to make a decision about a job offer and which direction she wants her career to head.

'But as I said, I loathe having to make decisons and this one is particularly difficult because on the one hand is a job I really enjoy doing but which offers no permanency and on the other is a job which is less in my field of interest but which is a permanent public service position. I am drawn towards the security of the permanent job because of my past experiences and not wanting ever to be in the position of being financially dependent. But at the same time I am also wary of it because I do not want to sober up.

'At some stage in their late thirties I think people make the decision about whether or not to get old. The way I feel about a forty-four-year-old woman is not the way I feel about myself. But I have always felt a strong pull towards security and I am a little anxious that this job may just make me fall over into my other, less desirable, sober self. Last night I threw the I-Ching, something I haven't done for a while, and it said, "There is strength in retreat." What am I to make of that?'

In one way the anxiety over the job decision has come at the right time for Chris: 'It has given me less time to worry about Katie. After all Berkeley is not Sydney. When we were all living together in America, the week we left was designated Condom Week. AIDS is not just something you read about or see in documentaries, it's right there. That was one of the things we talked about before she left. The fact is that promiscuity is just not on any more. Katie is a sexual person so it's an issue we had to discuss. I wanted to be as direct as possible without putting the fear of God into her. AIDS has moved into the heterosexual community and it's not going to go away. It can only get worse. When you and I were her age the biggest worry was getting pregnant. That seemed like a matter of life and death. AIDS isn't just *like* a matter of life and death, it *is* a matter of life and death.

'We, the three of us, have always talked a great deal about everything. We have always been very frank and open with one another. Me with them and them with me. I told her that if you are going to have sex with someone you can not be totally sure of, then use a condom. She has to be responsible for herself. The fact is women are more vulnerable, more physically vulnerable. You can't ignore that. Oh yes, I suppose if I had sons I would be anxious about them driving too fast, or getting into stupid and dangerous competitions with their mates. So I hope all this is not just a reflection of my own panic; it comes from a concern for her safety. I had to take the risk of appearing overprotective rather than sending her off unprepared.

'We also talked about drugs. But that's not something which worries me with the girls. We have also always discussed this frankly and they have both tried a bit of dope and know that along with cigarettes and alcohol it's a drug. They have been around it all, it's unavoidable, and show no interest in any of it.

Finally the best I could say to Katie was: "The first thing is to take care of yourself, the second is to make the most of it." Then I gave her a big hug and asked her to bear with me because it was difficult for me to let go.

'I also had to be very aware during this period that Joey didn't feel left out when so much attention was focused on her elder sister. They are very close, friends as well as sisters. They have rarely argued, in fact at one stage I was worried that perhaps they were abnormally pleasant and that this was due to my being unable to express anger.' The things mothers worry about!

'Katie has always felt Joanna is more beautiful than her and Joanna has always felt Katie was more intelligent than her. But neither idea is true. This year at school Joanna is doing better than she has ever done. In the past she's tended to be lazy, but now she is in Year 11 and she is at last finding the work interesting.'

Both her daughters are at an all-girls selective school. In other words they are super-bright. 'I was anxious about them going to an all-girls school because of living for so long in an all-female home environment. Sam, our fourteen-year-old dog, was the only male. We joke about it but I think that's why we've never had his balls chopped off!

'I've talked with various people about the pros and cons of single-sex schools, particularly for girls, and the general concensus has been that they are better for girls because when puberty strikes there is less distraction and no anxiety about competing with their own sex, whereas there is very real and destructive anxiety about competing with boys.

'The fact that they are gifted is the main reason why I feel so strongly about them going on to university. They have a responsibility to fulfil their potential. A university course will enable them to acquire skills which will render them more employable. And that means independence. I don't want them ever to be economically dependent. I want them to be viable members of the community.

It's been so difficult for me — to lose control, to let go of my responsibility for her. I've always been able to do something, to physically take care of her, to keep her safe, but now I can't do that. I have to rely on her.

'I have voiced all these feelings to Katie. But she is aggressively independent and clearly does not want to be told. So I try giving the information so that she can look it over herself and then make her own choice. Still I can't help trying to find out what her future plans are and when I fished around for an answer she was deliberately non-committal, which serves me right! Mind you she worked with me this summer for three months at the museum as a clerical assistant to earn some cash to go away with, and after one week she was saying she could certainly now see the point of going to university.

'She did well in her HSC,' — us stumblebums would think she had done excellently! — 'and has a place at university, which she has deferred for a year. She hasn't decided on what course she will study; marine biology, communications. She also wants to write and has dreams of being an astronaut. But right now she is planning on waiting tables in Berkeley. She is sharing a flat with a friend she made during the six months she was at school there. And she is out of my clutches!

'Joanna seems to miss her less than I would have expected. But this may very well just be her way of covering up how she feels. It is also because she is extremely busy with her own life. She has told me that she is enjoying school for the first time since Year 6. Not surprising seeing as how one of her classes has only ten students in it and another has just eleven. The quality of teaching they have received is very high.

'She is a very keen and competent gymnast and has been going to classes at the Police-Citizens Youth Club three evenings a week for the last three years. Last year she won an award for sportsmanship and this year she is also taking a coaching course. She has a full social life too and has had the same boyfriend for the last two years. She hasn't mentioned the possibility of taking a year off when she finishes school, and I have the feeling that she won't. But perhaps that is just wishful thinking on my part!

'Neither of the girls seem to have been put off men, which was another thing I worried about, with them having gone through the break-up of my first marriage. Quite the opposite, they both enjoy close friendships with boys. Mind you, whoever they bring home I won't think he is good enough! And you know what? I'll be right!'

Both the girls are talented in non-academic areas. Katie is an excellent pianist. 'And she also always had a job of some sort; serving in a chemist or a deli or delivering papers. That used to terrify me. I'd get up in the dark in the dead of winter with her just to see her across the road on her bike which was loaded with papers. She was twelve. But I couldn't help myself. I care about them so desperately. We'd laugh about it. Without being able to laugh we'd have been sunk!

'I didn't want to weigh them down with my caring so we'd talk about it and we had rules. We, the three of us, set the rules between us. We'd discuss them so they seemed reasonable to all of us. They agreed to a curfew, being home by a set time, and to always letting me know where they were and how they were getting home. It was a great relief when Katie learnt to drive. Oh yes, I do manage to have a selfish streak as well and it was wonderful that she could go and pick up Joanna!'

Joanna doesn't drive, yet. 'We thought it best to get Katie through and out of the way first. This year there will be more time for just Joanna and I am sure that will be good. I have to be very careful not to ask her to carry single-handed my sadness at not having Katie around. I've suggested to her that she may get cuddled even more often than usual and I've said, "Please put up with it, it will probably wear off!" But I won't let my tidy husband shut the door to Katie's bedroom. I want it left open so that I can feel she is still part of the house.

'She promised to write and I know she will. I am longing to get a letter. She also asked me not to phone her. I understand that. She wants to make this break on her own terms. She said she will phone every couple of weeks, reverse charges of course! But although the girls have been a major focal point of my life, they have never been my entire life, so I can already see that there are definite benefits in not having children living at home.' Pause. 'I think!'

Cynthia Stanley-Jones

'It was as if the sun had gone out.' That's how Cynthia Stanley-Jones describes what she felt when her oldest son, Michael, left home this year. 'It left an incredible hole. He and I are such good mates that when he came in from work we would sit and yarn together. He would tell me the details of his day right down to who said what to who and without me noticing it two hours would go by and the others would be coming in for their tea and we'd still be sitting there! That's what I miss most, the chats.'

But Cynthia still has people to chat to; her husband and her two other sons, Paul who is seventeen and Robert who is almost sixteen. Paul is an apprentice chef. Robert is still at school and plans to take his HSC and become a cadet journalist. Michael, who is twenty-one, completed his four-year apprenticeship as a carpenter and then decided to take a break. 'He is having a terrific time working as a porter at the resort on Hamilton Island. His girlfriend is working there as a housemaid. He writes great letters. But of course that's not the same as having him here. He's such a mate. And that surprised me. I had never envisaged my children developing into mates because I was a very strict disciplinarian when they were younger. I remember telling them once that they would never outgrow being smacked. I think I'm pretty old-fashioned in many way, about discipline and good manners and values, probably because I had a strict old-fashioned upbringing myself.'

Cynthia, the older of two sisters, was born in Cornwall, the county at the beautiful south-western tip of the British Isles. 'As a young girl I was not allowed out in the evenings, not that there was anywhere to go to even if I had been able to. It's a very quiet part of the country. I'm a bit of a basic soul and I had no great expectations other than to get married and have children. I left school at sixteen, did a secretarial course, and joined the navy as a writer. I wore a uniform and enjoyed the work, which was mostly clerical.'

Cynthia met the man she was to marry when he was on a visit to Cornwall to catch a few waves. 'He and his friends were among the first guys to surf off the coast of Cornwall, so they caused a bit of a stir. I was eighteen when we married. He was my first real boyfriend. He was twenty-four. That was it. It was as if I couldn't see past him. I've never been able to. I must have a one-track mind! Sometimes when I am at the football one of my girlfriends will say, "Ooh, look at him," about one of the players and I look and appreciate their good looks but that's it. I never even wonder what other men are like.' It's impossible not to pick up on this energy when you are together with the two of them. And it's difficult to pry Cynthia away from her spouse for long enough to get into a real conversation! They feel like two halves of the same whole. They complement one another. Her Libran equability and disposition the counterfoil to his mood swings.

The couple moved to Australia nineteen years ago. 'My husband's a maintenance fitter. There was no work for him in Cornwall and very little in the North, where he came from. For ten pounds we could live in a country which had everything we wanted, jobs, sunshine and surf! Michael was eighteen months old when we arrived, looking like a bunch of gypsies with all our possessions in a tin trunk, two suitcases, a sports bag full of wetsuits and flippers and this wooden chest.'

I had already commented on the chest when on my arrival Cynthia had shown me around her home. The entire house and garden gives off the same good energy as do Cynthia, her husband and her boys. There is a welcome, warm, homely feel. Every room is awash with family life, from the overflowing hatstand at the front door, to the kitchen wall collage of notes and stickers and funny pictures, to the cushion-smothered couches in the lounge. Many happy hours could be spent examining the wondrous array of Cynthia's collectibles; a tailor's dummy stands guard in a lace shawl at the top of the stairs, down the edge of which is a row of antique irons. On the walls, between the crowded bookshelves, are masks, unposed photographs of herself, her husband and her sons, all of them extremely attractive people, and paintings which would be overlooked at garage sales and yet in this setting their vibrant mystery commands attention. All of it melded together into a whole by Cynthia's ability to create a compelling atmosphere. And then there is the trunk.

Cynthia runs her hand over its oiled wood. 'I guess I like it so much because of its history. When we brought it from England it was covered in thick red paint. Awful. We kept it downstairs, out of sight, full of junk. Just before he left home Michael said he wanted to strip it back. It was a big job because there was so much paint on it and I didn't think he would have the patience. But he did.' The trunk gleams between us. 'He approached it in the same way as he did his apprenticeship. He set his mind to finishing it and even though there were times when it got tough he stuck it out. I am very proud of him.'

All her sons have known what they wanted to do with their lives even before they finished their schooling. 'Women have commented to me that I am lucky the boys have been so certain about their careers because their own children have no idea what they want to do right up to when they leave school and even afterwards. I think my boys are like this mostly because their

There's a freedom which I haven't had before and which I relish. But I am a bit anxious about being lonely . . .

father has always said to them that they should take up a trade, get into an apprenticeship and see it through so they will be able to find a good, well-paid job and have the freedom which comes from that. He was very strong on that point and I think he was right.'

Throughout the conversation it was obvious that the upbringing of the boys had been based on joint decisions. 'My husband wasn't at all keen on the boys when they were in nappies. Just not interested. But once they were old enough to do things with, from then on he was as involved as me, though not about the day-to-day running of things. We live what I suppose you would call an old-fashioned lifestyle. I run the house, do the cooking, cleaning, ironing, shopping. My husband doesn't do any of that. He goes to work and on the weekends he and the boys get into their various projects and sports. Over the years they've enjoyed fun runs, triathlons, football and surfing. The garden has always been the scene of one activity or another.'

Cynthia talks as if their lives are totally ordinary and normal. But that's not quite true. For starters it's seventeen years since she spent a night in bed with her husband, except on weekends and holidays! 'He found work almost as soon as we arrived here and within a year he was working for the same company he is with today; an envelope manufacturing company for whom he works the night-shift maintaining the equipment. He leaves for work at 6.00 in the evening and comes home around 4.30 am. He unwinds for half an hour or so, perhaps watches a bit of television and gets into bed at 5.00. When he was younger he was up again at 10.00 to go for a surf. But now he tends to sleep in till midday. We spend the afternoons together. It was good when the boys were young because it meant he had a couple of hours together with them when they came home from school but he was gone for that frantic period between 6.00 and 8.00 when they were all in the bath and eating and doing their homework.

'The fact that he was here during the day is the reason why I have never worked outside the home except on a very casual basis and then only in hours when he was sleeping. If I had gone off to full-time work during the day we would never have seen each other. I've always been quite content to organise my life around his and the boys. I've never had any ambition to have an outside career. So it suited us both. There's been enough to do mothering and looking after my husband. I think the boys liked having me here after school. But I wasn't one of those mothers who pick their children up from school and run them around to their friends's place or the beach or football practice. For years my husband had our only car and if the boys wanted to go somewhere they had to walk. I've been more than content to work around the house.'

That should not be taken to mean that Cynthia has spent the last twenty-one years just cleaning and cooking. Much of the furniture in her house she has lovingly repaired and restored herself. 'For a while there I would spend every Saturday morning at garage sales in the area. That's where practically everything in the house comes from! There was so much I couldn't possibly keep it all so I rubbed it down, mended it, oiled and polished and finished it and then sold it to friends or local antique shops. I loved getting out on the back patio in the sunshine, rubbing away with the sandpaper, bringing neglected furniture back to life. Very satisfying. I did the same by reframing old pictures and for a change of pace I painted walls and decorated. I get great pleasure doing this sort of thing. It doesn't make news but it's good fun!

'When the boys were little I did some voluntary work at the local hospital and for a bit of pocket money I have a little job as a companion-housekeeper. I've also done a bit of cleaning and babysitting but only during the hours when I wasn't needed at home. You see I am really happiest pottering around at home. I like to read, I read a lot. I like words and I like to write letters. The only career I would be the least bit interested in would be as a writer. And perhaps if I had to write for money and to deadlines that would take away the pleasure.'

Paul was born a year after the family settled in Australia and when the third baby, Robert, came along a year later and turned out to be another boy the Stanley-Joneses gave away the idea of trying again for a daughter. 'I have never minded in the least living in an all-male household. I have no yearnings to have a daughter. None at all. I don't know that I would have been an adequate mother for a girl. I'm not a frilly, tizzy type. I'm not much into fashion. I'm happiest in what is I suppose mostly still a man's world. I like going to the football. I'm a Warringah Rugby Union supporter. And I like going camping and living rough.

'I don't think the boys have missed anything by not having sisters. Actually I remember a couple of years ago Michael came home from a friend's house and said, 'You know Mum, I'm glad I don't have any sisters.' His friend had a teenage sister who was, well you know how teenage girls can be. I think she'd been a bit off towards her brother and Michael. And the more stories I hear from friends who have teenage daughters the more glad I am that I only have sons! Mind you there are worries that you have with boys which you don't have as much of with girls. Cars for instance.

'If girls drive they tend not to be as competitive as boys and to be more careful. Both Michael and Paul have written off cars. My cars! Not through driving too fast but through inexperience. Michael was first. He was saving up for his own car and he had never even asked to borrow my old Moke. But when he did I felt I couldn't refuse. He was seventeen and had just got his licence. The roads around here are very narrow. He came around a corner face to face with a bus which was coming along the middle of the road. He swerved to avoid it, lost control, ran off the road and into the back of an illegally parked car. He was very fortunate that apart from minor cuts he suffered only a badly broken wrist.

'I remember getting the phone call and having no vehicle to get to the scene of the accident. In the closest I've ever been to hysterics I ran from one end of the house to the other tossing up whether I should put on my running shoes and jog there or get on my bicycle. I decided to run but fortunately just as I was leaving the neighbour came home and I asked him to give me a lift. By the time we reached the spot, Michael had been taken to the hospital but I'll never forget when I looked into the wrecked Moke the sight of the blood swilling around on the floor. After that I was sort of prepared for it to be more awful than it was. Most of it was from a cut on his leg which took a while to heal, but could have been far, far worse.

'The second accident happened just a few months ago. Paul totalled my old Renault 12. His accident was much more frightening because both he and Robert were in the car along with a couple of their mates. He was also seventeen and had passed his driving test two months before. Again he wasn't speeding or doing anything crazy. It was the middle of the day and he was only going to the milkbar.

'That time I was at the football with my husband and when we dropped a friend home after the game her daughter came out and told us the police wanted us to go to the hospital. We arrived to a very frightening scene. Three of the boys were in wheelchairs. The fourth one was lying motionless on a stretcher. He was terrified because only just that week they had been shown a video at school about driving safety and what to do in the event of an accident. Immediately after the accident he refused to move from the car because he felt a severe pain in his back. The others had all tried to get him to climb out because they were worried the gas tank would explode. But in the video he had seen it had said that if you feel any pain in your spine you may do more damage by moving around so you are best to stay put, which is what he did until the ambulance arrived. It turned out that he had done the best thing because he had a crushed vertebra and it could have been made a lot worse if he had moved. He spent a month in hospital but he's back at school now. The whole event shook Paul up considerably.

'Both times I had lent the boys the cars because I was too soft to say no. But that won't be a problem with Robert because I won't have a car to loan him! It had taken me three years to save up for the Renault and it was only insured for third party claims.'

Shortly after the accident Cynthia phoned Michael, who was already working up on Hamilton Island. 'I told him, "Michael, I need you here. Please can you come home?" This year had been a bit traumatic even before the accident. We'd all been sick with a virus, Paul had decided to leave school without getting his HSC and was having trouble getting an apprenticeship and we'd had a flood through the back of the house. I felt I needed Michael home for a bit. He came straight away. He has a very sunny, up, disposition. He's an affectionate, open boy. He gives me bear hugs and kisses and I needed to have him around to talk to. He's a great mediator. When in the past they would all be getting together on a project, like renovating the house, his father would get worked up and Michael would smooth things over. Nothing phases him. I wouldn't like any of the boys to feel they have to hang around me out of duty. But on the other hand we are a close family and that's what families are for; to help out when things get tough.

'It was great to have him back just for those few weeks. He came with the girlfriend he has had for eighteen months. When he first started having girlfriends I didn't like it at all. Jealousy I suppose! I think I was pretty nasty to a couple of them! But I got over it and this one I get along with well. Michael has said to me, "You know Mum, I couldn't have picked a girl who was more like you. She even argues like you! She has a lovely nature but underneath that she's tough." I think he meant all that as a compliment.

'When he came back he thought about finding work down here. The last year of his apprenticeship he worked as a cabinetmaker and he is very talented at that, but he decided to wait a while before settling into a real job. Right now he's having too much fun.

'Things sorted themselves out. They always do. Paul was taken on as an apprentice in a restaurant a few kilometres away. He loves the work and he's very good at it. While he was at school he worked on weekends in the local seafood restaurant and also the cake shop. He has always been interested in cooking. Mind you he never cooks at home! If you had asked me six months ago which of the boys I was closest to I would have said Paul. I think it's because he is the only one I successfully breastfed and I think that bonding shows. He is also the one who is most like me. At school he was big and clumsy and uncoordinated.' — I protest strongly that Cynthia is none of these things. 'I can relate easily to his attitudes and moods. When he wants to do something he wants to do it immediately and he gets irritable if something prevents that from happening. That is just like me.

'At high school he was a very sociable child. I sometimes feel he grew up in other people's homes! The other two were always punctual and came home at the time they were told to. Paul always seemed to be a telephone call away at someone else's place. Now that he is working every night at the restaurant he's finding his social life is rather curtailed. Quite often at weekends he goes straight from work to a local nightclub and rages on there until it's almost time to go back to work, just dropping in here for a quick shower and a change of clothes on the way! I'm sure he has girlfriends but he doesn't bring them home or talk about them. He doesn't talk about much at all. He keeps himself to himself. He's always been like that. When they were younger and Michael and I would talk about sex and contraceptives he would listen and take it all in but he didn't join in the discussion. When he leaves home I'll be worried about what he's doing! It's always been like that. Michael tells you what he's up to so there's no need to worry. Paul doesn't and so I always imagine the worst!

'Not that I have ever worried about him or the other two getting into drugs. They none of them even smoke cigarettes and I always made it very clear how dangerous drugs are. All drugs. I expect they think I am very behind the times.

'As for Robert, I sometimes think he's missed out a bit by

I'm looking forward to having the time to develop skills which I'd been telling myself I will get to later. But I wonder if life will lose its purpose, its direction.

being the youngest. As yet we still have an unresolved relationship. Perhaps I've been too preoccupied with the older ones and now he seems to be almost grown up. He is quite determined about becoming a journalist and I shall be happy if that is what he does. I think now that Michael has gone and Paul has settled into his apprenticeship that there will be more time to spend with Robert.

'The three of them are very different from each other but they have always got along well together. And another thing is that I have always had an almost telepathic communication with them. Recently I phoned a friend up the coast for no particular reason except I felt I had to and just as she answered the phone Michael arrived at her place. Often when Paul was out and about I knew exactly where to contact him even though he hadn't told me where he would be. The same has happened with Robert. It's sort of odd. But it's as if they are an extension of me.

'How will I feel when the last one leaves?' Cynthia puts her hand to her mouth in a gesture of horror and then attempts to laugh the reaction off. Then she says, 'I'll be honest. It's not an original emotion but what I will feel will be sad, empty, lonely. After all they have been the fullness in my life. Yes, I am happily married, maybe even to an unusual degree, but I have been a mother and wife and soon, I guess within a few years, they'll all be gone and I shall be only a wife.

'I have to admit that I am a bit nervous about how that will be. We are approaching a big change in our lives. My husband is due for long-service leave. He's not sure what he will do after that. He may not want to go on with the same work. He's talked about a change of career. Nothing is definite yet. But I think when there is no longer the need to be financially responsible for the boys, when they are settled into their own careers, I guess that's a good time for a change. It would be quite a big adjustment.

'Right now I would like him to have a day job because we are well past the stage of the awful teatimes and he could enjoy having dinner with us. Also now it is quite often the case that they are all out. My husband at work. Michael up the coast. Paul at work. Robert with friends. And there is only me at home. When they were much younger one of us needed to be here every evening. But it's not like that now and I would like to live a more normal lifestyle.

'There are a few things that I am looking forward to getting into as I move into this stage of them leaving me. I want to learn to play the piano. I hope I'm not too old to be able to do that! I also want to learn to dance well, and I don't mean waltzing. I think I am having a second adolescence, probably because I didn't enjoy the first one much. I like rock music, especially going to live concerts with the boys. It's also good to be able to afford to buy a few things for myself. I've not been able to spend much on myself. I don't want to go overboard but I look at myself sometimes and think I should make the effort to be a bit more with it. And I want to travel. I've been back to England twice and I don't particularly want to go there again. I mean travel to interesting places. Go on the cheap, travel rough, camp out.

'I really do like the feeling of freedom which I am starting to get a whiff of. It's great to be able to go to the football and not have to worry about getting back to make dinner for everyone. I do still do all the cooking and washing and ironing for Paul and Robert and of course for my husband. I do it because I like doing it and also because I see that as what a mother and wife should do, but I don't make the boys' beds or clean their rooms. Every now and again when I can't stand the mess any longer I have an almighty turn out and tip everything into a heap in the middle of the room so they have to clean it up.

'When Michael came home a couple of weeks ago for his twenty-first birthday party I fed about forty of his friends here in the house and I really enjoyed doing it all myself. He stayed for a couple of weeks, which was great. To begin with he did his own washing and I was most impressed to see how well he could iron a shirt, but within a couple of days I had slipped back into doing this all for him. It was easier to put it in with all the rest. He commented on this and said he didn't mind at all doing it himself, but I went on doing it. He was terribly considerate. He gave me flowers every day and even bought me a sweater. I've never been a pampered person and I was very touched that he did these things. It was really lovely.

'When he left I steeled myself to saying, "We should go through all that stuff of yours downstairs because you won't be coming back except to visit." And he said, "Okay, I suppose you're right." So we did and I think I handled it quite well even though I knew this was it. When he took his little portable television I realised it really was goodbye this time!

'I suppose you could say that I have ambivalent feelings about them leaving. I have found myself thinking, if I liked I could go for a walk right now and for as long as I want. There's a freedom in that which I haven't had before and which I relish. But I am also a bit anxious about being lonely and not having anyone to chat to. My husband listens when I talk but he doesn't make conversation and I shall miss the interaction.

'I'm looking forward to having the time to be able to centre myself and to develop skills which for all these years I have been putting on the shelf and telling myself I will get to later. But I wonder a little if life will lose its purpose, its direction.

'Everyone says it of course, but that doesn't make it any the less true, that it seems so little time ago they were babies and now they are almost men. My greatest fear has always been that when they go out they will not come back, for whatever reason. When they were young boys it was that perhaps they would fall out of a tree or crack their head open with a surfboard and drown. As they've grown up it's that they would get a lift home from a party and have an accident. Now they will go simply because they have to live a life of their own. It's hard. I always knew it would happen one day. I didn't have a set age in my head when I thought that would be. I thought in general terms that it would be when they were ready. But it's happened sooner than I thought or like.'

Anne Wood

For his eighteenth birthday Anne Wood gave her son, Raymond, a beautifully embossed leather-covered photograph album. A labour of the great love a mother has for her son. One page for each year of his life, each one a collage of carefully chosen poetry and photographs of a baby growing through childhood to become a man.

From every one Raymond's clear, intelligent eyes and great, wide, warm grin jumps out. The look never changes, right through from tiny baby, toddler, the first day at school, the soccer player, surfer, to a student in Europe and looning around with his mates. In the last one he is wearing a dinner suit, his arm draped casually around his beautiful girlfriend. It was taken at the dance to celebrate his graduation from high school. A charmed life. A brilliant existence. But only when viewed from the outside. Two months after she gave her son his birthday present Raymond was dead. He died from an overdose of heroin.

The worst nightmare that a mother ever has about her child became a reality for Anne two years ago and she is just beginning to come to terms with it. 'One good thing is that whatever else happens during the rest of my life, nothing can ever be as bad as that. In a terrible, terrible way Raymond's death was almost a relief. That was it. Now nothing worse could happen. All the fears and anxieties, the sensation of constantly running in a futile attempt to keep up with him, the dread, the terror that something awful would happen; it all stopped. It was over. There was nothing more I could do.'

To anyone he met casually Raymond appeared relaxed, pleasant and happy, though brighter than many young men his age and with a wider spectrum of interests, but the truth was different. 'He was the most driven child I have ever known; obsessed with being the best, he was never as good as he wanted to be.

'Sometimes I think that the sheer intensity and absolute determination that went into creating him was the reason why he was the sort of person he was. Once he knew what he wanted, he locked onto whatever it was and moved relentlessly towards it. Even though neither his father nor I are competitive, we are both sort of laid-back, leftover hippies from the sixties, in some ways I could relate to his compulsiveness. I have streaks of it myself, it certainly was the reason why Raymond was conceived when he was.'

Anne had met her future husband when she was a twenty-year-old university student. 'The fact that he was ten years older than me, already married with a family didn't stop me falling in love with him. Terrible isn't it? But it's true and of course though we call it love it's really sexual attraction. It's definitely a primitive response. Nothing to do with logic. Something to do with my chemical make-up responding to something in his chemical make-up. Five months after we met he left his wife and we started living together. The good thing is that it turned out I had done her a favour! I realised that when, after fifteen years and two sons, my marriage also broke up. She was already remarried to a really great fellow and she and I have stayed good friends.

'For the first four years of our life together every second weekend I played stepmother to his young children. I hadn't wanted an instant family. In fact I hadn't wanted children at all. I'd had enough of that when I was growing up. For the first seven years of my life I was an only child, the product of a British wartime romance. When I was seven my mother decided to make a new start in Australia. On the boat out she met her future husband and that shipboard romance produced five children one after the other in quick succession! I remember telling my mother when I was a teenager that there was no way I was going to have children because I'd already raised five of hers! That's how it felt.

'I've always got along well with my mother, I still do. But I didn't get on so well with her husband. I didn't think of him as my father. I feel as though I've never had a father. From what I saw I developed the view that fathers didn't do anything. Perhaps that's the reason why men seem rather superfluous to me. I like men, but I've never thought of them as essential to either my spiritual or material well-being. And I think that attitude contributed a great deal to the eventual breakdown of my marriage.

'But that was a slow process, in the beginning things could not have been better. We lived together for four years and then totally unexpectedly I was overcome by this irresistible urge to have a baby. From being the thing I wanted least it became what I desired most. Compelled by my hormones, that's what it was. We think we are somehow higher than the animals but I don't think we are, not when it comes down to the urge to procreate. I wanted to be married before I had a baby so we got that out of the way first.

'I had it all worked out to a very definite timetable because I was determined to have a spring baby. That meant falling pregnant in late summer, but just at that time my husband suddenly developed severe kidney stones. He was in extreme pain and I was very concerned for him. He was hospitalised and they brought the pain under control but told him that he needed an operation. There was a week's delay before the surgery and my concern for him turned to panic as I saw the year slipping away. I thought, a week's wait, then he'll be a week in hospital and then at least another couple of weeks recuperating before he'll be fit enough. So I decided that I had to get him home for the week before the operation and get into it or it would be too late to make a spring baby. I was that calculating and determined!

'Well we managed it and nine months later, in the spring, Raymond was born. As I said before I've often thought the manner of his conception could well have influenced his personality. It was a quick delivery, only a few hours, he came in a rush, the way he was to live his life.'

Anne had planned on having two children in quick succession. 'I had not enjoyed being an only child for my first seven years and I was determined to have two. Even then, almost as if I knew, I was anxious not to put all my eggs in one basket.' But sometimes the best laid plans of mice and men come to nought. 'I had two miscarriages. The first one was pretty ho-hum but the second was not so good, in fact it was horrific. I was six months pregnant and there was a rush to hospital in an attempt to save it. It really upset my husband, who wasn't fussed about having another child. But again I was determined, and it had to be another spring baby. So when I became pregnant again I took all the advice about hormone injections and lying in bed with the result that Sean was born, three springs after his brother. Right from the word go he was a totally different personality. He was a laid-back character, perhaps due to all my lying around, whereas for Raymond yesterday was not soon enough.'

After the birth of his second son their father had a vasectomy. 'He wasn't taking any risks! But I think by then the damage to the marriage had already been done. In a way I think I must have made him feel no longer needed now that he had sired my children; that was another mistake, I always thought of them as my children rather than ours.

'In other ways too our marriage was moving towards its destruction. I think two people are really lucky or have worked tremendously hard at developing together if after ten years of marriage they still have compatible hopes and aspirations. My husband and I were developing along different paths. The physical attraction was still there but we were not supportive of each other's dreams and ambitions. Eventually I moved out when the children were in primary school and I had a full-time job.

'I thought about moving to New Zealand and making a fresh, clean start but again I thought, who am I to deprive two boys of at least being able to see their father on weekends? Out of guilt I went overboard. I found a two-bedroom place and I gave them a room each while I slept on the couch in the lounge. This really was a mistake. In always worrying about what was best for the boys, trying to atone for my guilt in depriving them of their father, I made their importance the central factor of my life, which is not the way it should be. Though they were only at that delightful pre-puberty age, I thought I should take their opinions into consideration when making decisions. I wanted mine to be a truly democratic family. But of course in this democracy I was outnumbered two to one and the chief manipulator in the power struggle was always my eldest son.

'Raymond was born competitive. He joined teams and more than anything else he wanted his parents to stand on the sidelines and shout encouragement. But this was foreign to both our natures. I remember the summer when Raymond was nine years old. Every Saturday morning he played cricket for the school team and when that finished at noon he would run, uphill for more than a kilometre, to catch the bus which would take him to the swimming pool where he would spend the afternoon in competitive races. He considered me the worst mother in the world because I wouldn't take him to training every morning before school. But I felt rather like my husband that yes, you learnt to swim or to play cricket, but then that was that. You did it for fun, not to be better than everyone else. That summer Raymond's cricket team gave him the best and fairest player award and in addition he scored more points at the swimming than anyone else; not by being the most brilliant swimmer but by turning up every week and swimming in every race and coming in second or third and sometimes first. But once he'd done that, that was it, he never went back. He was on to something else. Fresh fields to conquer.'

Anne bought a home on the coast. Raymond started at the local high school and began to surf from the area's wonderful beaches. Quite contrary to the image it has of being in harmony with the beauty of nature, the surfing scene is often quite hideously aggressive and overloaded with macho peer group pressure. It is, of course, also chock-a-block with drugs, though mostly nothing more than marijuana. Raymond took to the scene with a vengeance. He also took to high school with the same enthusiasm. He was a keen student, anxious to learn and forever pushing his limits.

When he was fourteen he met a man who was to have an enormous impact on his life. 'Harry told me that he was impressed with Raymond from the very first time he met him, when Raymond had asked him to explain all he knew about the stock and money market and investments. Harry was cultured and educated and well travelled and all this impressed Raymond, for whom he became a model to emulate. Naturally I was anxious about the friendship because I could see Raymond hung on his every word, but when I met Harry and he and I discussed this openly I felt it was all okay. I had a good feeling about him and his friends. That's all you can go on. He told me that he had never met a young man with such potential, and he said this in front of Raymond, which was great for Raymond's ego, which always needed building up. Raymond began spending a lot of his weekends with Harry and his friends and he always came back bubbling over with ideas and plans, talking about opera and classical music and other things, obviously stimulated and happy. Sean at this time was spending almost every weekend with his dad and he was happy too, so it was a good time for us all.

'There was only one problem and that was how the other boys at his school and his surfing mates reacted to Raymond's friendship with this group. To the surfing crowd anything that smacked of education, culture and the classics was definitely suspect and "poofterish". When he told me about their reaction I would say that he had to stand up to them, or at least ignore their prejudice, but that's difficult for young people. They want to be liked, and though they go to great lengths to be outrageous and different they really want to be the same, to be accepted. Raymond was torn between two very different worlds. I could see that but all I could do was be supportive.

'Then he started to talk about leaving school. He was anxious to start on the road towards making his fortune. This was the last thing I wanted. I wanted him to do his HSC because I knew that otherwise he was wasting his talents and he would very quickly become bored with the only sort of jobs he could hold down without any qualifications. He spent one school holiday working part time with a builder and decided this was the way to make big money. This made me very anxious that he really would give school away, so when Harry suggested that he could organise for Raymond to go to school in Europe it seemed like a great answer. Harry would have liked to have a son of his own and here was a young man with drive and determination just waiting to be channelled. The atmosphere at the school Raymond was at was very rough and ready and by contrast studying in Europe was a fantastic opportunity.

'I thought it would be just the thing for Raymond. I couldn't give him what he needed, the constant need to grow and experience, it was beyond me. Sharing a life with Raymond was like living in the middle of a hurricane. There was always something new he wanted to try. It was exhausting. By comparison Sean was such an easy person to be around. But because of Raymond's incessant demands Sean missed out, so I also thought that if Raymond went off to school in Europe I would have more time and energy to spend on his brother.

'I remember the day he left so well. He suddenly decided that because everyone in Europe would be very proficient on ice-skates he should brush up on his skating. His plane left at 2.00 in the afternoon and we spent the entire morning at an ice-skating rink with him going round and round, practising, so he wouldn't feel inadequate when he arrived. That says something about the sort of person he was. I waved him goodbye and he was as casual about going as if he was catching a bus into town.

'I felt very sad about him going. He was only fifteen. I felt my child had grown up and left me. I felt empty, lonely, even though I still had Sean. Raymond, because of his personality, had always been such a large part of my life. I felt it was more than a goodbye and I was right. He went away a child and came back as a man who was even more beyond my control and my understanding. I visited him once in Europe. We had a lovely holiday together. By then he had been there a year and he was speaking fluent French, very adequate German, and talked about whether he would go down to Florence when he finished school to polish up his Italian and study architecture, or go on to the Sorbonne in Paris and study languages, or to London and study economics. I was amazed at how well he had adjusted to living in Europe. He talked like a man of the world. There were so many challenges and opportunities for him, he revelled in it all. I realised then that I had lost my child son forever and that was sad, but I was also proud of him.

'He wrote me beautiful letters, which I am glad I kept. I remember one in particular, two pages of which was all about a violin concert he had attended in a church given by Yehudi Menuhin. "Mum," he said in the letter, "the music was so wonderful that I could do more than just hear it with my ears, I could feel it with my body." Was this the same child who, it seemed like just yesterday, was writing notes to the Tooth Fairy? It was hard to grasp.

'Sean spent the time Raymond was away going through the all too common horrors of early teenage years. Getting into strife at school, louting around with his mates, he was outrageous and obnoxious. But nothing too drastic! And I told myself a lot of it was a reaction to having divorced parents. He still spent a lot of time with his father, which I was glad about. I thought it was important that he stayed close to his father simply because he was his father.'

After eighteen months overseas Raymond took his O levels, the public examination which European students take at the end of Year 10. Then he came home for a holiday, with a French accent and a lot of polish and sophistication. It was summer, the beaches were crowded with attractive girls and the surf was up. Raymond slipped back into old friendships, including the crowd at Harry's place. At the end of the holidays snowbound Europe didn't have such appeal and he decided to give the local high school another go. 'I was glad to have him home and encouraged him to go back to the school. It must have been extremely difficult for him. He looked and behaved like a foreigner, but I think what made him stick it out was that he was a great hit with the girls.'

It was shortly after Raymond's return that Anne found the first evidence of drugs in her home. 'I found a bong and when I confronted them both with it Raymond said it was not his and I believed him because he had always been so health conscious. So although Sean also said it wasn't his I assumed it was, if for no other reason than the fact that a short while before he had come home with a grocery box full of tiny marijuana plants! He told me he had found it and wanted to show it to his dad. I decided this was one problem his dad could sort out so I drove him and the box to his dad's place. The things you do for your kids! Crazy. For the whole drive I was thinking, God what if the police stop me, how am I going to explain a box of marijuana seedlings!

'That box and the bong were the only evidence I ever saw of drugs in my house. But I became aware that Raymond had more money than I ever gave him and I sensed, you know the way mothers do, that it was to do with drugs. I could only assume that he was selling dope. Money was important to Raymond in a way it has never been important to me or to his father. Looking back I realise it was one of the factors which drew him into the drug scene. When I accused him of selling drugs he said, "Don't be ridiculous." He was working occasionally at weekends washing up in a restaurant and I never really knew exactly how much he earned.

'I told Harry I was anxious about drugs, but he assured me that there were never any around his place and I could only believe him. Whenever I confronted Raymond again and asked him how he had all this extra money he would tell me he had sold something he had brought back from Europe. He mentioned stuff I didn't know whether he had or not, so I couldn't pin him down. I began to feel him slipping out of my control. On weekend evenings he began going into town with his mates, some of whom were old enough to have cars or borrow their parents' vehicles. He went to nightclubs where alcohol was sold, even though he was under age, you know how easy it is for them to do that. It's an accepted social norm.

'I am not blaming anyone for any of this. I take the full blame. I thought about moving to the country to get away from the scene. But it's just as bad out there and anyway where would I find work? Even having been through what I have I still have no foolproof advice for other mothers. A lot of it is luck. That's a terrible truth. It depends so much on the personality of the young person. Some people can handle dope as a social drug and some can't. It's just the same as it is with alcohol. People are predestined by their physical and psychological make-up as to whether or not they will be able to cope with drugs. All drugs. From alcohol to heroin. Some people can try anything once and get away with it. For Raymond the choices were all at the other end of the line. I honestly believe, that because of his personality, from the very first time he used marijuana he was set on a one-track line to oblivion.

'When it came to the academically crucial last two years of high school it became obvious that the local state school could not offer the subject choices which Raymond wanted and he began to talk again about leaving school. He didn't want to return to Europe but he didn't feel intellectually stimulated by the school. We decided to try a private school and rang around setting up interviews. It was as if Raymond was interviewing the school and the headmaster. Eventurally we settled on one close to town.

'To begin with he travelled in every day by bus. But it's a long, long way from our place. The journey took over an hour and a half there, and even longer on the way back. He began to agitate about us all moving in closer to town. That would have meant uprooting Sean from the school where he was doing tolerably well, as well as me either changing jobs or also travelling. And I jacked up at that. I said, "No Raymond. Life cannot revolve around you entirely. There are other people to take into consideration."

'Then we thought of a young couple we knew who had just moved into a flat in the eastern suburbs. We arranged for Raymond to spend the week nights there and come home at weekends. This really was the beginning of the end. He couldn't resist the nightlife. He was out practically every night at Stranded or The Berlin Club or at some private party or other. I wasn't there to try to impose some rules and control. And of course I couldn't expect this young couple he was staying with to play that role either.

'The trouble was that he was doing well at school so I didn't have any reasonable excuse to complain. It was about this time that I threw in my hand and gave up. I had tried everything I knew of to keep a rein on him and I hadn't been successful. But while I was anxious about the direction he was headed he was making his mark in his own way at school. It's a very academic school so although Raymond was a well above average student there was no way he was going to set himself up against that sort of competition.

'Also it's a very traditional school and only boys who have been at the school for the whole of their school life and who probably had fathers who had attended the school too had any chance of becoming a prefect, let alone a house captain. So he stood no chance of recognition in that arena. He didn't fancy himself as a hero on the Rugby field either; not his scene. But he was driven by his personality to make his mark. And that he did in the area where no one else could touch him, the trendy scene. When he was awarded the Decore Wow-Look-at-Me-Now Award he had won all the acclaim his nature craved so much.'

For the last term of Year 11 Anne was so anxious about her son's headlong flight along the fast-track of Sydney nightlife that she insisted he live with his father, whose home was near enough to the school for Raymond to be able to manage the journey. But during the Christmas break his father moved out into the country to start over with a new wife. So for Year 12 Raymond was back again living close to town and the speed at which he was travelling became increasingly dangerous.

'I knew that during the previous year he had tried cocaine and pills in addition to marijuana. We had talked about it and I had tried reasoning with him. But I'd got nowhere. He had all the answers. Or so he thought. All I could do was hang in there. It was like having a tiger by the tail. Or being dragged along at speed underwater. It was terrifying. Raymond. Raymond. Raymond. It was all Raymond. He took over my entire life.'

The stage was set for the final seemingly unavoidable act. 'At the beginning of the year he started dating a wonderful girl. Marie was a few years older than Raymond and worked as a receptionist at a big hotel in the city. For the first term of that year he seemed to be far more settled than he had been ever since he was in Year 8. He was staying in at night and doing his homework and I really thought that with Marie he had turned the corner and things might really settle down. You know as a mother you cling on to any tiny little spark of hope.

'He took his driving test and persuaded me to finance a second-hand car. Then he promptly had an accident and smashed it up. Foolishly I thought, well, that's that, at least now he doesn't have a car that's one less thing for me to worry about. But without me or anyone else knowing about it, he went up to Gosford and paid a man a $100 deposit on a big motorbike, for which he didn't have a licence. He drove it back to Sydney, picked Marie up from work on it, did an illegal U-turn in the middle of the main road and collected a car. The bike, which was uninsured and not even in his name, was a write-off. Marie's ankle was broken and he went with her to the hospital. When the police came and asked for details he gave them another fellow's licence, which he had obviously stolen. Now he was in deep trouble and he knew it.

'He stayed with Marie until she was released and then they went home to her place and that night someone said to him, because he was so obviously shaken up and frightened, "Here try some of this. It'll make you feel better." It did. It was heroin.

'Raymond was addicted from the first hit. My very first words when he told me he was using it were, "My God Raymond, that's a one-way street." But of course he didn't think so. He told me how terrific it made him feel. How he need never feel depressed now. How it helped his creativity. How he wrote far better essays after a hit. He went on about Coleridge and other poets and writers and painters who used it to enhance their talents. And how he was in control of it; only using it at weekends. That was Raymond's way; always the bush lawyer. The wonderful girl who stood by him through all his problems was also paying for his addiction. Most of her wages went on heroin for Raymond.

'The ridiculous thing is that to a degree he was right. His grades went up. He stayed home during the week to study and he seemed calmer and more at ease. Less frantic. But it was all an illusion which quickly became apparent even to him. In the beginning I had insisted that he come with me to see people. The doctor we saw prescribed tranquillisers. The psychiatrist suggested a course of therapy to build up his self-confidence and the drug referral centre told me that until he admitted he needed help there was nothing they could do. I felt totally helpless and panic stricken. I had no one close to me that I felt I could confide in.

'I couldn't burden Sean with his brother's troubles. He had enough of his own. I was glad their father wasn't in Sydney because I didn't want to tell him. I felt I was to blame. Now my greatest regret is that I didn't confide in him and thereby give his father a chance to try and save his son.'

At the end of the second term Raymond himself made the move. He went down to the snow for a skiing holiday with Marie and suffered such severe withdrawal symptoms he realised the extent of his dependence on the drug. He came back to Sydney willing to seek help and determined to break his habit. He and Marie moved in to stay with Harry in his city apartment during the crucial period of the HSC exams, but just when he was most in need of support Harry was injured in a traffic accident and was hospitalised. Raymond was left alone in an apartment in the very heart of Sydney's drug area.

'Straight people can walk through the Cross and not even see what is really going on because we don't know what to look for. To recognise a dealer you have to be another dealer or a user, or a police officer. For an addict to have any chance at all of breaking the habit it's necessary to get away from the place where the drug is available. As soon as he had finished his exams he went up the coast to a friend's farm. Marie went with him and so did a woman whose boyfriend had died of a heroin overdose. She was very strongly anti the drug and she knew Raymond wanted to get off it. They all stayed up there for three weeks and Raymond went cold turkey. I know it was hell for him because he phoned me often and we talked about how he was feeling.

'When he came back, a week before Christmas, he was off the stuff but he was so frightened that with all the inevitable parties at that time of year it would be impossible for him to stay clean he begged me to take him to Europe for a holiday. Perhaps if I had. No. That's not so. I know that really. It would only have delayed the inevitable. At the time I felt great resentment towards him that he could make yet another demand and somehow make it appear as though it was what a caring, loving mother would do. I said, "No. Enough is enough, Raymond." Then some friends offered to take him to Bali.

'They were supposed to stay away for ten days and come back on New Year's Day. For some reason I shall never know the answer to, he came back a day early, ahead of the others. I didn't know he was back. He didn't tell anyone. I heard later from people that they saw him that night; the night before New Year's Eve. They saw him in various nightclubs and at a couple of parties. He told them he had come back early to surprise Marie. But he never saw her. Somewhere during that evening he must have had a hit, perhaps more than one, and the first thing I knew that anything was wrong was a phone call early in the morning of New Year's Day from Harry. He had come back and was at his flat. He told me that Raymond was very sick and that I should come as quickly as possible.

'I drove into the city and outside the apartment I saw a police car. I panicked, rushed into the flat and when I saw there were no police there I distinctly remember thinking, oh well, if the police are not here then everything must be okay. It's funny how memories like that stick in your mind. When I went in a doctor was there and he told me, "Raymond is dead." But I am sure I didn't really register what he said. I just felt as though I had been kicked in the stomach. My very first thought was, so quickly? It was just six months since the first time he used it. I went down to the basement where Raymond was still lying. The police told me that the caretaker had found him there with a young woman who had been in a coma and had come to and found Raymond dead in her arms. He had died in his sleep. Peacefully. I am grateful for that. I couldn't bear to think of him choking to death on his vomit. Or knowing that he was dying and trying to struggle to live. At least he died peacefully.'

It is peaceful too where Anne and I are sitting, in her tiny basement flat overlooking the water. We sit for a while listening to the sounds of silence. Thinking about Raymond and how easily it could have happened to my son or yours. There but for the grace of God. I apologise, inadequately, for stirring up all these extraordinarily difficult emotions. 'No. I'm glad to talk about it all. It has helped me. I couldn't have done so until now but talking to you has made me realise I am coming out of the end of the tunnel.

'I don't feel lonely. What I feel more than anything else I think is a sense of relief that it is all behind me. Nothing could ever be worse than what I have been through. So I know I will survive whatever the future holds. I know the eventuality is never as bad as our fear of uncertainty. Everyone, without exception, was very kind and supportive. Every single woman who either phoned me or wrote or came up to me in the street, said the same thing:" I am a mother too so I know how you must feel and I want you to know that I feel for you, as another mother, a great deal of sympathy." It made me realise how much good there is in the world. The other thing which I learnt was a degree of heightened awareness, a spiritual sense. I can quite understand how at such times people become born-again Christians. I have never believed in God or in a life after death so I haven't had that option.

'It is always comforting to know someone who has been along the same path ahead of you. A friend of mine lost her husband, after a battle with cancer, just twelve months before my loss. I have spent a great deal of time talking with her, sharing emotions and being strengthened by her strength. I remember how amazed I was at the funeral of her husband; how she radiated warmth towards others at a time of immense grief. Now I understand that she was in fact reflecting the comfort and support given to her by others.

'One other good thing which has happened is that I know Raymond's death had a profound effect on several of his close friends. It shook them up, made them realise they are not immortal, that Raymond died because he took stupid risks. If his death does nothing more than protect those young people from

We can never be sure that what we think is right, really is. We just do the best we can.

throwing their lives away in the same manner then it won't have been a total waste.

'Looking back over my life as a mother I recall battling with my natural instinct to be very overprotective of the boys when they were young. I couldn't bear to watch them climb trees. I had to go away to stop myself from trying to hold them back. I knew that as young men they would want and need to experiment with life. The other thing is that looking back, if I had a second chance, the opportunity to do it all again, but without the benefit of hindsight, I don't think I would do anything differently. I did what I thought was best at the time. I really did. And if motherhood has taught me one thing, it's humility. We can never be sure that what we think is right, really is. We just do the best we can.'

The last poem in Raymond's birthday present album is by the Russian poet Yevgeny Yevtuschenko:

> Mother, let me congratulate you on
> the birthday of your son.
> You worry so much about him. Here he lies,
> he earns little, his marriage was unwise,
> he's long, he's getting thin, he hasn't shaved.
> Oh, what a miserable loving gaze!
> I should congratulate you if I may
> Mother on your worry's birthday.
> It was from you that he inherited
> devotion without pity to this age
> and arrogant and awkward in his faith
> from you he took his faith, the Revolution.
> You didn't make him prosperous or famous,
> and fearlessness is his only talent.
> Open up his windows,
> let in the twittering in the leafy branches,
> kiss his eyes open.
> Give him his note book and his ink bottle,
> give him a drink of milk and watch him go.

Before heaven and earth
There was something nebulous
    silent isolated
    unchanging and alone
    eternal
    The Mother of all things.

LAO-TZU, THE *TAO-TE CHING*